Trading the Future

TRADING THE FUTURE

Farm Exports and
the Concentration of
Economic Power in
Our Food Economy

James Wessel
with Mort Hantman

Institute for Food and Development Policy
1885 Mission Street
San Francisco, California 94103

Library of Congress Catalog Card Number: 83-20512
ISBN: 0-93528-13-7

Printed in the United States of America
1 2 3 4 5 6 7 8 9

To order additional copies of this book, please write:

Institute for Food and Development Policy
1885 Mission St.
San Francisco, CA 94103 USA
(415) 864-8555

Please add 15 percent for postage and handling ($1
minimum). California residents add sales tax.
Bulk discounts available.

Distributed in the United Kingdom by:

Third World Publications
151 Stratford Rd.
Birmingham B11 1RD
England

Wessel, James.
  Trading the future.

  Bibliography: p.
  Includes index.
    1. Agriculture and state—United States. 2. Agriculture—Economic
aspects—United States. 3. Food industry and trade—Political aspects—
United States.   4. United States—Economic policy—1981–   .
5. United States—Commercial policy. I. Hantman, Mort. II. Title.
HD1761.W422   1983   338.1'0973   83-20512
ISBN 0-935028-13-7

Design: Nancy Guinn
Type: G & S Typesetters, Austin
Printers: McNaughton & Gunn, Ann Arbor
Text: Aster
Display: Americana

To the love, friendship, and support that helped make this book possible.

Table of Contents

List of Figures and Tables

Acknowledgements

To my principal collaborators in this effort I owe the greatest debt. To Mort Hantman, my deepest appreciation for steadfast support, solid intellectual contributions, and a shared commitment to this work without which it might not have been possible. And to Frances Moore Lappé, my heartfelt gratitude for our three-year association and for important contributions throughout this project.

I owe a special debt as well to Phil LeVeen, director of Public Interest Economics–West, whose great depth in this subject matter and critical understanding of the issues was an invaluable resource.

I would also like to thank those who reviewed the manuscript in its various stages: Nick Allen, Medea Benjamin, Rebecca Bogdan, Richard Borowitz, Tony and Shirley Bos, Fred Brauneck, Tom Brom, Fred Buttel, Joe Collins, Bruce Coleman, Diana Dillaway, Roxanne Enerson, Marilyn Fedelchak, Bill Freese, Harriet Friedman, Bill and Virginia Genzen, Roy Gesley, Richard Gilmore, Gretta Goldenman, Steve Goldfield, Merle Goldman, Nancy Guinn, Tracy Helser, Carol Hodne, Quentin Hope, Laura and Lester Joens, David Kinley, Betty Lamplot, Cathy Lerza, Daniel Levitas, John McCormick, Dale Malmberg, Pam Mickler, Tom Miller, John Moore, Julie Neal, Jan Newton, Michael Perelman, Mike Pincus, Don Reimund, Mark Ritchie, Pam Roberts, Tom Saunders, Ed Schafer, Melvin Schneider, Susan Sechler, Pat Steffes, Marty Strange, Catherine Taylor, Wendy Walker, Seph Weene, and John Young.

I would like to recognize the special contribution of a number of Institute colleagues during my three-year tenure there: Jan Newton, for unwavering support of this work; Nick Allen for help in preparing the final manuscript; Nancy Guinn for straight shooting as publications coordinator; Steve Goldfield for work on the word processor and a sharp editorial eye; Stephen Slade for effectively filling the role of Institute general manager; Art and Pat Bergeron for the title of this book; David Kinley for support of this project at crucial stages; David Ritchie for work on the footnotes, bibliography, and final details; Michael Samuel and Chris Nihan for daily help with administrative matters; and Wendy Ward for her help as Institute librarian.

The wide-ranging research that formed the foundation for this book would not have been possible without the dedication and talent of those who gave their time as members of "the U.S. Ag. team" at the Institute. Their personal support and commitment to this project was an inspiration to me, and my work with them was uniquely rewarding. My deepest thanks to all.

In addition, I would also like to thank Catherine Taylor for her very fine editing on the final draft and Tom Brom and Seph Weene for their extremely helpful editorial hand on earlier drafts.

Special thanks for the Columbia Foundation, the Field Foundation, and the Shalan Foundation, whose contributions made possible both the research and publication of *Trading the Future*. Thanks also to the thousands of members of the Institute for Food and Development Policy whose support makes the Institute's work possible.

Two closing acknowledgements in a more personal vein: To my mother, Mildred Wessel, I owe that unique debt of life, love, and the wisdom of a growth-centered parenthood. Her grass-roots activism gave me an early awareness of things political and showed me the importance of working for social change. Finally, to Jennifer Lovejoy, a former colleague at the Institute and now my partner in life, I wish to acknowledge a very special indebtedness for her patience, support, love, and understanding that words cannot fully express.—J. W.

The author would like to give special recognition to the following people who, as members of the "U.S. Ag. team" at the Institute, made major contributions to the research of this project.

KATE ALBERT
FRED BRAUNECK
CLIO FISCHER
MERLE GOLDMAN
TRACY HELSER
MARILYN McGREGOR
PAM MICKLER
JEFF REEL
DAVID RITCHIE
ERIK SCHAPIRO

1 A Time of Crisis

As the decade of the 1980s unfolds, Americans watch developments at home and abroad with increasing uneasiness. Uncertainty and crisis often leave us feeling confused and at the mercy of a world not of our own making. As we go to press in early 1983, more of us are out of work than at any time since the Great Depression, and most of us are losing ground to economic forces seemingly beyond our control or understanding. Poverty and hunger are growing at home and the evening news reports threatening political and economic developments abroad. Neither political leaders nor the experts offer more than Band-Aids for problems that seem as intractable as they are difficult to define. As both spectators and participants in this unpredictable social drama, we often succumb to cynicism and a sense of powerlessness.

The Tip of the Iceberg

News headlines trumpeting recent developments in our farm and food economy reflect both the crisis atmosphere in which we live and the contradictory nature of the problems we face:

"Bankruptcies Soar, Farm Depression Worst Since 30s"

"Tons of Cheese Warehoused as Soup Lines Lengthen"

"Agricultural Exports Set New Record While Farm Prices Drop"

Behind these paradoxical headlines lie even more disturbing facts.

- As American farmers brought record harvests to market in the early 1980s, they also faced the highest rate of bankruptcy since the Great Depression. The costs of producing most major crops were much higher than the prices farmers received for them. For many farmers, the more they produced, the more money they lost. A river of red ink engulfed the farm economy as net farm income was sharply reduced—cut in half from 1980 to 1982. Farm families all over the country struggled on the edge of survival, and growing numbers went under, unable to shoulder rising debts, skyrocketing interest rates, and falling profits per acre. The consequences have been more farm auctions all across rural America and concentration of farm ownership into fewer hands. By 1982 the 1 percent of farms with incomes above $500,000 a year were receiving two thirds of all farm income, while those with sales below $40,000, on average, were operating at a loss.[1]

- As the economic crisis on the farm deepened, so did an environmental crisis that continues to threaten the basic resources needed to produce food upon which future generations rely—soil and water. On two thirds of American cropland, topsoil is being lost faster than nature can rebuild it. Nationwide, our current average erosion rates surpass those of the Dust Bowl period. This soil loss is especially severe on some of our country's richest, most productive farmland. Much of our groundwater, upon which a significant portion of agricultural production depends, is used so extravagantly for irrigation that the western U.S. water table is dropping an average of three feet annually. In north Texas, for example, groundwater reserves have effectively been consumed in one generation, and in other key farming areas reserves are rapidly being depleted. The combined effects of erosion, urbanization, and desertification render more and more land useless or unavailable for farming and raise the question of whether we will have enough farmland to meet our future agricultural needs.

Our massive agricultural output over the past decade, culminating in the record harvests of the early 1980s, has failed to result in a net gain for consumers. Even with inflation abating in the face of the worst recession since World War II, food prices continue to rise in the supermarket while farm prices stand at record lows. Since 1972, more of workers' average weekly wages have gone to buy food—reversing trends in the 1950s and 1960s. Tighter food budgets caused most Americans to shift their diets, while growing poverty left more and more people with minimal food budgets. In 1980 more than 3 million people were added to the ranks of the "officially poor," and soup lines lengthened across the country as the portion of those living below the poverty line rose to levels higher than any year since 1966.[2]

- While the farmer, the consumer, and our food resource base have been increasingly pressed over the past decade, this has not generally been the case for the handful of giant firms that dominate key sectors of the food economy. These large firms are able to protect themselves in ways foreclosed to others. When profits have not been sufficient at home, they have gone abroad, taking jobs with them. Even when recession strikes worldwide and business slumps, they are able to cut their losses at the expense of others—laying off workers and passing on increased costs to consumers. Over the past decade, while net farm income has stagnated and then dropped precipitously, the half-dozen major grain companies that sell the farmer's produce have reaped enormous profits. And while consumer purchasing power has steadily eroded over this same period, the food industry has become more tightly held by a few firms whose profitability has dramatically increased. From 1969 to 1981 the top fifty food companies increased their share of industry assets from 52 to 66 percent and their profits (as a percentage of equity) rose from 11.4 to 15.1 during the 1970s.[3]

- Since 1970, U.S. farm exports—mainly grains—have tripled in volume and risen more than sixfold in value, to an astonishing $44 billion in 1981. By 1980 over half of cash crop receipts came from sales abroad, and over one third of harvested acreage was exported. The U.S. Department of Agriculture and the multinational food processing corporations continue to promote U.S. farm exports "to feed a hungry world." In reality, over two thirds of these exports feed hungry animals, whose meat is too expensive for hungry people to buy. (Most of the remaining exports go to relatively well-fed consumers.) As Marty Strange of the Center for Rural Affairs points out, the United States might better be characterized as the world's "restauranteur" than as the world's breadbasket.

- The government and food industry giants also promote farm exports as the antidote to the negative U.S. balance of trade. In fiscal year 1981, for example, the United States exported $26.5 billion worth of food more than it imported. However, U.S. farmers spend the equivalent of 40 cents' worth of imported oil to produce each dollar's worth of farm exports. This calls into question the comforting equation of "wheat for oil."

These recent developments in our farm and food economy support an unfolding drama of relatively few winners and many losers that at first appears bewildering. How can we have record harvests and an economic crisis in farming at the same time? Why does our agricultural bounty disproportionately benefit a few giant corporations? Why have sales of our farm products overseas neither reached the hungry nor substantially improved our economic position in the world?

The purpose of this book is to delve beneath the surface of the issues and contradictions raised in this chapter and expose the root causes of our farm and food problems. We hope to show how these problems inevitably result from the basic forces of growth that govern our food economy—forces that run counter to majority interests and threaten our future food security. By providing a framework for understanding how our farm and food economy works, we can begin to make the connections between the headlines and the structural problems they reflect. Then we will be able to ask the right questions as a first step toward building a food and farming system that will serve both farmers and consumers, here and around the world.

To examine the roots of our current food crisis, we will

investigate the boom in farm exports that began in the early 1970s. While the export boom is not the source of our problems, its enormous impact has accelerated trends already underway, such as concentration of control over farmland, and has exacerbated preexisting problems such as soil and water depletion. By examining the impact of stepped-up exports on our farm and food system, we will bring to light the inner workings of our economic system and begin to understand the panorama of forces that shape our daily lives.

The Doughnut Solution?

In 1982 U.S. Secretary of Agriculture John Block traveled to China. In Peking he stopped for a doughnut at a U.S.-equipped bakery—one of dozens of international projects designed to relieve U.S. agriculture of its grain surpluses. "I never saw so many people in my life," Block said on his return. "If they would just eat one doughnut a day. . . ."[4]

John Block had been assigned the strange mission of unloading the largest cornucopia of food in world history. But the secretary's good humor masked the increasing desperation of his task. With wheat stocks at their highest level in two decades and the 1982 grain harvests straining U.S. storage capacity, grain prices sank as low as 40 percent below the estimated average cost of production.

While the dual problems of chronic oversupply accompanied by low farm prices are of crisis proportions today, they are hardly new to American agriculture. Nor are efforts to promote exports, such as Secretary Block's. These recent efforts are part of a history of government programs since the New Deal designed to rescue American agriculture from the disasters of its own bounty by supporting farm prices through subsidies or controlling overproduction through "set-asides." Since the PL–480 "Food for Peace" program began in the 1950s, and especially since the 1973 Soviet grain deal, government policymakers have pursued foreign markets for U.S. grain with the almost religious conviction that "greater exports will save us."

Ironically, this strategy has succeeded famously in

boosting exports. In just one decade, agricultural exports tripled in volume and shot up nearly sixfold in value, reaching $44 billion in 1981.[5] (See figure 1–1.)

These figures should warm the heart of any sales executive. But have they had the desired effect of helping farmers earn stable, higher incomes, while keeping consumer food prices—and farm subsidies—low? The answer clearly is no. Despite flourishing exports, farm income is at its lowest point since the mid-1930s, food prices continue to rise even as farm prices fall, and farm subsidies are expected to top $18.8 billion for 1983.[6]

The deepening crisis in U.S. farming, which is causing growing numbers of farmers to sell their farms every week, and the failure of decades of farm policies aimed at increasing demand for crops or reducing supply call for a fundamental reassessment of our food production system. As we will see throughout *Trading the Future*, we must break free of the conventional views that have defined "the farm problem." We must look beyond the market questions of supply and demand and examine the basic forces that govern production in our farm and food economy. For it is only in the deeper exploration of how production works in our system that we will find the root causes of the dilemmas we face.

While this book has a relatively narrow topic—farm exports—its scope is broad in terms of the field it covers and the issues it raises. In tracing the impact of the export push, we survey a large part of our farm and food economy, focusing primarily on domestic developments but also examining the international sphere that has become so indispensable to understanding the problems we face. The rise of export agriculture in the United States signifies the integration of our farmers into a global food production and marketing system that is leading to increasingly similar patterns of agricultural "underdevelopment" in the third world and here at home. As we will see, the increasing concentration of control over farmland, the rapid loss of soil and water resources, and the growing dependence on a narrow range of export crops that characterize third world agriculture are also occurring in the United States.

But there is another, perhaps even more important, parallel. Throughout the world—be it the United States, Gua-

Figure 1–1
Increase in U.S. Agricultural Exports, 1960–1981

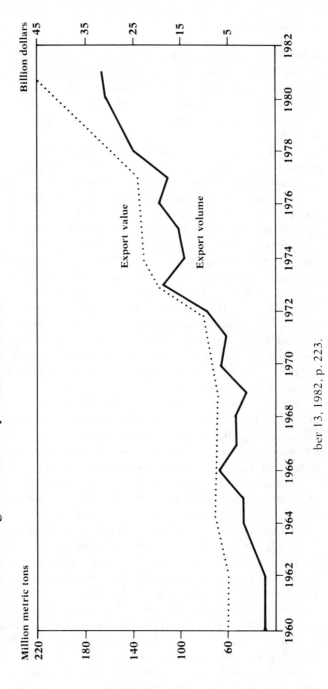

ber 13, 1982, p. 223.

temala, France, or the Soviet Union—the crisis of food and agriculture indicates an unwillingness to confront fundamental causes. Instead, government and corporate decisionmakers are allowed to administer—in ever larger doses—the deadly potions that created the illness in the first place.

The narrow interest groups that benefit from current economic arrangements continue to work their will, while the majority of us find it increasingly difficult to look critically at our own system and locate the source of our problems. Often, we defer to those in power simply because it is so difficult to judge the real costs of our present course, particularly since many such costs are hidden. Our major tasks in this book, therefore, are to uncover these hidden costs and to show how the basic forces that define growth in our agricultural system are destroying our food security.

In preparing this book, we made some important discoveries. First, *a few benefit at the expense of the many in our farm and food economy*. This is the central message of our book. How and why this occurs is the story we tell in these pages—a story whose lessons are crucial to securing our personal and global welfare.

Second, as we evaluate the winners and losers in a decade of rising exports, we find that ours is not a search for villains. We will see that winners and losers cannot be simply explained by conspiracies or the abuse of economic power. To truly understand the root causes of our farm and food problems we must probe the very foundation of our economic system and trace how the ground rules governing its operation create winners and losers in an increasingly inequitable, unstable, and inefficient manner.

Third, our country's failure to address problems at their source means that we have dealt only with their surface manifestations. Cause and effect have been confused and solutions such as the export push have diverted our attention from more basic issues and masked the underlying forces that hurt the majority in our society and abroad.

Fourth, these underlying forces determine the way *growth* occurs in our farm and food economy, through basic rules of the game governing how profits are accumulated—unevenly, and at the expense of most who participate in the economy. As we realize that this process works in self-reinforcing fashion, we see that understanding and changing the rules that perpetuate it is the key to real solutions.

Fifth, given the unbalanced way our mechanisms of growth operate, a production push such as the export boom serves only to strengthen the dominant position of a few better-off producers and to intensify a range of existing problems inherent in how this mechanism works to the disadvantage of the many. Thus, the export push of the 1970s is a powerful tool for understanding this process. It serves as a lens through which we can see how our system works and how the solutions advocated by policymakers actually exacerbate the problems they claim to be solving. *The export boom itself is not the cause of this basic problem.* These causes lie elsewhere, deeply embedded in the very structure of the food economy itself and in the economic ground rules that determine its path of growth.

With these basic points as a guide, let us begin our journey toward a deeper understanding of the food crisis we face by sketching the main features of our food economy and the basic dynamics that animate it. Soon we will see why John Block ended up in China, believing that the solution to America's farm depression lay in creating a billion new doughnut lovers.

2 The ABCs of the Food Economy

Pushing a basket down the supermarket aisle, few of us are likely to give much thought to the food production system that brings us the bounty we see on the shelves. While we notice the rise in food prices each time we pass the cash register, most Americans are not aware that something is very wrong with our farm and food system. We read disquieting headlines, but have difficulty piecing together the full story.

This chapter provides a framework for understanding how our farm and food economy works so we can begin to untangle the contradictions and probe the roots of the problems highlighted in the last chapter. Armed with some basic tools to demystify our system, we can trace the impact of the export boom and the economic processes it has reinforced. In presenting these basics as a foundation for the rest of the book, three major points are of essential importance.

First, the farm economy cannot be understood in isolation from the rest of the food economy. In particular, the relationship between the agricultural and industrial sectors of the food system is central to this understanding.

Second, we must consider this relationship as it has developed historically. This allows us to identify the root causes generating the imbalance of power between these sectors and to understand how this imbalance has persisted—leading to the current crisis.

Third, these root causes go to the very heart of how our economy is organized. We must identify how the basic ground rules of profit accumulation have shaped growth in both the farming and industrial sectors to systematically benefit a few at the expense of the many.

An Introduction to Our Economic Ground Rules

Certain elementary facts of economic life are so obvious that we can easily fail to appreciate their significance. We must start with these basics—the ground rules that shape growth in our economic system—to see how they have operated over time and how they connect with the problems we review in later chapters. In defining these elements as "ground rules," however, it is important to realize that they are not in any sense "made up" by the participants in the economic activity they govern. Rather, they are a product of history and embody the fact that we have an economy organized by a set of social arrangements called capitalism. As such, our ground rules are the basic determinants of how we do business as a society.

In America, the fundamental ground rule (the "bottom line" so familiar to all of us) is that we have an economy of people in business to make money. We have a system of private enterprise in which owners of businesses make individual decisions about what to produce based on the quest for profits—profits realized by selling their wares in the marketplace. A second ground rule governs how the first is pursued. Owners accumulate profits by widening the gap between what it costs to produce a commodity and the price received. They also increase profits by expanding sales so that a "growth imperative" is built into the way production is organized and producers are rewarded.

Our first two ground rules lead to a third. In order to successfully compete in this system, bigger enterprises are needed. For individual firms the growth imperative becomes a size imperative because technological innovations increase the scale of operations required just to meet the competition and stay in business. Greater use of technology both cuts costs through labor-saving devices and boosts output by increasing the total production from each worker—making more sales and bigger profits possible. Finally, this third ground rule produces a fourth. The size imperative results in a pattern of economic growth through consolidation within industries that gives a few large firms an ever bigger share of total sales and profits. Because operations unable to expand generally cannot survive the competitive struggle, they are squeezed out of business, often absorbed by their larger rivals.

Particularly in the major industrial sectors of the economy that rely most heavily upon technology, a handful of giant enterprises eventually come to dominate the industry. They grow to account for such a large share of total production that, as we will illustrate in the case of the food industry, they gain control over the market to influence price, supply, and demand to their mutual advantage. While competition among these giants remains, it becomes increasingly based on complex market strategies, such as advertising, packaging, and the introduction of "new" products, rather than on competitive pricing.

The strengths of our economic system in promoting efficiency, innovation, and growth are widely touted in our society. Our nation's productive capacity is generally regarded as the cornerstone of our country's greatness, as well as the foundation of our individual freedom and welfare. A glance at our crowded supermarket shelves seems to confirm the wisdom in our way of doing business.

But the impressive economic expansion that has characterized our nation's history can easily divert our attention from a clear view of what is wrong with our system and where the root causes of the problems it creates actually lie. Precisely because its vast outpouring of goods has come to represent "progress" in our economic life, "more is better" almost by definition. To most of us, "economics" is primarily a numbers game—pages of dry statistics and jagged lines on graphs. It is easy to forget that at bottom economics is about real people, the relationships among them, and the interests that guide them in their pursuits of material goals in life. The mathematical world of the economist encourages us to view the operation of our ground rules in cold, abstract terms that ignore the *relative positions of power* between groups within the economy—relationships crucial to understanding how things really work and who benefits.

To understand these power relations in our food economy and appreciate their implications, we must examine how our ground rules shape growth within its major sectors and how this growth affects the relationships among them. We can think of the food economy as consisting of four distinct stages or sectors that trade among themselves: *agricultural inputs*—the manufacture of those items, such as tractors and fertilizer, used by the farmer; *farming*—the food-raising process itself; *food processing*—the manufacture of raw food commodities into consumer items such as wheat into bread; and *food wholesaling and retailing*—the distribution chain that moves food from farmer to consumer. The relationships among these sectors and the terms of trade that define them determine whether our food economy stays in balance (i.e., whether it benefits one group more than another) and, more generally, how well it meets human needs.

We must ask how farmers as a whole fare in their transactions with other sectors of the food economy from whom they buy supplies and to whom they sell their produce. Within farming, how do the ground rules of our economic system determine which farmers are better off and which are struggling to survive? In international trade, how do they determine the distribution of food and its profits among the groups that participate: farmers, corporate enterprises in the other segments of the food economy, and people all over the world?

We will start by tracing how our ground rules have shaped growth in farming and in the industrial sectors of the food economy with which the farmer does business. The unequal economic power between the agricultural and industrial sectors of our food economy and the way this has systematically placed farmers at a disadvantage provides a key to the problems we review throughout this book. To fully understand how this uneven development has occurred, we must jump back in history well over a century to sketch the emergence of commercial agriculture in this country.

Our Economic Ground Rules Take Hold of Agriculture

In the early 1800s the United States was primarily a nation of farmers. Even as late as 1840, nearly 70 percent of the labor force were farmers,[1] and the bulk of farm produce went to feed the families that harvested it. Except for slave-based commercial agriculture in the South, American agriculture was dominated by small landholders and tenants who made most of the implements they needed to farm and in the main did not produce for the market.

But even in this early period, farmer indebtedness had created pressures for commercial agricultural activity and had begun to impose on farmers the ground rules governing business enterprise. As the frontier was pushed back during the first half of the nineteenth century, land speculators working with banks stayed just ahead of new immigrants, buying up land cheap and then reselling it for high profits. Many settlers went into debt to pay the high prices. This eventually created a pattern of heavily mortgaged ownership among farmers, who began producing more crops than needed for their own self-sufficiency. A cash crop was needed to pay creditors and prevent losing the land upon which their survival depended.[2]

The Civil War served as a major catalyst for the growth of commercial farming and ushered in a period which historian Wayne Rasmussen has called "the first American agricultural revolution." In the North wartime and foreign demand for food combined with labor shortages and high farm prices to fuel the shift from human power to horse power and to encourage a greater use of machinery on the farm to replace farmers who joined the army. By 1870 the boost in productivity from these developments, together with the postwar industrial expansion in the East, reduced the portion of those gainfully employed in farming to just over half of the total labor force. As the growing population of hungry factory workers created a new demand for food in the cities, farmers turned increasingly to production for urban markets. The shift to commercial agriculture was under way.[3]

It was to prove a revolution indeed, both for the farmer

and the rapidly industrializing nation the farmer increasingly served. Like factory owners and other businessmen before them, as farmers produced for the market they fell under the ground rules of profit accumulation that govern all successful enterprises in our economy. For farmers, it was a move deeper into an economic setting in which the cards were increasingly stacked against them.

First, in contrast to nearly all other businesses, farms were by far the most vulnerable to nature. In the nineteenth century, before government crop insurance, just one year's drought could throw a farmer into a lifetime debt cycle. Since nature, not market projections and the regulation of factory output, determined the timing of a farmer's production, farming was tied to seasonal cycles in which all production hit the market simultaneously, pressing prices downward.

Second, farmers depended on others to transport their goods long distances to market. Throughout the nineteenth century, and particularly after the Civil War, canals, river transport, and the developing railroad system provided access to markets, but at high shipping costs. In 1869, for example, an eastern canal syndicate, the "Erie Ring," made $12 million on the nation's wheat crop while farmers earned only $8 million.[4] During the second half of the nineteenth century, the growing power of the railroad barons to charge high freight rates put increasing pressure on farmers to produce more crops to make the shipments to market worthwhile.

Third, farmers' indebtedness was exacerbated by their dependency on local merchants for essentials such as cloth, sugar, shoes, tools, wagons, etc. In the South following the Civil War, for example, local merchants sold goods on credit to farmers with no cash, taking a lien on the farmer's crop for security. The effective prices charged were often double what the cash buyer paid, leaving many farmers in a state of perpetual debt bondage.

Farmers trying to survive and succeed in the mid-1800s had to compete among themselves for urban markets that were controlled by powerful eastern mercantile interests or for sales to the food processors who served those markets. Meat packers such as Phillip Armour and Gustavus

Swift and millers such as Charles A. Pillsbury began to work with the railroads to control the commodity markets by using their combined storage and transport arrangements to affect bidding and to control the prices of grain and beef.

The lower prices farmers received put more pressure on them to increase their harvests, and other businessmen began to invest in the production of farm implements to take advantage of such pressures. By the 1850s, John Deere, Cyrus McCormick, and others started to produce major types of agricultural machinery, and by the beginning of the Civil War they were providing customers with steel and chilled iron plows, horse rakes, seed drills, corn planters, disk harrows, cultivators, mowers, binders, and threshing machines.[5]

Such developments in food processing and farm machinery reinforced the earlier pattern of farm indebtedness begun by the banks and land speculators. Frundt describes the results of this "first agricultural revolution":

> Many farmers purchased these machines to increase production, hoping to avoid foreclosure on their mortgages. By the first half of 1865, for example, they had bought more than 250 thousand reaper-mowers. To make full use of their machines, however, they needed more acreage. Thus they borrowed more funds to buy the machines and the additional land to be cultivated by machine agriculture. A farmer's share decreased still further as the railroads and grain dealers took more of a chunk from the selling price. As in the past, this forced the farmers to increase production at even higher rates in order to avoid losing their lands through indebtedness. Thus a vicious cycle reinforced the growth of commercial agriculture.[6]

This cycle in the 1800s foreshadowed the continuing unequal relationship between the farmers and the rest of the food economy.

Agriculture vs. Industry: No Contest

The pattern of industrial expansion in the last half of the nineteenth century created financial panics and economic crises. To boost profits, industrialists cut costs by employing hungry and unorganized immigrants at miserably low wages. Unfettered by antimonopoly law, for those with capital this "was a period of cutthroat competition in which the big fish swallowed the little fish and then tried to eat one another," according to historian Samuel Eliot Morrison. Trusts froze out competitors by cutting prices below costs and giving illegal rebates. In the words of Theodore Roosevelt, "the industrial overlords . . . increased with giant strides."

As the nascent farm supply, food processing, and marketing sectors of the food economy expanded, the quest for profits and the imperative to grow in order to survive led to consolidation of operations under ever larger corporate umbrellas. Beef and grain trusts emerged and began to engage in monopolistic practices that placed farmers at an ever greater disadvantage. Writers such as Hamlin Garland, Frank Norris, and Upton Sinclair graphically portrayed the links between the railroads and food processors and their tightening control over the food economy. By deliberately timing grain deliveries to produce price-depressing gluts on the market, for example, and by charging small growers exorbitant freight rates, these corporate giants padded their profits at the farmer's expense.[7]

During this time, as settlers moved westward to homestead new land, the number of farms and farmers continued to grow, even though as a percentage of the work force they continued to decline. With more acres put to plow and with the boost in productivity provided by new agricultural technology, total farm production increased well beyond domestic needs. Price-depressing gluts coupled with the growing economic power of those with whom farmers did business only intensified the vicious cycle of overproduction that had encouraged the growth of commercial agriculture during its first revolution.

Agricultural surpluses served vital purposes for the urban industrialists, who came to increasingly dominate the economy during this period. Low farm prices helped keep food cheaper for workers in the city, allowing factory owners to keep workers' wages low and their own profits high.

In addition, the cheap surplus food proved an attractive item on the world market and made it possible to pay for foreign raw materials and capital goods needed to fuel industrial expansion at home. Agricultural exports nearly tripled between 1870 and 1900, while urban industrialists successfully lobbied for tariffs on the importation of manufactured goods to restrict foreign competition and boost their own prices in domestic markets. As historian Louis Hacker observed, the farmer became both the tool and the victim of the rise of American industrialization. As a tool, his surpluses helped industry develop during this period of high tariffs; as a victim, he paid higher prices for protected goods as well as high interest and freight rates.[8]

Farmers did not stand by passively. Nineteenth-century farm history is the story of farmers' attempts to join together and thereby reduce their dependence on banks, railroads, manufacturers, and merchants. By 1890 the National Farmers Alliance boasted a million members and had begun to organize farmers by establishing farmer-run marketing and supply cooperatives and by planning a farmer-controlled banking system. But within two decades the movement was in disarray. Farmers failed to gain the necessary support of unorganized workers in the city, and the "democratic promise" held out by the agrarian populist movement collapsed under the "economic, political, and moral authority [of] . . . 'corporate capital,'" as historian Lawrence Goodwyn has pointed out.[9]

The Vise Tightens

As the American economy matured in the late nineteenth and early twentieth centuries, the different patterns of development that characterized the corporate and farming sectors of the food system became increasingly evident and problematic. Underlying both patterns, however, were the same ground rules of profit and growth. The drive for profits led both farmers and industrialists to cut costs and boost output. Both increased their use of technology to achieve these ends. But the adoption of labor-saving devices on the farm and in the corporate sphere had different results. Farmers were squeezed in the vise of the farm supply industry's growing economic power on the one hand and the food processors and marketers on the other.[10]

The few large firms that emerged from the decades of cutthroat competition quickly learned to avoid price cutting by tacitly cooperating in a policy of "administered pricing" that kept their profits high. By 1936, for example, four firms sold more than three fourths of all important farm implements. Since a few firms controlled the bulk of production, they could control the market by agreeing to "follow the leader" in price hikes during booms and to hold prices rigid during downturns by cutting back on production. For example, during the Great Depression, industry cut its production of farm equipment by 80 percent, resulting in a wholesale price decrease of only 15 percent. But farmers were able to cut their production by only 6 percent; so the prices they received for farm produce dropped 63 percent.[11]

These figures illustrate the contrast between the administered prices of the corporation and the free market prices of the farmer in the twenties and thirties. Unlike industry, the drive for profits in agriculture did not result in monopoly growth. The population of corn and wheat producers was not narrowed nearly to the same degree as were manufacturers of major industrial goods. Farmers continued to face highly competitive markets that pitted many producers against each other, forcing them to take whatever price was offered.

In the period just prior to and during World War I, foreign demand for agricultural exports and a growing domestic population supported increased farm production, resulting in a rough balance between the incomes of farmers and those of the rest of the economy. After World War I, this brief respite in farmers' fortunes reversed, and the vise that had slowly tightened on American agriculture for decades became a stranglehold. Europe could no longer afford to buy much American food, and foreign demand for our agricultural surplus declined sharply. In addition, the rate of growth in the domestic market contracted. With the end of heavy immigration, the American population was no longer rapidly increasing. Even when per capita incomes rose, the portion spent on food did not rise proportionately, since demand for food is limited physiologically while demand for industrial goods is not.

In the summer of 1920 farm prices collapsed and sent American agriculture into a decade of depression that only worsened when the Great Depression hit the rest of the economy in 1929. During the 1920s, cash receipts from farming plummeted by 75 percent. By the year of the big crash, per capita income of farmers was just one third that of the rest of the population. Mortgage debt as a percentage of farm value more than doubled. By 1930 only a quarter of all farm operators owned mortgage-free farms, compared with over half in 1890. In the decade after 1925, almost a third of all farms changed hands by involuntary sale.[12]

Individual farmers responded to shrinking profit margins by redoubling efforts to expand production—hoping to make up in volume what was lost in price. This drove them further into the arms of industry—not only as the major outlet for their produce, but also for products that would help them raise output on the existing land base. Continued overproduction further depressed farm prices and made agriculture even more vulnerable to the pricing power of the farm supply industry.

Witnessing how increased production meant lower returns to farmers, journalists began to speak of the "farm problem"—a term that remains in use to this day. Something had to be done. This was obvious even to industry— but not out of charitable concern. The imbalance of power between agriculture and industry benefited industry but not if that imbalance became too extreme. For if the squeeze on farmers undercut all incentive to produce for the market, industrial interests would be hurt, too, since the price of food would go up and force wages up as well.

Government to the Rescue?

After the 1920s decade of failed attempts to enact legislation protecting farmers from contracting markets and rising costs, the government took a decisive step with its New Deal farm programs of the thirties. Through the Agricultural Adjustment Act of 1933, the government introduced a program of agricultural price supports and production controls to mitigate the twin problems of over-production and low farm income. The Commodity Credit Corporation was set up to purchase surplus farm commodities, support prices with loans to farmers, and enter into production contracts with farmers to control output.

In general, New Deal policies reflected an effort to do what the competitive "free market" for farm commodities could not—protect agriculture by giving farmers the same kind of shelter from market forces that the farm supply and food processing industries developed through their monopolistic control over the price and output levels of their products.

But there were limits to the government's efforts. Sectors of the food economy dominated by shared monopolies had a vested interest in current arrangements. And the economic power they had gained over the last century gave them a growing influence over government policy. This is vividly illustrated by the fate of a critical provision of the 1933 farm legislation.

The provision legislated a tax on food processors to underwrite the new farm programs. The tax seemed appropriate as a means to return to farmers a portion of the financial loss they experienced as these firms disproportionately profited from low farm prices. But this step amounted to more than a government prop for the farm sector. It amounted to a direct redistribution of the relative economic benefits between the agricultural and industrial sectors. While the food processing industry was clearly interested in preserving the basic health of the farm economy, it was not prepared to achieve this in a way that seriously transgressed the mechanisms of profit accumulation that supported its own economic growth.

The constitutionality of the tax was appealed to the United States Supreme Court. The court's decision is revealing. The high court found that the tax provisions of the 1933 law unduly penalized one branch of industry for what it preferred to see as a broad "social problem." In 1938 the financial burden for New Deal farm programs was shifted to the taxpaying public—where it has remained.

Government and Our Ground Rules: No Contest

In comparative historical terms, the New Deal went far in addressing the chronic overproduction and resulting low farm income synonymous with what had come to be called the farm problem. It set the basic parameters of farm policy to the present day. But its limitations are the key to understanding what it did and did not do. Under the New Deal, government attempted to resolve contradictions in the nation's economy that had brought it to (and beyond) the brink of disaster. Left untouched, the dynamics of growth in the food system—to say nothing of the entire domestic economy—had demonstrated a capacity for instability and human deprivation too painful to leave to its own devices to repair. But rather than a fundamental redesign of the engines of growth, government policy instead tried to put the existing economic machinery back into operation—preserving the basic mechanisms that held it together.

The implications were crucial for the future of American farm policy. For New Deal farm policy set as its task the overall adjustment of supply and demand for agricultural commodities. In so doing, it defined a policy arena that stopped at the boundaries of the farm economy itself. It dealt only with the adverse market *effects* of the vise that had closed in on farmers and failed to address the basic ground rules of growth that were the *cause* of the vise and of the problems in the marketplace because of its tightening squeeze.

As a result, farm policy became trapped by the same forces that had created the need for such policies in the first place. The ground rules of growth-through-greater-profits that had fueled industrial expansion and its consolidation into mammoth operating units lay outside the purview of New Deal legislation. By addressing only the unequal market power between these giants and farmers, and leaving the process that created that inequality intact, the government resigned itself to the Sisyphus-like task of continually trying to roll farm prices upward, only to watch them roll back down again because of forces beyond its control. Thus, in spite of government attempts to soften the blows, farmers remained increasingly caught between the rigid, noncompetitive prices for farm supplies from industry on one side and ever lower prices for their crops in highly competitive markets on the other.

The bind in which both farmers and policymakers found themselves by the time the Great Depression hit reflected an *overall* pattern of development in the food economy. This had profound implications for the way our ground rules of profit accumulation and growth perpetuated a set of key mechanisms *within* the farm economy that defined the continuing plight of farmers over the next fifty years. These mechanisms—the cost/price squeeze, the production treadmill, and the boom/bust cycles of agricultural production—determine the day-to-day economic realities farmers face as a consequence of the way our society does business.

The Cost/Price Squeeze

Since the New Deal, the growth dynamics fueling the monopoly power of industry, together with government policies that stopped short of directly intervening in these dynamics, have effectively institutionalized the weak position of farmers. The ground rules governing development in the corporate and farming sectors of the food economy kept farmers in the role of *price takers*, at the mercy of the large enterprises with whom they did business, who had become *price makers*. The result has been a cost/price squeeze on farmers that intensifies as costs of production rise and crop prices remain inadequate. Figure 2–1 graphically illustrates this squeeze, tracing the worsening relationship between prices paid and prices received by farmers from 1910 to 1982 (except for brief periods during war years).

Even today a wheat farmer in Kansas competes with hundreds of thousands of farmers throughout the world who produce the same crop. By contrast, as we explore in more detail in chapters 5 and 6, a grain trader, farm equipment manufacturer, or food processor has only a handful of other giant firms to contend with. In a sense, farmers may be the last of the true competitors in a society that holds free competition as an article of faith.

Figure 2–1
Index of Prices Paid and Prices Received by Farmers, 1910–1981
(1910–14 = 100)

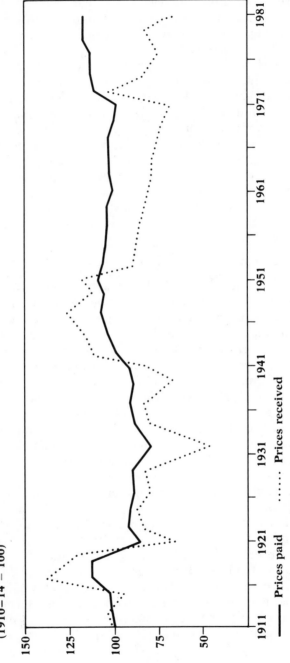

Data from USDA, *Agricultural Prices—Annual Summary, 1980.*

In this position, they reap no permanent gain. Even when increased demand pushes up prices for agricultural commodities, prices for fertilizers, tractors, combines, seeds, and irrigation equipment also rise, reducing farmers' real incomes. And the prices for these farming inputs remain high even when the prices farmers are getting begin to fall. Because the farmer cannot individually influence total output and engage in administered pricing, the prices farmers receive have no relation to their costs of production.

Farmers are squeezed, not just by the rising costs of supplies, but by two other rising costs over which they have no control. First, the price of a farmer's basic raw material—the land itself—climbs, not just because of pressure from farmers seeking to expand on a land base that has become fixed with the closing of the frontier, but as outside speculators seek a safe investment as well. This was especially true in the 1970s, as we will see in chapter 3. The net effect of this process is to transfer returns that would otherwise go to farmers as income into rising farmland value that disproportionately benefits the few who own most of the land. Second, the more farmers depend on costly industrial inputs, the more they need credit. So farmers have become more vulnerable to bank policies and interest rates.

In addition, rising costs have also tightened the squeeze by indirectly putting downward pressure on farm commodity prices themselves. The increased pressure on farmers to raise output to make up for slimmer profit margins has intensified the problem of overproduction and further lowered their earnings. Farmers are caught in a vicious circle of low farm income, which exacerbates chronic overproduction and leads to lower prices still, while the government wrestles with the problem of what to do with the farm surpluses that have piled up year after year.

The Production Treadmill

Since World War II, and particularly after the Korean War, the cost/price squeeze has placed the entire farm sector on a "production treadmill," forcing farmers to run faster just to stay in the same place financially. Wartime

Figure 2–2
Net Income of Farm Operators as a Percentage of Gross Income, 1910–1981

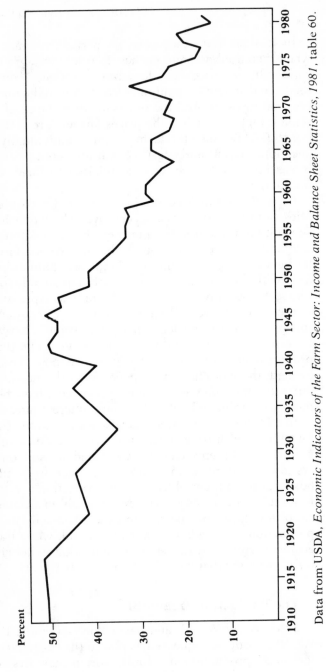

Data from USDA, *Economic Indicators of the Farm Sector: Income and Balance Sheet Statistics, 1981*, table 60.

demand, high food prices, and the end of production controls opened the way for the adoption of farm technology that, after the war, left American farmers fully committed to a "technological imperative" in agricultural production. Between 1940 and 1977 the share of such technological inputs rose from one third to two thirds of all farm expenses—widening the farmer's exposure to the price-rigid markets of industrial suppliers and allowing them to take an ever larger chunk of the fruits of the farmer's labor. (See figure 2–2.) Meanwhile, the overproduction stimulated by technology cuts profits per acre and puts all farmers in a race to "grow or die" that few can survive, much less win.

This treadmill not only hurts many farmers. The technological imperative that quickens its pace is blind—and blinds us—to the devastation of natural resources such as soil and water that results from intensifying production, as we will see in chapters 4, 7, and 8.

The Boom/Bust Cycle

Dependent on the weather and harvest cycles, farming has always been subject to good and bad times. The production treadmill, the technological imperative, and the cost/price squeeze have exaggerated a "boom and bust" agriculture. Despite government production controls and farm price supports since the New Deal, agricultural commodity markets have remained highly competitive and subject to widely fluctuating prices. Periodic gluts of farm produce hit the market and cause busts in farm prices. Even after prices drop, farmers step up production and oversupplies can drag on and deepen the trough. Since nothing farmers can do individually will get them out of a bust, it is likely to continue until some outside force—such as a major crop failure—jacks up the price again.

These peaks and valleys in the market from year to year further complicate survival in farming. As boom period profits contract or disappear during busts, farm income bobs up and down. (See figure 2–3.) At the bottom of these cycles all farmers are pressed. But larger producers and those with the most volume and equity in their land are better able to make it. As we document in the next chapter,

Figure 2–3
Net Income from Farming—Per Farm, 1940-1981
In Constant (1967) Dollars

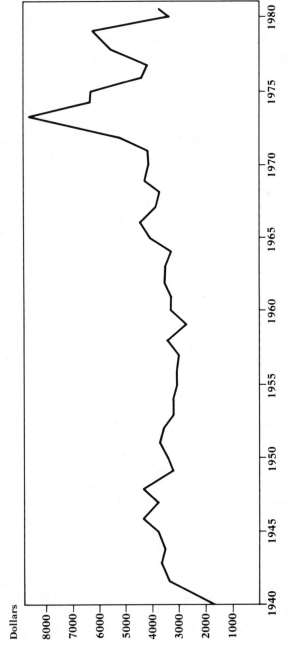

Data from USDA, *Economic Indicators of the Farm Sector: Income and Balance Sheet Statistics, 1981*, table 62.

it is not necessarily their superior efficiency but their larger cash flow and borrowing opportunities that allow such farmers to survive. Smaller and less established operations are more likely to be absorbed into the shrinking minority of larger operations in an increasing concentration of farm ownership that parallels the earlier fate of other profit-seeking enterprises in the farm input, food processing, and marketing sectors of the food economy. Since the mid-1930s farm numbers have steadily fallen from almost 7 million to less than 2.4 million today, while average farm size has increased from less than 150 acres to over 500.[13]

Government Policy as "Mission Impossible"

Farm policy since the New Deal has continued to seek ways out of the farm problem that have only reinforced the mechanisms perpetuating it. After World War II various programs designed to dispose of the burgeoning farm surpluses and subsidize flagging farm income characterized government policy. The production treadmill, fueled by higher yielding seeds and vast increases in pesticide and fertilizer use, resulted in a level of overproduction so high that by 1959 it had put the equivalent of a full year's harvest in government storage bins. By the 1960s the cost of farm programs that made the government "buyer of last resort" and a major subsidizer of agricultural prices had become increasingly difficult to justify. The annual budget for farm programs had risen from an average of $2 billion in the 1950s to over $5 billion by the mid-1960s, and a new system of direct payments to farmers made these costs much more visible. Urban legislators were increasingly reluctant to vote ever larger subsidies to a shrinking constituency in rural America—particularly as it became more obvious that these subsidies were disproportionately benefiting the largest producers.

Clearly, a reassessment of the New Deal farm package was needed. But how could government deal with the twin dilemmas of low farm income and overproduction now that the limits of its intervention had apparently been reached?

Exports to the Rescue

In 1965 President Johnson convened the Berg Commission of agribusiness executives and like-minded academics. The commission struck upon one central bright idea: turning to commercial markets abroad as the salvation of the farm sector.

Commission Chairman Sherwood O. Berg and his collaborators can hardly be credited with originality. While prior to the 1920s agricultural exports played a key role in promoting domestic expansion as an important source of foreign exchange to buy raw materials for industry, by the 1960s, the old export strategy had a new rationale. Now the urgent goal was to get government out of the business of shoring up agricultural prices. Exports would do that, concluded the Berg Commission.

But where were these markets to be found? After the Korean War, the U.S. government came up with the PL–480 program to dispose of agricultural surpluses on less than commercial terms as food aid to third world nations. A combination of foreign trade barriers and domestic price support policies in the post–World War II era had rendered U.S. farm output both unattractive and unavailable to world commercial markets. But now, with the reconstruction of postwar economies abroad, the time seemed right to tap potential overseas demand for U.S. farm commodities.

This approach had particular appeal for corporations like John Deere and International Harvester. Greater production for foreign markets held out the prospect of stronger demand for the wide range of technological inputs on which the farmer had become increasingly dependent in the struggle to get more out of each acre. Rising exports also suited the strategies of food processors and retailers in the late 1960s. They were discovering limits to the variety of food products they could inventively package and convince American consumers to buy. They saw correctly that U.S. agricultural exports could help provide the raw farm commodities needed to support a shift to the American meat- and processed-food-centered diet that would create new consumers abroad.

What remained, then, was to lower trade barriers and phase out domestic price supports to permit the free flow of U.S. farm commodities into foreign markets—precisely the key policy recommendations of the Berg Commission.[14] But foreign demand did not materialize in the late 1960s, and by 1968 farm income had plummeted to historic lows not seen since the Great Depression. Although the Berg proposals fell flat, the farm export push had been officially revived. It was now an articulated policy at the highest levels of government, ready to claim a central role in U.S. strategies for coping with the global economic crisis in the following decade.

The Farm Problem: What It Is, and Isn't

The export push was successfully launched in 1972 with the Russian wheat deal, as we discuss in greater detail in chapter 9. The export push and the greater-markets-will-save-us premise it embodies simply reflect the continuing failure of policymakers to see the farm problem for what it really is—chronic overproduction and low farm income caused by the ground rules governing *production* in our food economy, rather than inadequate markets to absorb the resulting farm surpluses. In this sense, the export-oriented policies of the past decade fit neatly with traditional supply and demand prescriptions pursued since the New Deal, even as they attempt to extricate the government from subsidies historically associated with such farm programs.

As long as the imperative of growth through profit accumulation continues, so will overproduction. As chapter 3 details, seeking bigger markets abroad does nothing to alleviate this cycle. On the contrary, by *encouraging* greater production, the export push actually *accelerates* the cost/price squeeze, production treadmill, and boom/bust agriculture that contribute to the farm problem.

The inability to appreciate the actual distribution of rewards within this system has led some farm economists—both in and out of government—to turn the farm problem on its head and proclaim that since fewer can survive in farming it simply means there are too many farmers! For them, the demise of the "family farm" only reflects the necessary shakeout of inefficient producers. Rising farm debt, the increasingly unfavorable relationship between prices paid and received by farmers, and falling net farm income can easily be minimized or explained away. In the words of one such observer, published during the depths of the farm depression in 1983,

> None of these trends are indicative of a progressive impoverishment of the farm sector. The ratio of prices received to prices paid by farmers is falling because productivity in U.S. agriculture (output per unit of input) is rising faster than the rest of the economy. Total real farm income is misleading because that income is now divided among fewer farms and far fewer people (less than one fifth the number of people are engaged in agriculture than forty years ago); and because farmers now derive a larger (and still increasing) portion of their total income from nonfarm sources (55 percent, on average, in the past five years as compared with 30 percent forty years ago). Farm debts in 1982 were still only 18 percent of real assets—slightly higher than in 1970 and about the same as in 1940.[15]

These observations, while typical of apologetic views of the farm problem, are nonetheless remarkable—both for the facts they ignore or distort and for the realities they refuse to face.

First, the attempt to dismiss falling total real farm income by suggesting it is divided among far fewer people (while certainly true) is itself grossly misleading. As figure 2–4 shows, real net farm income *per farm* has *also* stagnated since World War II (except for a few boom years). In the early 1980s it stood at levels, adjusted for inflation, that were lower than all but a handful of years since 1940 and lower than any year since 1963. Moreover, the fact that this stagnant income situation has been increasingly supplemented by off-farm income backhandedly proves the key point: unable to rely on farming as a sole source of income, more and more farmers have had to turn to outside jobs to remain in farming. That hardly establishes the health of the farm sector; it simply underlines the basic problems we have described in this chapter.

Further, the comparison of debts and assets overall is

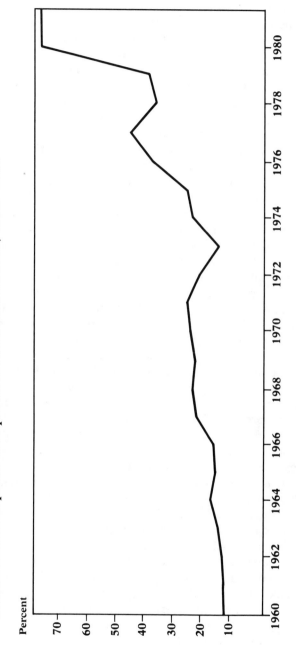

Figure 2–4
Farm Interest Expense Compared to Net Farm Income, 1960–1981

Data from USDA, *Economic Indicators of the Farm Sector: Income and Balance Sheet Statistics, 1981*, tables 41 and 60.

also seriously misleading and ignores the extremely uneven distribution of both within farming. As we will more
fully explore in the next chapter, tightening control over
asset ownership—5 percent of farmers now own half the
land—means that relatively few receive most of the benefits from the land price inflation most responsible for the
rising value of assets. On the other hand, growing debt hits
the majority without a large asset base the hardest. Interest payments alone rose to 80 percent of net farm income in
1980—up from 24 percent in 1970—a fact buried in the
celebration of the inflated paper value of assets. Tragically,
the rise in the value of farm assets has increased the ratio of
debt to income, as more farmers have borrowed against
equity in a desperate effort to cover increased yearly operating expenses and still have enough left to live on. As this
avenue has been exhausted for many during the farm depression of the early eighties, bankruptcy has resulted.

And finally, the claim that the chronic decline in the
ratio of prices received to those paid by farmers simply reflects growing productivity in the farm sector as compared
to the rest of the economy confuses apparent efficiency
with the results of unequal economic power in the food
economy that puts a cost/price squeeze on farmers. Thus
the "productivity" that results is largely a reflection of the
way this "grow or die" squeeze produces chronic overproduction and functions to disproportionately benefit
other sectors of the food economy in their transactions
with farmers. The cold mathematics of "greater output per
unit of input" ignores the fact that the key "input" is the
farmer's labor—kept cheap by the production treadmill.
Further, as we will show in more detail in the next chapter,
this treadmill has actually pushed the size of farms that
now produce over half our food *beyond* the scale of operations which can be justified on the grounds of efficiency.

At the root of these problems lie our economic ground
rules. As we hope to show throughout this book, the growth
and size imperatives they define produce a pattern of development in which a few systematically benefit at the expense of the many in our farm and food economy. Before we
can seek lasting solutions, we must understand how the
profit accumulation at the heart of our economic system

inherently results in this outcome. By creating huge corporations that depend on monopoly profits to enable them to grow, our ground rules mandate a circle of wealth creating more wealth. Thus simply "righting the balance" in our farm and food economy (as government since the New Deal has attempted) will not work. The imbalances that generate the cost/price squeeze arise from a concentration in ownership of productive assets that is *built into* the process of economic expansion and cannot be "righted" under the current ground rules.

Once we understand this, we can begin to make sense of it all—even of the apparent paradox of soaring farm bankruptcies after a decade of record sales. We are armed against government policymakers and others who will tell us that the farm problem is "too many farms" or simply "overproduction" and have some basic tools to expose these issues as only the surface manifestation of much deeper problems—problems based in the ground rules at the very foundation of our economic system.

Our Challenge—Asking the Right Questions

In this chapter we have raised basic questions regarding how our food economy works, and in whose interests. In exploring the impact of the export push on our food production system, we need to look critically at the very assumptions that defend our economic ground rules:

- *They're fair because anyone can compete.* In the next chapter we'll begin to examine this issue in more detail, tracing the fate of farmers over the past decade as they've been forced to run ever faster on the production treadmill just to stay in the same place. In later chapters we'll explore competition elsewhere in the food economy to answer the question, Is this a fair and open system or one closed to virtually all but those with the wealth and sales volume to compete?

- *We all gain from the resulting productivity.* In chapter 6 we will take a look at where our food dollar goes and why it buys us less. In other chapters we will ask, Who benefits and who is hurt by the cornucopia of food we produce?

- *The marketplace reflects the majority of individual preferences.* As we trace the impact of rising exports, we'll explore to what degree the market is governed by individual choices and to what degree by the interests of producers with greatly varying power. Does the marketplace ensure that production for profit is also production for human need?

- *Any destructive or unfair side effects are worth the price because the system is so productive.* But are we even informed about the price—not just in individuals losing the opportunity to farm and the destruction of rural life, but in the natural resource costs that go with all-out production for export?

- Most important of all, *our system ensures that those who produce are given full reward for their efforts.* In examining the winners and losers in a decade of rising exports we are forced to ask, Is this really true or are a few benefiting at the expense of the many who are systematically robbed of the full fruits of their labor by a process that ensures that wealth begets more wealth?

By encouraging Americans to look critically at these widely accepted economic rationales, we hope this book will open the door to a new understanding of our food problems. We hope to focus attention squarely on the most important question of all: How do we begin to build a society that holds human justice and welfare paramount and affords all opportunities to work toward achieving it?

3 Export Boom and Bust: How the "Stompers" Win*

"We've worked hard for thirty years to build this farm. Last month we filed bankruptcy. My husband was so depressed we had to stay with him all the time. He blamed himself. He felt like he'd let the kids down."—Iowa farmer, 1983

"I know farmers who are building fires in the kitchen sink and turning to food giveaways for help."—Iowa farmer, 1983

"I'm going to fight this [foreclosure]. I will not be stolen from any more. I used to think this was such a great country, but I'm not so sure any more. I used to think so but we're losing it."—South Dakota farmer, 1983.

These farmers tell of hardship, disillusionment, and anger as tens of thousands of efficient farmers are losing their life's work. Their defeated dreams reflect a decisive step in an economic and cultural transformation that is both historical and contemporary. It is rooted in the last century, as we have just seen, but the mechanisms driving it have intensified during our lifetimes, even in the last decade. In this transformation:

- The size and wealth of an enterprise are rewarded above efficiency, sacrifice, and good management.
- Ownership rights come to rest in fewer and fewer hands.
- Decision-making power is increasingly removed from those who do the work.
- opportunity is closed to all except those already economically established.

*By Frances Moore Lappé.

But how can we be moving in such a direction—one that undermines the well-being of tens of thousands of farmers and would-be farmers and belies the structure of work and community life widely associated with a democratic society?

To find an answer, we will trace American agriculture through the farm export boom of the 1970s and the bust that followed. We will examine what has happened to American farmers during a period, not of market stagnation, but of great market *success*—a sixfold increase in the value of farm export sales and almost a tripling of volume in just one decade. We will ask, Which farmers have benefited from this striking growth? Which farmers have been most hurt by the bust? What meaning does it have for the rest of us? The answers to these questions have much to do with two forces—*inflation* and *risk*, both heightened by the massive expansion in farm exports. In this chapter we will discover the consequences of the underlying ground rules of our economy that were suggested in the last chapter.

Inflation and economic risk are not like the weather, hitting big and small alike; they discriminate. Those at the top of the farm ladder—with gross sales of $200,000 and over and those with considerable equity in their land—are able to handle inflation and economic uncertainties in ways denied to mid-sized farms—those with $40,000 to somewhat over $100,000 in gross sales.

Most proponents of export market expansion claim that it is a great boon to overall farm income. Therefore, before we look at the impact of the export boom *within* agriculture, let's look at its impact on the agricultural economy as a whole.

The Glorious Promises

In the early 1970s, the government told farmers that expanding export markets would finally bring their long-awaited prosperity. Plant "fence row to fence row" for booming exports, was Secretary of Agriculture Earl Butz's famous advice to farmers in 1973. And, the promises came true! Sales and prices did rise. After the 1972 Soviet purchase of 18 million tons of wheat and the next two years of tight supplies, the prices of feed grains more than doubled and food grain prices tripled by 1974. Sure enough, the boom did come for farmers. Compared to 1971, net farm income doubled by 1973. In fact, 1973 was among the best years for farm income in this century.[1]

But, throwing the fate of American farmers into the international sales arena, the government lifted production controls and set price supports too low to protect most farmers from low commodity prices. By 1976, while exports continued to climb, farm income staggered. After a moderate boom in 1979, farmers in the early 1980s were sinking into the worst farm depression since the 1930s— even though production controls were periodically reintroduced after 1975, price supports raised, and a record $12 billion was put into government payments made to farmers in 1982.

How could a decade of high sales—exactly what would lead to prosperity for, say, the auto industry—lead to depression for farmers? To understand, we must look at the repercussions set off throughout the economy by this sudden farm sales boom.

Fallout from the Export Boom

First, *food prices shot up*. Between early 1972 and mid-1975, the consumer price index for food rose 48 percent. Most of this increase did not reach the farmer. The portion of our rising food prices that went to nonfarm labor, packaging, transportation, corporate profits, advertising, etc., rose more than three times faster than the portion going to farmers. The amount Americans were paying for food that actually went to the farmer increased only 8 percent during these years.[2]

When commodity prices are high, food processors and retailers pass on their costs through higher consumer prices, often adding enough to ensure higher profits for themselves. Between 1973 and 1975, after-tax profits of food corporations rose by 54 percent, more than any other component of the nation's food bill. But when commodity prices drop, consumer prices are miraculously insulated. They do not fall. Food prices still pushed upward even after commodity prices began to fall in 1975.[3]

Second, *prices of farm supplies soared*, as farmers rushed out to purchase needed production supplies with their new income. "I bought a tractor with equipment in 1952 for $3,600," recalled cotton farmer Herman Lorenz of New Deal, Texas. "Now you can't even buy the wheels for $3,600!"[4] Lorenz was largely reacting to the way prices leapt upward in the 1970s. Arriving in unexpected big chunks, rather than steady, reliable increases, the new income appeared to many farmers as perhaps their only chance to buy that long-wished-for piece of equipment.

Then, along with inflation in the rest of the economy— caused by higher petroleum prices, devaluations of the dollar, and so on—rising food prices forced workers to demand higher wages just to maintain their purchasing power. Higher wages, added to the rising costs of petroleum used in manufacturing meant higher production costs for farm supply industries. But they were not about to see their profits shrink. Highly concentrated (two firms control half the tractor sales and four corner almost 60 percent of all pesticide sales), the farm supply industry—like food processors and retailers—could pass on its rising production costs to farmers through what economists call "cost-plus" pricing.

Given both the sudden spurt in demand and rising costs, it's little wonder that prices of tractors, combines, trucks, pesticides, and fertilizers climbed faster than the general inflation rate. In the six years prior to 1973, the price of tractors rose 37 percent; in the five years following 1973, the price jumped by 200 percent.[5]

The farm supply industry found it easy to make these higher prices stick because farmers were eager purchasers. Many had "received incomes never imagined before . . . [and were] challenged to find ways to reduce their taxable income," explained Lyle Schertz of the USDA.[6] Buying new capital equipment was a smart way to take advantage of tax incentives, such as the investment tax credit and the accelerated depreciation allowance.

Third, *the price of farmland tripled* in nominal value during the 1970s and rose by 60 percent (after adjusting for inflation). Farmland prices climbed twice as fast as overall inflation. "They ain't making any more land so we'd better get ours while we can—that's what people were thinking," said one Kansas farmer, explaining why some farmers rushed to purchase additional acres in the mid-seventies with their hefty new export-generated incomes. Given historically falling income per acre, buying more land, if you could, seemed like a necessity to some. Others no doubt saw the chance to make a killing by expanding their operations to take advantage of booming markets abroad.

In the ten states with the greatest export growth over the 1970s, all but three saw land values climb significantly faster than the national average for farmland. In the big export states of Minnesota, Iowa, Illinois, and Indiana, for example, land values increased from 18 percent to 38 percent above the average national increase between 1967 and 1979.[7]

But farmers were not the only buyers pressing farmland prices up. Increasing uncertainty about long-term profitability in other sectors of the American economy led outside investors, including several major insurance companies, to take advantage of farmland values, which appeared to be rising indefinitely.

Fourth, *farm debt quadrupled*, totaling over $200 billion by 1983 as farmers sought bigger-than-ever loans to buy increasingly expensive land and equipment. With the heady prospect of ever-growing export markets, major farm lenders expanded their credit, facilitating farmers' increased demand for new equipment and farm real estate.[8] Credit from the Farmers Home Administration and the Federal Land Bank, with softer than commercial terms, grew from about one third to represent about one half of all farm real estate debt.[9] In fact, over half the total dollar volume of the Farmers Home Administration loans made since the agency's beginning has been loaned since 1975.[10]

Many farmers claim that lenders actively pressed farmers to expand. Iowa farmer Virginia Genzen said, "The lenders told us, 'We can't lend you any money if you stay static. You have to grow.'"[11] Other farmers were even more blunt: "They [Farmers Home Administration] almost hauled you in and stuffed the money down your shirt," observed Michigan farmer Merrie Kranz.[12]

Fifth, *interest rates more than doubled*, for reasons only partially linked to greater credit demands within agriculture. By 1982, on larger, capital-intensive farms, interest payments were accounting for as much as 30 percent of all expenses. "The lenders should have warned farmers that these interest rates—running as high as 20 percent— would kill them," said Melvin Schneider, former Iowa farmer and retired farm credit officer. "But, of course, a banker is not about to say that his product is going to give you a problem."[13]

These five dramatic changes—not caused by the export boom, of course, but clearly aggravated by it—begin to explain how a great surge in sales, which would mean prosperity to any highly concentrated industry, could help precipitate the second greatest depression of this century for the highly competitive farm sector.

Then, the Bust

Given the increased costs of farm supplies and rising land values and interest rates, is it surprising that export expansion failed to bring the golden era of American farming promised since the Nixon administration? While exports soared, net farm income stagnated or declined in seven of the nine years following 1973.

The export boom itself, as we've just seen, contributed to an inflationary spiral from which most farmers were hard pressed to protect themselves. Every industry on which farmers depend was able to pass on its mounting costs to farmers, and farmers competing for farmland pushed costs up still further. *Even by 1978, income per farm in real purchasing power was no greater than during the early 1960s.*[14] So all it took was a slowdown in the growth of exports— and a drop in the value of exports in 1982—to bring on disaster.

By 1982, net farm income per farm had sunk in real (1972) dollars to half of what it was in 1979.[15] Even by 1980 profit per acre had dropped to less than a third of the peak export boom year 1973, reinforcing a long-term trend.[16]

(See figures 2–3 and 3–1.) Average disposal personal income of the farm population plunged to 88 percent of the nonfarm population, from being approximately 100 percent during the late seventies.[17] "Farm depression" was no overstatement. In 1981, Minnesota's net income per farm dropped to just over $1,000; in Georgia, to $758.[18]

Not to worry, said the Reagan administration. Farmers' fortunes will rise again! In the fall of 1982 Secretary of Agriculture John Block reminded farmers that "we are in a growth market. Our potential—the human population—is growing all around the world. . . . I am confident we can turn the 1980s around and make them profitable."[19] What Block conveniently overlooked is that the human population is not a market; *only people with money to spend are a market.* In fact, the world population had been growing throughout the 1970s, and the United States still ended up with price-depressing surpluses.

The Reagan administration was quick to blame faltering prices on the slowdown in exports caused by the Carter administration's 1980 embargo on grain sales to the U.S.S.R. The embargo, it claimed, was responsible for the U.S. share of Soviet grain imports sliding from 70 to 30 percent over the following two years. But, according to Iowa State University economist Robert N. Wisner and his associate Massoud S. Denbaly, "The embargo probably reduced U.S. grain exports less than generally believed. . . . Contrary to popular belief, the share of U.S. farm products shipped to the Soviet Union has increased in the past five years."[20] Reagan's administration also pointed its finger at other countries' protectionist policies, the growing strength of the dollar (making our exports relatively more expensive), and the worldwide recession.

But debating why exports began to flag ignores the more basic question. Would sustained growth of sales alone have brought higher real income for farmers? Even *before* the slump in export growth, farmers had reaped no real income gain from booming exports. Between 1978 and 1980, *with export values still climbing,* net farm income sank by almost 40 percent. In 1967 dollars, 1980 net farm income was lower than half its average during the peak 1972–74 period. The answer is now in. Never has the greater-

Figure 3–1
Average Net Income per Acre from Farm Marketing, 1945–1979
In Constant (1972) Dollars

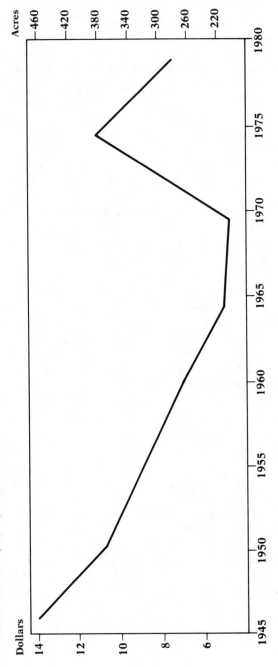

Adapted from US General Accounting Office, *An Assessment of Parity as a Tool for Formulating and Evaluating Agricultural Policy.*

markets-will-save-us strategy been so thoroughly tested as during the 1970s. And never has it so dramatically failed.

Others, including some farm organizations, blamed the 1980s farm depression on our government's failure to ensure that commodity prices cover the costs of production. But, considering the farm supply industry's ability to pass on its costs to farmers and that land prices inflate when agriculture looks profitable, would not such a commitment by the government, if nothing were done to make farmers less vulnerable to rising prices of land and farm supplies, just lead to a nightmare of forever-escalating costs for farmers? Unfortunately, yes. Thus, stable prices that cover the costs of efficient production must be seen as just one aspect of any strategy to protect farmers.

John Block says he's confident "we can turn the 1980s around and make them profitable." And he may be partially right. True, economists are predicting a slow recovery for agriculture. But if nothing else, as the Iowa Farm Bureau's president reminded us in early 1983, there's always the chance of a weather disaster somewhere else in the world wiping out current price-depressing grain surpluses.[21]

But the issue is not whether there will be an end to the current farm depression. Yes, there will. What John Block neglected to address is the real issue—the tragic price we as a nation, and many farmers very personally, are paying for accepting the economic ground rules that cause boom and bust farming. What is that price? To answer, we must look at the impact of the export boom *within* agriculture.

Before the Boom

We can't understand the impact of the export boom and bust unless we know what American agriculture looked like *before* the boom began. Already by the early 1970s, the number of farms in America—about 3 million—had been reduced to half of what it was twenty-five years earlier. By 1970, a clear pattern of consolidation of returns from farming had emerged.

Over 80 percent of American farms were small, part-time operations, selling less than $20,000 in farm commodities annually and getting half or more of their income off the farm. There were over 2 million such small farms, but they earned less than 20 percent of net farm income.

In the middle were the significant producers in our farm structure, farms selling from $20,000 to $99,000 a year. These mid-sized family farms relied on farming for most of their income. Although they represented about 16 percent of all farms, they earned about half of net farm income.

At the top were farms above $100,000 in farm sales. Less than 2 percent of all farms were this large, but they reaped a third of net farm income in 1970.[22]

Thus, even before the export boom began, income from farming had become considerably concentrated. During the sixties the share of net farm income captured by the biggest farms had already increased fivefold. At the top, fewer and bigger farms were thriving. Many still called themselves family farms because, with the help of hundreds of thousands of dollars of machinery, one family could still do most of the work. At the other end, smaller farms were increasingly having to rely on income from jobs off the farm.

In our economy, this process of concentration is often taken for granted and is justified on the grounds of efficiency. So, before we look at how the boom and bust decade of the 1970s accelerated the tightening of control over agricultural resources, let's look at this justification.

Weeding Out the Inefficient?

An editorial in the *New York Times* in early 1983 expressed one of the most widely held assumptions about how our economy works. The government should not rush to aid struggling small farmers, it warned, because "that would only retard the transition to efficient farm size."[23] Boom and bust cycles weed out the inefficient, so the theory goes, and because those who survive are the strong, the whole process strengthens our economic system.

When virtually all farmers were hurting during the last great farm depression, it was easier to see through this assumption. But the more differentiated our agriculture has become—with a tiny group of superfarms now at the pinnacle—the harder it is for farmers, and all of us, to question the assumption that concentration is justified on the grounds of efficiency. On the surface it seems so clear—if some farms are thriving, then those who aren't must be doing something wrong.

Moreover, when newspaper coverage of the early 1980s farm crisis regularly reported that commodity prices were below the average costs of production, it was hard for the lay reader not to assume that *all* farmers were losing money. Indeed, by early 1982, delinquencies and defaults on farm loans from the Farmers Home Administration were running at 33 percent, double the 1979 rate. News stories of farm auctions touched the sympathies of the nation: "A wake is less sad than a farm sale," Iowa swine farmer Jack Ryan told the *Minneapolis Tribune* in early 1982. "And the thing that's so rotten about it is it's happening all the time. Used to be a few a year. Now twenty a day is nothing."[24]

But all farms weren't on the brink of bankruptcy. In 1982, for example, in a farm management training program in Minnesota, 342 farmers filled out questionnaires about their income. The top 5 percent reported a $40,000 income, while the bottom 5 percent reported more than $30,000 in losses that year.[25] But *which* farmers were in trouble in the early eighties? "It's scandalous that no government agency is even bothering to find out," charged farm advocate Catherine Lerza of the Rural Coalition, a Washington-based public interest group.[26]

National media coverage of the farm crisis focused on farmers who had expanded aggressively during the 1970s. Hoping to take advantage of the promised bonanza from growing export sales, they got locked into a debt cycle. Then interest rates soared while the value of their loan collateral—their land—stagnated by 1980 and then slipped by 1982. "How did I know the world was going to flip upside down?" asked Eugene Smith, an Indiana farmer who had acquired 16,000 acres betting on the export boom.[27] "Serves 'em right," was probably the reaction of many Americans to the plight of these big operators.

But media focus on these dramatic cases obscured the broader picture. There is no official accounting of which farmers were going under, but we've pieced together an answer by talking with farmers and their representatives throughout the Grain Belt.

Not all of the big expanders were in trouble, insisted Iowa farmer Melvin Schneider in early 1983. "I call those guys the 'stompers' because they don't care about anyone else. All they care about is getting bigger. Most of them aren't suffering. They'll make it through. A lot of them have outside income and can use farming as an income tax deduction."[28]

"Only a small percentage tried to make a killing by expanding," said Iowa farmer Bill Genzen. "Sure, many did buy some land or try to rent more . . . but it was because of the financial pinch, and the lenders advised them that more land would help them—or maybe they needed more land to bring a son into the operation."[29] Schneider interviewed one hundred financially troubled farmers in early 1983. According to him, the majority of those most hurt by the bust are mid-sized family farms without significant off-farm income and without a lot of equity in their land to borrow against.

Moreover, renters were particularly hard hit. "It's the renters—those who don't own any land—who are really in trouble," said Quentin Hope of the small farming community of Pierceville, Kansas. "They just can't bear up under the high costs when they have to hand over a third of their crop to the landowner."[30]

Some of the mid-sized farmers going bankrupt in the early 1980s had been farming for decades. But within this group were also heavily indebted young, new farmers who had purchased land in the 1970s, when agriculture looked bright indeed. They were then saddled with huge debts with high interest. Julie and Bobby Neal are one example. In 1978 they bought an eighty-acre farm across the road from where Julie had grown up near Cincinnati. Since then they have worked from before dawn into the night, with no vacations. "But we're not even breaking even," reported Julie Neal in early 1983. "The main thing is the worry—it's constant. Bobby's ulcer got so bad he went to the hospital twice last fall." The Neals are right on the edge of losing their farm. "If prices don't get better we may not make it through '83," she predicted.[31]

It is the squeeze on these mid-sized farmers, including young newcomers like the Neals, with which this chapter is primarily concerned. Many of the "stompers," as Melvin Schneider calls them, will make it through the bust of the early eighties because they have advantages of size and wealth that we'll document throughout this chapter. And the USDA predicts that many small farmers will survive because of income from jobs off the farm, although many of these jobs are also threatened by the farm depression.

In this mid-sized category are the majority of all farmers in America who make most of their income from farming; yet they captured only about 15 percent of net farm income in 1981. This mid-sized category consists of between 400,000 and 500,000 farms with gross sales between $40,000 and about $150,000. On average, they rely on farming for most of their income and are large enough to be economically viable, when prices are good. Farm income per farm for this group in relatively good years, such as 1978, is near the national family income average; adding off-farm income brought the average net income for this group to between $20,000 and $30,000 per farm that year.[32] These mid-sized farms have been the foundation of rural community life throughout much of the country.

Now that we have described *who* is most threatened by boom and bust, let's return to the question: Are they the inefficient? And the corollary question:

Are We Rewarding Efficiency?

Since concentration of farm ownership has increased while agricultural productivity has improved, many readily leap to the conclusion that this shakeout is inevitable and indeed beneficial from society's point of view. "True, farms have gotten bigger, as has nearly every other type of economic enterprise," wrote Stephen Chapman in *Harper's* in October 1982. "They have done so in order to take advantage of the economies of scale offered by modern production techniques." By implication, we all gain in the process because our food is produced more cheaply.

"Economies of scale" means simply that each bushel can be produced more cheaply if fixed costs are spread over a large number of bushels. It seems like common sense, and that's why commentators like Chapman use economies of scale to rationalize growth in farm size. But Chapman overlooks the fact that economies of scale in every industry have an upper limit. After a certain size, there is no increase in efficiency from continued growth.

That upper limit had already been reached by the late 1960s on the farms that produce most of our food. "Growth you now see in farm size has little to do with efficiency," concluded agricultural economist Tom Miller, author of the USDA study *Economies of Size in U.S. Field Crop Farming.* "Above about $40,000–$50,000 in gross sales—a size that is at the bottom end of the medium-size sales category— there are no greater efficiencies of scale," according to Dr. Miller.[33] (The exceptions, he noted, are in cattle, poultry, and specialty crops.) Indeed, not one single economic analyst we've encountered in our research has claimed that the dramatic concentration of production during the last ten to fifteen years is either motivated by or results in greater efficiency.[34] "Medium-sized family farms are as efficient as the large farms," concluded a 1980 summary USDA report. "About 80 percent of these farms likely have costs *below* the national average cost of production."[35]

Thus, farms have grown, not to achieve greater efficiency, but primarily because expansion has been the only way to maintain their incomes, given rising costs that relentlessly shrink profits per acre. Moreover, those farmers who can, will expand to continue increasing their incomes. "For after all," explained Dr. Miller, "if you have the same efficiencies and double your volume of sales, you will double your income." Tax and credit policies that encourage capital investment have also encouraged farm growth, as we suggest below. As a result of these pressures, over half of the agricultural commodities produced in America are now grown on farms *larger* than can be justified on grounds of efficiency.[36]

Of course, being an efficient manager *is* critical, and few would survive in farming if they weren't. But the history of our farm economy shows that being a good manager is no guarantee of survival. Other factors—particularly *size* and *wealth*—are rewarded more. Our point is that while rising costs, lower commodity prices, and high interest rates aren't good for any farmer, they are devastating to some. Others can ride through the busts ready to cash in on the booms. Who survives depends on how different farmers are affected by two key forces—*inflation* and *risk*—as they interact with the economic ground rules. Both have been aggravated by the massive farm export boom. In other words, while our national ideology holds that "boom and bust" weed out the inefficient, in reality they weed out the vulnerable, those with fewer assets and less volume. This has nothing necessarily to do with efficiency, and therefore is no gain for society as a whole.

Land Inflation Rewards Wealth

Every year since 1973 capital gains on farmland (that is, the rising value of farmland) have been greater than net farm income, rising an average of almost 26 percent each year of the 1970s. Thus, many observers of the changing face of American agriculture concluded that farmers were doing all right—their income may have looked bad, but they were getting substantially richer every year during the past decade. (Remember that only in the early eighties did farmland values begin to slump.)

Less often are we reminded that, of course, only farmers *who already own land* benefit from its inflation. Only about half of American farmers own (or, are buying) all the land they work. One in ten owns no land.[37]

Of those farmers who do own land, only a small minority own most of it. Nationally, 5 percent of farmland owners own almost half of the land; but in the Mountain and Pacific states, the share of the top 5 percent is over two thirds.[38] To appreciate how inflation rewards the minority who own most of our farmland, consider that in the mid-1970s, even a moderate-sized farm with 80 percent equity (typical of that class) enjoyed a $34,600 annual increase in the value of its assets—almost twice the year's net income from farming![39] Moreover, the land of the largest owners increased in value more rapidly than the average during the 1970s,[40] perhaps because they had the most desirable land to begin with.

Most important, if you own land, inflation makes it easier to buy still more. For inflation increases the collateral you have with which to secure a loan for expansion. At the inflated prices of the 1970s, only those with sizable collateral could even consider buying. A typical Illinois corn grower in 1976 needed the income from three acres, or the equivalent, to finance the purchase of one more acre.[41]

"Under these conditions," explained Marty Strange of Nebraska's Center for Rural Affairs, "simply owning land comes to be rewarded more highly than producing food on it—and unearned wealth becomes a bigger factor in farm expansion than is earned income from farming."[42]

Farmland inflation also pushes would-be farmers without other significant sources of income out of the market. A new farm family can't meet the payments if all it has is income generated from the purchased acres. "Farming doesn't earn enough to pay for farmland," one Iowa farmer lamented.[43] If an aspiring farm family had bought a 200-acre farm in 1979 at a relatively low 9 percent interest from, for example, the Federal Land Bank, it would have lost twenty dollars on every acre that year, according to a government study.[44] Without other income, this family could not hold on.

Inflation in land prices not only rewards those who already own land and excludes all except wealthy newcomers. It favors the absentee owner over the farmer-owner.[45] Sure, the farmer-owner's land inflates in value and can be used as collateral for loans. But, the farmer-owner is also hit by the adverse consequences of land inflation. Over a third of all farmers are "part owners," meaning they must rent part of their land. With inflation, their rents rise. Moreover, owner-operators must pay the higher land taxes out of declining farm income.

By contrast, inflation means absentee owners can charge higher land rent to help offset higher land taxes. In early

1983 *Fortune* magazine explained the landlord's logic in raising rents: "Midwest land prices skyrocketed 300 percent to 400 percent during the seventies; since the asset the landlord supplies is worth more . . . he's entitled to take more."[46] Most important, the absentee owner can sell the land at any time to take advantage of the capital gains. Unlike the farmer-owner, selling out does not mean sacrificing a way of life and a livelihood.

Not surprisingly, absentee owners with lots of capital did well during the 1970s. Ashby Bladen, investment vice-president for Phoenix Mutual Life Insurance Co., boasted in 1982 that his company "made a lot of money buying and improving farms during the farm price inflation of the last decade." While Bladen's company installed drainage systems on some of the farms it bought, "buying and watching the land appreciate" might more aptly describe the source of Phoenix Mutual's profits.[47]

Heightened Risk of Boom and Bust

We've seen how bust followed boom as farmers' costs soared—how farmers are trapped into a position of actually contributing to their own demise as their survival and expansion strategies press up the costs of land and farm supplies. The export thrust only added to this cycle. For, in addition to accelerated inflation, the last decade brought heightened risk to farmers—risk from four changes linked to the export surge: greater *specialization* of production on the farm; a quadrupling of *farmers' indebtedness*; greater *market instability*; and *stress on storage and transport systems*.

"I'm concerned whenever there is the loss of a farmer," said Robert B. Delano, head of the American Farm Federation Bureau in early 1983. "But agriculture is a risk business. You risk the opportunity to make a profit, and you risk going bankrupt."[48] Stated this way, the process sounds almost like a lottery in which every bettor stands a chance. But as head of an organization representing some of the country's biggest farm operators and nonfarming agribusiness interests, Delano is hardly likely to tell us how risk, like inflation, favors those with considerable equity in their land and those with large sales volume, and threatens those without.

Exports Narrow Farmers' Options

As export markets surged for certain crops, farmers have specialized increasingly in those favored crops. In one decade, the top three export crops—corn, wheat, and soybeans—grew from one half to cover two thirds of our harvested cropland. (See figure 3–2.) Not only have export markets tended to narrow farmers' crop options, they have encouraged farmers to accelerate a shift from mixed livestock and crop production toward specialization in corn and soybeans, especially in the North Central states.

According to agricultural economist Philip M. Raup, we are "creating a pattern of one-crop, export-based agricultural activity in the corn, soybean, wheat, and sorghum regions that is very similar to the type of monocultural dependence formerly associated with colonialism. In an important and sobering sense, the grain belt of America is acquiring the characteristics of a colony."[49] Nothing more characterizes the economy of a colony than boom and bust linked to fluctuating world market prices for primary exports. Also, in a colonized economy the rewards of production are captured primarily by the largest producers, as well as by commercial interests off the farm.

When farmers produce a variety of crops, or both livestock and crops, they have some built-in protection against losses when prices decline. If feed grains hit a price slump, farmers can always feed part of the crop to their livestock. And when farmers produce a variety of crops, they are somewhat protected if prices fall for one. With greater crop specialization, such back-up protection is lost.

Greater Debt—Greater Risk: But Who Can Live with Debt?

Mounting indebtedness has also drastically increased the risk in farming, as growing interest payments add ap-

Figure 3–2
Use of U.S. Cropland, 1969 and 1980

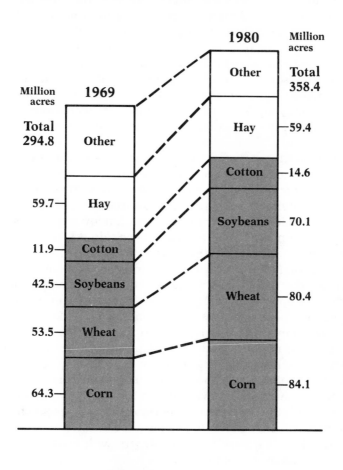

Data from USDA, *Field Crops: Estimates by States, 1969–74,*
and *Crop Production: 1980 Annual Summary.*

preciably to a farmer's fixed costs. In 1970 the interest on farm debt equaled about 24 percent of total net farm income; a decade later, 80 percent.[50] The USDA gives us a simple example of how greater fixed-payment obligations heighten farmers' risk: "If a farm has $100 in gross receipts and expenses of $70, and expenses increase 10 percent, then net cash income is reduced by 23 percent ($7). But if its expenses are $90, the same 10 percent increase in expenses cuts net cash income by 90 percent—from $10 to $1."[51]

If mounting payments on debt eat up more and more income, who can make it through the busts?

First are farmers with considerable *equity*. They can use their equity to go on borrowing to cover family living expenses. Included in this category are landowners without any debt on their land at all—indeed, almost half of all farmland is owned by those without land debt. Most of these owners are not farmers themselves, but landlords, renting out their land to renters and sharecroppers.[52] The critical importance of equity was highlighted in a 1982 study by University of Missouri economists. Of the farmers studied, only those with high equity made a profit in 1981. They were not the most efficient producers, however. In fact, the high-equity farmers had lower value of production per hour and per acre than the low-equity farmers.[53]

Second are farmers with gross *farm income big enough* that even after subtracting enormous interest payments, there is still enough left to live on.

Third are farmers and landowners with considerable *off-farm income*, notably those smaller farmers—below $40,000 in gross sales—who get most of their income off the farm and nonfarm investors.

But, while the high-equity farmer, the debt-free landlord, the very large volume producer, and the farmer or landowner with significant off-farm income are *not* wiped out by debt, mid-sized family farmers often are.

Laura and Lester Joens farm 480 acres near Manning, Iowa. They've been farming for twenty-seven years, but in the fall of 1982 their local bank ordered them to liquidate everything except their home to pay off their debts. "When my husband's father died in 1980, we borrowed to buy 66 acres of the estate. Then in 1981 my brother-in-law wanted to sell the land we'd been renting. We decided to borrow again to buy 130 acres," Laura Joens told us. "It was either that or lose the land we'd been farming for twenty-seven years. They say farms are in trouble because of bad management, overexpansion. But we didn't want to expand; we just wanted to keep what we had. . . . My husband really blames himself. But how could we have known that prices and land values were going to fall so low? This year is going to be a turning point for lots of people like us."[54]

In the early 1980s, however, many were claiming that "the producers in most danger" were the ones "who've expanded rapidly in recent years and borrowed heavily," as *Farm Money Management* editorialized in the spring of 1982. One imagines those in trouble to be, not people like the Joenses, but the really big operators such as Eugene Smith above, who tried to add on 16,000 acres in the mid-seventies. What is often overlooked is that the very size of their loans often helps protect the biggest operators.

"It's like the big banks with Argentina or Mexico. They just can't afford to foreclose on these big borrowers. They'd lose too much," explained Jerry Hansen, a Nebraska farmer who counsels farmers with debt problems. "It's the farmers who don't owe that much who are really under pressure." Data on the Farmers Home Administration gathered by the Center for Rural Affairs in Nebraska confirms these impressions. Although 83 percent of the value of delinquent loans was held by the big operators, less than half of the agency's collection goal for early 1983 was targeted at this group.[55] Marty Strange, codirector of the center, believes that this bias reflects an underlying shift in government farm credit programs.

> Farm credit programs have been reshaped to fit the emerging farm economy in which a handful of farms dominate production . . . Their main purpose is no longer to help small and beginning farmers establish themselves in farming, but to insulate expanding farmers from the risks associated with expansion.[56]

On the Export Market Roller Coaster

In how many businesses do producers have no notion from one day to the next what the selling price of their product will be? That is the position of American farmers, and their growing dependence on export markets has only heightened the uncertainties.

Farmer dependence on exports doubled over the 1970s. In 1970 the value of farm exports amounted to 14 percent of cash receipts from farming; by 1980, about 30 percent. Greater dependence on export markets means greater price fluctuations simply because more variables come into play. Agricultural economist John Timmons observed, "Foreign demands for our agricultural products are very fickle and unreliable, depending upon such events as a drought in Russia, the Anchoveta catch in Peru, or a political change in China."[57] Export markets are determined not only by weather over the entire globe but by our own government's decisions to embargo agricultural exports and by many other governments' farm export policies. For example, because of the European Economic Community's aggressive marketing and export subsidies, its wheat exports had swollen to one third of our wheat exports by 1982, up from only one seventh of U.S. wheat exports in 1977. (Of course, the United States competes by subsidizing its farm commodities, too.) This growing competition obviously adds to the uncertainties about future U.S. farm export sales.[58]

Less immediately obvious, the international market in grain is volatile simply because most nations produce 95 percent of what they consume. Since they import only a 5 percent margin, a very small change in domestic production could either double or eliminate entirely a nation's import needs. But what amounts to a small change in a single nation's production can move prices by as much as 25 to 50 percent once the news hits the international market.

The United States probably insulates its farmers and consumers from the vicissitudes of the international market less than any other major food exporter. As a result, the United States has become what economists call the "residual" supplier to the rest of the world. This means that our exports are excluded when they threaten other countries' producers, and they are imported only when needed to make up for those countries' domestic shortages.

Thus, it is not surprising that the Department of Agriculture reports that "the prices of major farm commodities were much more unstable during the seventies than in any other recent period." During the 1972 to 1978 period, variation in the prices received by farmers for all crops was five times greater than during the 1964 to 1971 period—and six and one half times greater than in the late fifties.[59] Figure 3–3 shows these heightened price swings.

Since other countries appear to be becoming more protective of their domestic interests, the USDA predicts that the United States will be forced to swallow even more market instability in the future, which could double annual swings in foreign demand for U.S. grains and soybeans.[60]

Who Can Stay on the Roller Coaster?

Superficially, the biggest producers appear to be hardest hit by the heightened risk associated with expansion for export—increased indebtedness, narrowing of crops, and greater price fluctuations. A bigger share of their total income comes from the farm and their income from farming changes more dramatically than the income of smaller farmers, undoubtedly because a larger portion of the crops these farms produce are export crops. Plus, farms in the $100,000-and-up-sales category have much higher cash production costs for every dollar of sales—about 35 percent higher than the average of smaller farm categories. This is primarily because big farms hire more of their labor; smaller farms use more family labor.[61] Moreover, these larger farms have higher debt-to-asset ratios than their smaller neighbors.

No wonder many analysts who look only at the statistics suggest that price fluctuations most threaten large farms. They often overlook crucial differences *within* the most commonly used $100,000-and-up-in-sales, large-farm category and how size itself serves as a buffer. All are not equal, even at the top. A Kansas wheat farm in this category might have 1,000 acres and $138,000 in sales—a relatively modest family operation. A California cotton farm, how-

Figure 3–3
Season Average Prices per Bushel of Wheat, Corn, and Soybeans, 1950–1980
In Current Dollars

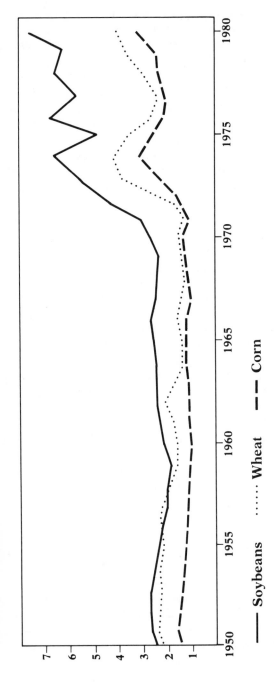

Data from USDA, *Agricultural Statistics, 1972*, tables 1, 38 and 189, and *Agricultural Statistics, 1981*, tables 2, 39 and 178.

ever, might have 8,000 acres and $3.4 million in annual sales.⁶² Obviously, price fluctuations would affect these two farms very differently.

The first, with a 1978 income of about $26,000, would have a tough time paying bills and meeting basic family expenses if prices slumped—and certainly if prices were bad for three straight years as in the early 1980s. "When these family farms get squeezed between rising costs and low prices, it's what I call their 'family baggage' that breaks them," observed Melvin Schneider. "Maybe they add some land to try to have enough to pass on to a son. Or maybe they try to put a child through college. Or maybe someone in the family gets seriously ill. The squeeze is already so tight when this additional stress is added in, they can't hold on any longer. Now a commercial operation will just fire someone when they're sick, but in a family farm operation, it comes out of the profits."

One long-time Iowa farm family with heavy medical expenses a few years ago told us why they doubt whether they'll make it through. "For three weeks in January we survived on $2.98 worth of food," the family told us. "Now we've applied for food stamps."

But a farm at the very top of the big farm category, with an annual income of $636,000, would be better able to ride out price drops and could take in stride the weather or "family baggage" that puts smaller farmers under. If prices fall, this farm could shift what had been net income for the family to pay fixed costs without hardship. In addition, this family's land assets mean it could also more easily borrow additional funds.

Thus, the enormous difference in assets and income mean that the heightened price swings of the 1970s affect even so-called "large" farmers very differently. The tiny 1 percent at the top had an average income of $500,000 by the end of the 1970s. They are, by their very scale, more immune to threats that price fluctuations pose to their smaller neighbors.

But to understand how increased risk affects different sized farms we must look not just at relative debt burdens. We must also explore how the biggest farms can reduce risks. For when the uncertainties increase, strategies for mitigating the uncertainties take on even greater importance.

Commodity Futures Markets: Do They Reduce or Heighten Farmers' Risks?

According to conventional wisdom, commodity futures trading—markets in which primarily grain traders, major agribusiness interests, and speculators buy and sell grain contracts for future delivery—is supposed to reduce market instability and, therefore, farmers' risks. (Chapter 5 describes more fully how futures trading operates.)

The volume of commodity futures trading multiplied sevenfold during the 1970s, spurred no doubt in part by the exaggerated price uncertainties associated with the export boom. Inflation itself pushed businesses and speculators into the futures market. Because of inflation, investors began looking for "alternative investments that would produce a real return on their money," and businesses looked "frantically for ways to stabilize prices and lock in profits," according to *Commodities* magazine.[63]

Again, according to conventional wisdom, increased volume in trading should lessen price fluctuations. But the volatility of the market can be compounded instead of lessened through futures trading, according to Albert Wojnilower, the chief economist of First Boston Corporation. He believes that, in principle, futures are a good idea during stable times and when there is a predictable range to prices or interest rates. But in times like these, "because no one has the foggiest notion of what the price of gold will be three weeks from now, the futures markets become a vehicle for embodying that uncertainty and for enormous bandwagon movement in all directions."[64]

Only a tiny minority of larger farmers, however, try to reduce their risks by hedging through the commodity futures markets. ("Hedging" means taking a contract position as a buyer in the futures market that is the opposite of the farmer's position as a seller in the cash market, so that if the farmer loses in one transaction, he will gain in the other.) In 1973, only 5.6 percent of farmers bought or sold futures contracts.[65]

Although most farmers do not directly participate in the futures market, they are forced to invest indirectly. Farmers sell their grain to elevator companies, both private and cooperative. Some of these companies not only use the market to hedge but also to speculate on the market. And speculation in the futures market has been a major factor in elevator bankruptcies over the past few years. In 1980, one Iowa co-op lost $460,000 in seventy-one days on the futures market.[66] And when a grain elevator goes bankrupt, often the farmers are hurt the most.

Information Is Power

Information is yet another key to coping with heightened risk associated with export expansion. Information is power for those who deal in commodity markets, and, as the export push has intensified, that power has come to be shared less and less equally, as chapter 5 details. Changes brought with the export boom are reducing the farmer's accessibility to information flows in the market—information which is crucial to profitable decisions on when to buy and sell farm commodities.

First, as global markets increase in importance, more grain flows to major port terminals (large elevators), bypassing traditional inland terminals, on which farmers have traditionally relied for price information. As trading has thinned out at the inland terminal markets, they have become increasingly unreliable sources of price information. So the farmer must engage in a costly information search, which only the biggest farmers can afford.

Second, in the wake of increased foreign sales, the domestic market has generally eroded as a source of timely and accurate information on grain prices for the farmer and other "outsiders." Farmers are thus forced to sell in relative ignorance of what the "true" price is. A recent government study noted, "These farmers who are taking the prices . . . which they are offered are actually going out of business. It may just turn out because of that disparity [of information], and because of the transfer of profits based on lack of knowledge, there may very well be a large adverse effect upon our whole farm system."[67]

Farmers increasingly feel that, given their lack of access to adequate market information, the production figures they give to the government are used against them. The Department of Agriculture compiles data on farmer-held grain stocks and planting intentions which is helpful to the grain traders. But it does not offer the reverse service of supplying farmers with information about how much the grain traders are holding here and abroad or their buying intentions.[68]

The cycle becomes self-reinforcing. As farmers' skepticism of valid price information grows, so does their resistance to providing crop data to the USDA. As more farmers refuse to divulge crop information, the reliability of domestic markets is further eroded, increasing the instability of the farm economy.

Contracts Reduce Risk for Some

Income, wealth, and access to information all help protect farmers from increased price fluctuations.

Large volume helps, too. Big volume producers are better able to contract directly with food processors for delivery at a fixed price in the future, helping protect themselves against unpredictable price changes. Forward contracting, as this practice is called, became a major part of the marketing strategy of certain grain and cotton producers in the 1970s. Even by 1974, 11 percent of soybean and 20 percent of cotton production was under contractual arrangements, according to the 1979 USDA report *Status of the Family Farm*. In that year, the average farm using contracts in the production or marketing of its output had sales nearly two-and-a-half times greater than that of a typical commercial farm. "You've got to have big quantities to sell now or you are more or less being forgotten in the market," Iowa farmer Bill Genzen told us.

But do large farms result in contracting or does contracting result in large farms? The Department of Agriculture concluded that "it is probable that the relationship goes both ways." While contracting may not be a "primary factor" in increasing farm size, it is "significant." "To the extent that contracting is an effective means of reducing some of the risks inherent in farming, it increases the advantages of large farms relative to small farms." The trend is self-reinforcing; "the growth of large farms leads to contract production, which encourages the further growth of large farms."[69]

"The growth of contracting has major implications to the continued survival of small farms," warned the report. Through individual contracts, the processor coordinates the production of many farms. These separate farms then function as a single farm under the direction of one contractor. When contracting becomes the prevalent marketing arrangement for a given commodity, traditional open markets, on which the smaller producers depend, will die away.[70]

The point is that while all farmers are hit by increased uncertainties from the latest export era, big farmers are better able to protect themselves.

Who Gets Squeezed When Transport Is Tight

In yet another way, the export boom heightens the risks of farmers, some more than others. With almost triple the volume of grain flowing toward the ports, storage and transportation networks have been stretched to their limits. All farmers are not equally disadvantaged by this strain. Those who can protect themselves include:

- Farmers who have large on-site storage capacity. These are likely to be the bigger operators.

- Farmers closest to the major waterways of the Mississippi and Missouri basin and nearest the major rail lines. They will likely have first crack at what rail and barge transport is available. (Moreover, their land values rise simply due to their proximity to the major grain transport routes.)

- Farmers with large enough volume either to have influence with the local elevator or to bypass it. In a 1980 survey of over 35,000 farmers in sixteen states, more than one third reported that they were unable to sell their grain when they wanted because the local elevators were full.[71] The Department of Agriculture states that "very large grain producers can, in some cases, more economically transport grain over long distances to terminal elevators and processors." Not only does this mean they can escape the local bottleneck, but they can "capture the country elevator's share of the price at the next stage for themselves."[72]

The greatest transportation crisis for farmers is the closing of branch rail lines, a byproduct of the major rail mergers following government deregulation of the industry in 1980. One third of the rail mileage in such key agricultural states as Iowa and South Dakota has been abandoned in the last ten years.[73] Farmers' increasing reliance on exports has made them more dependent on access to major ports and, therefore, more vulnerable to these cutbacks and unequal access to terminals.

The development of unit trains (discussed in chapter 5) has also hurt some farmers because it has hurt country elevator operators who don't have the track to accommodate these huge 125-car trains. As country elevators go under, often farmers must ship their grain greater distances to the major terminals. Only the large volume producers can afford to do this.

Most important, the power of the rail and trucking corporations—their ability to shut down branch lines, increase rates, and offer volume discounts—affects different farms very differently. Again, those with greater volume, higher incomes, and more equity in their farms are better able to cope.

Public Policies, Too

This chapter began with a look at how the export boom has heightened the squeeze on the farm sector as a whole, but we have focused on how that squeeze affects different farmers very differently. For example, farmland inflation rewards the already well-established, and heightened risk hurts the mid-sized farmer more than others. Choosing to focus on the underlying economic forces that are often diffi-cult to perceive, we have still to consider the public pol-icies—most important, tax and credit policies—that also selectively benefit the biggest producers. The *New York Times* reported that in 1978 only 3 percent of all farms re-ceived almost half the total benefits from tax and credit policies relating to agriculture.[74]

A special USDA report on tax policy concluded, "Gener-ally, tax policy has led to upward pressure on farmland prices, larger farm sizes, incentives for farm incorporation, altered management practices, and increased use of farm-land as a tax shelter—by both farmers and nonfarmers."[75] In its 1981 report *A Time to Choose*, the USDA concluded that our tax laws not only have "abetted the trend toward fewer and larger farms" but have encouraged absentee ownership as well. One tax provision, for example, selec-tively benefits those better off by allowing farmers to sub-tract a portion of the price of new equipment from their taxes. The higher the tax bracket of the farmer, the more the deduction is worth.[76]

Because we cannot do justice to these issues here, we refer you to the Center for Rural Affairs in Walthill, Ne-braska. Its publications provide up-to-date analyses of the impact of both tax and credit policies.

The Chickens Come Home to Roost

We've seen how the export boom contributed to rising costs and fluctuating prices, which intensified the trend of shrinking profits per acre. By the early 1980s, profits per acre were half their mid-sixties level. Just to maintain fam-ily income, a farm had to grow. This pressure for growth went hand in hand with the lure to growth. The promise of ever-expanding markets fed our "only growth proves suc-cess" ideology, encouraging most farmers *who could* to get bigger. They grew by buying out their failing neighbors. "Every time one of us loses our farm, someone else is getting bigger," Nebraska ex-farmer Dale Malmberg reminded us.

One telling indication of this process—what some econ-omists call the "cannibalization" of American farms—is a striking shift in the purpose of farmland sales. In the 1950s

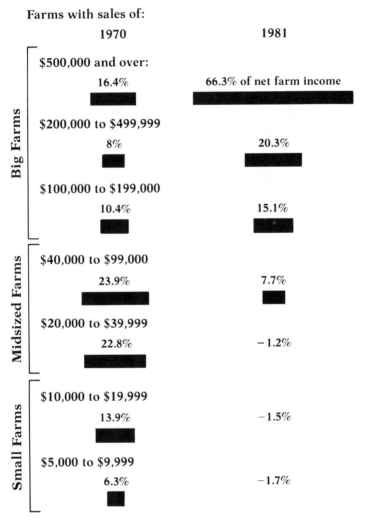

Figure 3-4
Percent of Net Farm Income and Net Income
per Farm—by Major Sales Category
In Current Dollars

Farms with sales of:

	1970	1981

Big Farms

$500,000 and over:
16.4%   66.3% of net farm income

$200,000 to $499,999
8%   20.3%

$100,000 to $199,000
10.4%   15.1%

Midsized Farms

$40,000 to $99,000
23.9%   7.7%

$20,000 to $39,999
22.8%   −1.2%

Small Farms

$10,000 to $19,999
13.9%   −1.5%

$5,000 to $9,999
6.3%   −1.7%

Data from USDA, *Economic Indicators of the Farm Sector:
Income and Balance Sheet Statistics, 1981.*
Sales classes below $5,000 in gross sales were deleted for
simplicity; thus percentages do not total 100 percent.

Farms with sales of:

	1970	1981

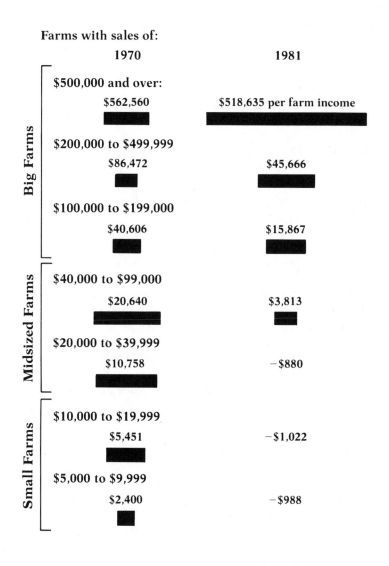

Big Farms

$500,000 and over:
$562,560
$518,635 per farm income

$200,000 to $499,999
$86,472
$45,666

$100,000 to $199,000
$40,606
$15,867

Midsized Farms

$40,000 to $99,000
$20,640
$3,813

$20,000 to $39,999
$10,758
−$880

Small Farms

$10,000 to $19,999
$5,451
−$1,022

$5,000 to $9,999
$2,400
−$988

almost two thirds of farmland sales resulted in the birth of new farms. By the mid-seventies only one third resulted in new farms—the bulk of sales were to *expand* an existing holding.[77] By 1982, in at least one state—North Dakota—80 percent of farm sales resulted in the expansion of existing farms.[78]

Now, looking back over the decade, we can see the consequences of these pressures.

When the bust hit in the early 1980s, the advantages held by the biggest farmers—all those advantages we've outlined in this chapter—became dramatically obvious.[79] By 1981, inflation's reward to wealth and the selective protection that wealth and size offer from the risks of boom and bust were strikingly evident. That year a mere *1 percent of all farms in America—those with sales of $500,000 and over—reaped two thirds of net farm income of all farms in the country*! (See figure 3–4.) In just one year, from 1980 to 1981, these farms increased their share of net farm income by 25 percent, and in one decade their share had leapt fourfold.

Melvin Schneider's view is borne out by the statistics. The "stompers" were doing all right. In fact, in 1981, only one sales category showed a *gain* in net income. It was made up of 25,000 "superfarms," with *minimum sales* of $500,000 a year and *average annual profit* also of $0.5 million. While the per farm average income of this group did not show a gain that year, as a group they added another $100 million to their collective income, reflecting an increase in the number of farms in that category. Indeed, since the beginning of the boom-and-bust export decade, the increase in the number of superfarms has been dramatic. In 1970 only 4,000 farms ranked in this sales category; by 1981, there were 25,000—an increase of almost 50 percent, even after adjusting this figure for inflation. "If we keep going like this, the stompers will be producing most of our food," said Schneider. "And there'll be only a handful of farms in each county."

On the other side, income for farms with sales below $100,000 sank disastrously over the decade. Whereas in 1970 farms selling from $20,000 to $99,000 earned a decent family income and captured close to half of all net farm income, by 1981 most farmers in this category either lost money or netted virtually no income from farming. These mid-sized to medium-small farms—viable in 1970—had always been viewed as the backbone of family farm agriculture. Yet by 1981, they captured only 6.5 percent of net farm income, one seventh of their share in 1970. (All smaller sales classes were losing money by 1981.) While the number of mid-sized farms increased over the decade, even after making adjustments for inflation, we concur with the USDA prediction of the "disappearing middle," a trend that will no doubt be clear after the shakeout of the early eighties.[80] No family can support itself on the less than $4,000 farm income this group averaged in 1981. These farmers will either grow, go under, or become part-time farmers getting most of their income off the farm.

One Business Lost for Every Seven Farms

One caveat here. We don't want to leave the impression that farmers unable to survive on their low farm incomes can simply take a job off the farm to compensate. "Jobs in rural communities are getting scarcer and scarcer," warns Dan Levitas of Rural America, "just as increasing numbers of desperate farm families are looking for off-farm jobs." Many small-town businesses that traditionally supplied jobs for farmers "are being destroyed by the same process of concentration that is happening on the farm. On average, every time seven farms go under, one business serving a rural community folds," according to Levitas.

Creston, Iowa, is such a farming community. The county seat, Creston has a population of 8,500. In just one year, 1980–81, Creston lost twenty-two small businesses. And that was *before* the worst of the farm depression.[81] In Manilla, Iowa, "almost every business on Main Street is for sale!" farmer Virginia Genzen told us in early 1983.[82]

New Kind of Specialization?

More farm income in fewer hands and the destruction of rural communities still does not tell the whole story of the changes under way in American agriculture, sped up in the last decade. Economist Lyle Schertz of the USDA predicts that the tremendous capital gains realized by established farmers as their land values rose in the 1970s will lead in the next two decades to what the government calls "separation of ownership from land use."[83] In common parlance, it's farm tenancy—renting and sharecropping from absentee landowners, a tenure pattern common in this country in the last century and throughout much of the third world today.

Schertz predicts a new shift toward absentee ownership because farmers whose wealth swelled due to inflation in land values will not pass on their farms intact to only one child. Tax laws, combined with the enormous land values, make it more likely that farms will be divided among several offspring, not all of whom may desire to stay on the land. The next stage: The child of the beneficiary of the seventies export boom becomes the landlord of the eighties and nineties, living in the city and collecting rent from tenant farmers.

According to the USDA, 27 percent of U.S. farmland is owned by nonfarmers.[84] This average figure does not reveal the extent of absentee ownership in certain key farm states. In late 1982 the Kansas Rural Center published a report documenting the "separation of ownership and use" in six Kansas counties.[85] In none were owner-operators the majority, and in one county they constituted only a fifth of all owners. "On over half the farmland in five out of the six counties studied, the functions of ownership and operation are *not* held in the same hands," concluded the report.

In the early eighties a coalition of church and farm interests conducted a similar study of forty-seven counties in Iowa.[86] They discovered that over 57 percent of the farmland acres were rented, not owner-operated. The counties with the highest land values had the lowest percentage of owner-operators. In one such county, nearly 73 percent of the land was rented. And this is in Iowa, supposed heartland of the owner-operated family farm.

Levitas, who collaborated on the study, noted, "Although right now most of these absentee landlords live within the county and many are retired farmers, more and more of this land is going to fall into the hands of wealthy absentee landlords—doctors, lawyers, grain elevator owners, well-to-do people looking for a tax break. In my home county of Adair, Iowa, I know of one law firm that owns 1,500 acres scattered in several townships and several thousand additional acres in neighboring counties. This is the first step away from family, owner-operated farms. In the second stage," predicted Levitas, "these wealthy individuals and small firms will sell out to big industrial and insurance corporations."[87]

Ironically, agricultural economists and government foreign aid specialists have for decades seen tenancy as symptomatic of third world underdevelopment. In fact, they have promoted "land reform" giving operators direct control of the land as a solution to agricultural problems in the third world. Yet today government officials and academics seem to take a sanguine view of the same development here at home.

In 1979, former USDA official and respected authority on American agriculture Don Paarlberg denied that becoming a tenant is a loss either to the farmer or to society. "As it becomes increasingly difficult for the farmer to supply all the factors of production, he will gradually slough off providing the capital, owning the land, and even supplying the labor. *He will retain to the last that most precious role of all, entrepreneurship—the decision-making function.*" (Emphasis added.)[88] Paarlberg did not explain how a farmer could retain decision-making power when someone else controls the land and capital and does the work. In his vision, a farmer becomes a foreman, not an entrepreneur.

In the same spirit, John Lee, director of the USDA's National Economics Division, suggested in 1980 that increased tenancy should be viewed as just another type of specialization, no different from other specialization in our economy. "Some could specialize in land ownership and in seeking the returns to the ownership function, whereas others might concentrate on being farm operators." Lee concluded, "Such tenure arrangements no longer carry the social stigma they once did."[89]

A 1983 article in *Fortune* gives us a taste of what these

new "specialists" can look forward to.[90] With unconcealed admiration, *Fortune* explains the success of Farmers National, a company that manages 3,200 farms throughout the Midwest on behalf of absentee landlords. Analyzing how Farmers National "Makes Farming Pay," as the title of the article reads, *Fortune* notes, "The tenant's pocket is a good place to start looking for those additional dollars." The company's real coup has been to find a way around the traditional "crop-share lease" in which the landlord shares the risk and the tenant almost never gets less than 50 percent of the crop. Since farmland is now worth more, Farmers National argues that the landlord should get more.

But how to overcome the tenant's fear of "being jeered down as a sucker" by his neighbors if he settles for less than the traditional cut? Farmers National has the answer. Its "net share lease," says *Fortune*, is "really a way of concealing from the neighbors that a tenant has settled for less than half; he [the tenant] can brag that he's only giving the owner 45 percent of the actual crop, but what he doesn't say is that the landlord isn't putting up a dime of the production costs." Lest we wonder for a moment why any tenant would give up so much, the article reminds us that "prospective tenants are always bidding against each other to get new leases." *Fortune* makes no bones about its delight at this accelerating shift toward the separation of ownership, management, and work. "One of these days the farm may be a place only for the efficient, like those foursquare fellows at Farmers National," the article concludes.

Perhaps *Fortune*'s view of the direction of American farming should not surprise us. But could the learned academic and government spokespeople we cited above truly be unaware of the evidence from around the world and within our own country documenting the superiority of agricultural organization in which those who work the land have direct control of it?

In several books by the Institute (see our publications list at the end of the book), especially *Food First: Beyond the Myth of Scarcity* (Ballantine Books, revised, 1979), we discuss the "the inefficiencies of inequality." Both production and resource conservation are thwarted by land tenure systems that concentrate decision-making power in a minority, who are often unfamiliar with the day-to-day demands of farming. How can tenants be expected to conserve and improve land, for example, when they aren't sure of holding onto the land? Just as important, tenancy often denies those who do the work the satisfaction of a real say in production or full reward for their efforts.

When tenancy is abolished, security of tenure is guaranteed, and decision-making power devolves to those who actually do the work, not only can production increase but the fruits are often more widely shared. The most striking example in this century is China. Forty years ago most observers were certain that because of its population density, China could not avoid widespread, ongoing starvation. Yet, by removing control of production from an elite landlord group and vesting it increasingly in village-level production teams who directly benefit from what they grow, China has alleviated the tragedy of hunger, a tragedy that continues to plague third world countries still dominated by small land-owning elites. Of course, the Chinese system is very different from American family farm agriculture. Our point is that the goal of both is for those who do the work to have a strong say in the organization of production and to directly benefit from their labor. Rising absentee ownership makes both goals more remote.

Where Are We Headed?

In early 1982 President Reagan soberly observed, "Some farmers will not make it through this difficult period of readjustment." Of course, if President Reagan had bothered to look at previous administrations' predictions, he would not have been surprised that over seven hundred farms were going out of business each week in the early 1980s. In 1975, for example, the USDA produced a study showing that if farmers were left to the vagaries of the international market, the nation would lose over one and a half million farmers in the following ten years. Of those remaining, only 9 percent would be owners of all the land they worked, compared to a third in the mid-seventies.[91] A similar report was released in 1980.[92]

In other words, the path we're on has been clear for decades. What we have lacked is an understanding of the driving forces behind it and an appreciation of the real costs. Without this, farmers rally behind strategies—the export push, for example—that speed their own demise, and the rest of us accept the loss of family farms as an inevitable part of our economy's drive toward efficiency.

Part of the difficulty in awakening Americans to these changes in our agricultural system is that they are not immediately visible to the general public. We do not foresee the "Californiazation" of the country, with 10,000-acre industrial farms emerging across the Midwest. The changes are hard to see and therefore hard to confront.

First, doors are closed to new farmers. The start-up costs for a new farmer, close to $1 million, preclude all but heirs and the very wealthy.

Second, the concentration of land ownership continues, and as land values continue to inflate, landowners become increasingly wealthy compared to nonowners. We head toward what former Secretary of Agriculture Bob Bergland warned us against—the rise of a "landed aristocracy" in America.

Third, hired labor increasingly takes the place of family labor. During the last decade hired labor rose from a quarter to almost half of total farm labor. For the first time in U.S. history, most people who work on farms do not live on them.[93] In early 1983, for example, the young Neal couple told us that if they lose their farm, they will probably move to Illinois and take a job managing someone else's big sow operation.

Fourth, farm tenancy rises. It begins as retired farmers hold onto their increasingly valuable land, renting it out. In the next stage these ex-farmers sell the land to nonfarm interests.

Fifth, rural communities are destroyed as businesses, schools, and churches lose the farm families they served.

These five changes describe a profound economic transformation. But what is its meaning?

Our Loss

Today about 200,000 commercial farms produce most of the food we eat. In 1980, the government predicted that by the year 2000 only 50,000 farms would produce most of our food.[94] Sure, 200,000 farms, or 50,000, or even 5,000 farms could produce all the food we need. That's not the question. What, then, is at stake?

Some argue that fewer farms mean our food supply is less secure. They claim that once farming becomes purely a big commercial operation, food will be produced only when it's profitable. Under such conditions, food prices would have to rise, they predict.

Others insist that that fewer, bigger farms mean more environmental destruction because only the personal concern of the family farmer will protect the soil. "When corporations with farm managers take over, all they will care about is profits," said Nebraska farmer Betty Lamplot. "They'll let the land go."

Still others point out that continued concentration means more energy consumption because the biggest farms tend to rely more heavily on energy-intensive inputs such as fertilizers and pesticides.

Yet another point of analysis has been central to our Institute's work: The conflict between the concentration of economic power (wealth in land being one source of economic power) and the accountability of our political democracy to majority interests. Situated in California, we have seen firsthand the power of mammoth land interests make a mockery of the law. Throughout most of this century they blatantly ignored a law reserving the benefits of taxpayer-subsidized irrigation water for small family farms. After small farmers protested, these large agribusiness interests succeeded in altering the law so they would no longer have to break it![95] This is just one example of what one sees in many third world countries—the power of a landed elite to manipulate political structures in its favor.

While each of these arguments is persuasive and many are addressed directly in later chapters, we insist that other, less tangible questions are just as important:

Why, we ask, has the idea of the family farm captured the imagination of so many Americans? Why has every administration felt it had to promise to "save the family farm," even though farmers make up only a tiny percentage of our population? Could it be because the farmer appears to retain the dignity and self-direction so many Americans, locked into mammoth corporate structures, long for?

"No matter how stressful farming is, it's less stressful than working for someone you don't like," remarked Melvin Schneider. Ohio farmer Julie Neal echoed, "No matter how hard it is, the good outweighs the bad. You're close to what you are doing. It's not like the assembly line. There, you work and get that paycheck, but who cares? In farming you can *see* what you have done." While many of us increasingly produce nonessentials affordable only by those better off, farmers know they are producing what is vital to life itself.

For many people farming also represents strong family ties based on common experience. "I like having the kids see how hard we work. They get a better understanding of what life's all about," Julie Neal commented. "The whole family works together—so we communicate," said Nebraska farmer Betty Lamplot. The comfort of small town, face-to-face relationships—"people know when you're sick and care when you die"—also appeals to many Americans alienated by big-city life.

"Being close to nature" is another value that farmers cherish. "But how can you explain that to a city person?" one farmer asked me. "The warm air in your face in the spring. The soil in your hands . . . you can see life in it that no city person could ever see."

Thus, the death of the family farm is more than an economic question. It forces our attention on the *quality* of our lives. The family farm represents more than a livelihood that many are being forced to abandon. It symbolizes a sense of connectedness to one's work, of serving a purpose larger than one's own survival. It seems to offer the chance to integrate economic, family, and community life.

Many have claimed, as did Stephen Chapman in *Harper's* magazine, that such a vision of family farm America "has always been largely mythical."[96] Certainly family farming in America has been far from idyllic, given all the pressures and uncertainties we've touched on in these last two chapters. But deflating the romanticization of the family farm is much less important than attempting to understand why that myth-mixed-with-reality has held our national imagination. If in it we find qualities that most Americans yearn for, why dismiss the family farm as passe? Why not instead use the vision of the family farm—myth and reality—to reflect upon the kinds of lives we want and to ask how can we begin to envision economic structures *throughout our society* that will afford more Americans the opportunity to live these values?

Just as important, we must grasp a sad irony. Given our economy's basic ground rules, some of the values family farmers most cherish have actually contributed to their own demise. First is the drive of each individual farm family to make the most of its resources—to build their farms up with more acres and the latest technology.

"We added in the hog operation because we wanted to keep our sons busy on the farm. We bought almost 200 acres because we wanted to have enough so at least one son could start farming," one Iowa farmer told us. "But our daughter told my husband after he filed bankruptcy, 'If you'd just hung out in the bar downtown instead of working so hard to build up the farm, you might be better off today. It's just not fair.'" This family's desire to pass on a good life to a child—a loving and responsible act in the eyes of most Americans—actually contributed to its downfall.

In our economy, the push to expand, whether motivated by desire for more material wealth or the widely shared view that growth is what hard-working and responsible people are supposed to do, leads to overextension and dissolution for many. There is only so much farmland.

Similarly, their very willingness to accept the many hardships and uncertainties of farming—traits many farmers value in themselves—keep farmers from perceiving how the rules are stacked against them. "Farming doesn't have to be so stressful," said Melvin Schneider, but few farmers would likely agree. "Everything in farming is do or die," farmer Bill Genzen told us. "Stress becomes a natural thing." Farmers often become resigned to circumstances and feel powerless to change them.

Finally, the belief that our food benefits the hungry abroad moves many farmers to accept their own difficulties without complaint.

As individuals struggling to produce in an economy dominated by highly concentrated industries over which they have no control, farmers defeat themselves. They must compete, clinging to the belief that somehow they can beat the odds.

Such is the tragedy of our economic structure. It's not simply that it penalizes the competitive farm sector and favors highly monopolized industrial sectors. It's not simply that it encourages the already wealthy to keep expanding or that it entices speculators to try to make a killing. The real tragedy of our farm economy is that well-meaning, hard-working Americans, simply pursuing what they believe to be their legitimate self-interests, wind up jeopardizing their own or their neighbors' interests. For our economic system offers no mechanism through which we Americans are able to perceive how our individual well-being is linked to the well-being of all—no mechanism for acting on our *mutual* interest in widely dispersed land ownership, the union of ownership and work, and stable rural communities.

Thus, as the family farm is destroyed by underlying economic forces that squeeze agriculture as a whole and selectively reward wealth and size, we are all challenged to ask: How can we develop economic structures that will allow the individual, for the first time, to pursue his or her own livelihood within a context of concern for the needs of all?

Too many Americans perceive the forces transforming American farming as inexorable. So I was impressed when Melvin Schneider told me simply, "We can choose how many farms we want to have in America." His remark seemed to hit straight to the heart of the matter. Right now who can farm is being decided by invisible economic forces beyond public scrutiny. But we Americans must decide that the economy—which determines so much of our lives—is in our hands. Even those forces which now seem virtually God-given can be drawn out into the light of day. They can be seen for what they are—deeply rooted but capable of being changed to serve the values we choose to live by.

4 Wheat for Oil: Is It Really a Bargain?

"A big solar energy factory" whose products enable the U.S. to buy ten barrels of foreign oil for each barrel used to produce and export them—that's how a recent USDA pamphlet describes American agriculture.[1] Champions of farm exports point to the large surplus in agricultural trade—in 1981 $26.5 billion more in farm exports than imports—to prove that agriculture contributes to the nation's balance of payments. This surplus has steadily increased over the last decade, reaching 34 percent of the cost of imported oil by 1981.[2]

The message to farmers is clear: even if you aren't doing so well, your efforts serve the nation. The sale of agricultural products abroad provides the foreign exchange needed to buy OPEC oil—"wheat for oil."

Even after their spectacular rise during the 1970s, farm exports today comprise only 19 percent of overall U.S. exports, no larger a share than in the late 1960s. But the erroneous view that agriculture has a special mission in correcting our trade imbalance is still promoted and keeps us from questioning the farm export push.

Most important, wheat-for-oil propaganda obscures the basic questions: *Why* did our economy become so dependent on increasing exports in the first place? Could we have dealt with the rising cost of energy import by importing less, instead of pushing to export more? We'll return to these questions in later chapters.

In this chapter we will take the wheat-for-oil rationale at face value and question whether it is really a bargain. We discovered that both critics and proponents of increasing exports fail to appreciate the true dimensions of a crucial variable in the wheat-for-oil equation. That variable is energy—the energy used to produce our farm exports. As agricultural exports have risen over the past ten years, so have the amounts of fuel, fertilizers, and pesticides used in farm production, almost all of which are derived from fossil fuels.

Few policymakers who support increasing exports have addressed the hidden energy costs of exports. And no one, it seems, has analyzed the impact of these hidden energy costs on the U.S. balance of payments.

When we undertook such an analysis, we expected to draw from a well-developed literature and data base to determine the energy costs of producing farm exports. To our surprise, we found that the issue has not been directly studied and that literature dealing with energy consumption in the U.S. food system is woefully inadequate.

The data and assumptions we used are specified in detail in the Institute for Food and Development Policy's research report, "Export Agriculture: An Energy Drain."[3] We hope our efforts to realistically assess the energy costs of American agriculture will spur the additional research needed to obtain more definitive estimates.

Energy and Agriculture: How Much Oil for the Wheat?

Agriculture uses energy for two purposes. Energy can replace labor: Using fuel-burning machinery, a single farmer can work hundreds of acres that would otherwise require many farmhands. Second, energy can increase yields: Fertilizers and pesticides—produced from petrochemicals—increase the productivity of each unit of land.

Until the energy crisis of 1973, relatively low energy prices encouraged farmers to consume fossil fuel in their race to produce under the cost/price squeeze. Between 1950 and 1970, farmers became much more dependent on petroleum inputs. So, when the export boom hit and the cost of energy inputs simultaneously soared, farmers were already hooked. Most felt they had to continue energy-intensive farming techniques, in spite of rising energy costs.

Between 1970 and 1979, farm machinery use increased by 29 percent; use of fertilizer and irrigation rose by almost 30 percent; and the overall application of agricultural chemicals jumped by almost 60 percent.[4]

What do these figures reveal? Does energy used in agriculture represent a significant portion of our total energy consumption? Is U.S. agriculture becoming more or less energy intensive? Finally, does the energy used to produce our farm commodities eat up a significant portion of the energy we import?

To answer these critical questions, we had to start with a realistic assessment of agriculture's share of total U.S. energy consumption.

The most recent general accounting of energy use in the U.S. food system was done by Steinhart and Steinhart in 1973, and much of the data came from the 1960s.[5] To reach an approximate answer, we constructed estimates based on incomplete data and on extrapolations of trends since these early studies. Some studies omitted key direct elements, such as the energy used to transport farm goods. Others failed to take into account energy use for capital goods, such as the amount consumed to manufacture tractors.

The most frequently cited study eliminated the energy used in farm production for export, because its focus was limited to the domestic food system.[6] This resulted in the extremely low estimate that farm energy consumption totaled only 3 percent of U.S. energy use. Nevertheless, this estimate has been cited so often that, over the years, it has become "fact."[7]

Rechecking the primary sources and using data compiled by the Booz-Allen Hamilton consulting firm in 1973 for the Federal Energy Administration, we arrived at a more complete estimate for the late 1960s. This estimate is shown in Table 4-1.

Before the export boom and the oil crisis, agriculture was using about 6.3 percent of the nation's energy. To evaluate how the export push and the oil crisis influenced agricultural energy use, we studied the recent history of agri-

TABLE 4-1

Direct *	1.9 percent of U.S. consumption
Indirect * *	2.5 percent of U.S. consumption
Capital	
Depreciation	.75 percent of U.S. consumption
Transport	.98 percent of U.S. consumption
Maintenance	.15 percent of U.S. consumption
TOTAL	6.28 percent of U.S. consumption

Note: Adapted from Booz Allen Hamilton and Hantman. Booz Allen's calculations for transport were increased by 0.15 percent to account for transport of inputs to farms. The energy used for maintenance of farm capital equipment was added by Hantman.

* Energy used directly on the farm, such as fuel and electricity.

* * Energy used in producing farm inputs, such as fertilizer.

culture's consumption of the four major components of its energy use: fuels, fertilizer, electricity, and farm machinery.

Using USDA data, we learned that on-farm energy use had risen from 6.3 in 1967 to 7.1 percent of our nation's total energy use by 1981. From a low in 1973 to a high in 1981, farm production's share in our total energy budget had increased 40 percent.[8]

Clearly, the farm economy was out of step with the rest of the economy. As the energy crisis deepened, energy consumption nationwide began to level off and even decline in many sectors of the economy. But, as the export push took hold, the reverse occurred in agriculture.

As a share of total national energy use, 7.1 percent may seem minor. But in light of the wheat-for-oil rationale for mounting agricultural production, that 7.1 percent takes on new meaning. For example, in 1980, to keep our farm economy chugging away required the equivalent of *half* of net energy imports for the entire nation.

The Energy Price Tag for Exports

After working out the total energy bill for U.S. agriculture, we divided it between energy used to produce food consumed at home and energy used for export crops. As farm exports soared during the 1970s, the energy costs to produce those exports grew to represent a bigger share of the value of the exports themselves.

Between 1970 and 1980 the value of farm exports rose from $7.2 billion to $41.3 billion, and the export share of total agricultural output rose from 18 percent to nearly 37 percent. Meanwhile, the cost in barrel equivalents of oil for the energy to produce these exports increased over thirty-fold, from a mere $325 million in 1970 to over $11 billion in 1980.

Thus, energy costs as a percentage of total value of farm exports rose from 4.6 percent in 1970 to 27 percent in 1980—a sixfold increase. In other words, by 1980, *for every dollar of farm produce we sold abroad, we had to spend the equivalent of 27 cents for imported oil to produce it.*[9]

Even this sizable chunk of energy expense does not fully reflect its true price. We must also consider the billions expended because of decreased energy efficiency in agriculture associated with our all-out-for-exports strategy.

The Price of Expansion: Less Efficiency

During the 1960s, when exports were a smaller and fairly stable portion of total farm output, energy efficiency in American agriculture was gradually increasing. Between 1967 and 1971, energy productivity (the amount of farm output per unit of energy input) rose by about 5 percent.[10] But in 1973, the first year of the export push, the increase turned into an actual *decrease*. Energy productivity continued to decline every year through 1979. By 1980 energy productivity had registered a decline of 22 percent below the peak levels of 1973, as the table below shows.[11]

Not only did energy consumption in agriculture increase; it passed the point of diminishing returns. Additional energy inputs no longer resulted in proportionately larger output. This is perhaps the most serious and startling energy effect of expansion for export.

A full accounting of the energy price tag associated with rising exports must include the costs of increasing inefficiency *throughout* the farm sector because of the produc-

TABLE 4-2: Falling Energy Productivity in Agriculture (Farm Output per Unit of Energy Input)

Year	Energy Use* Index	Output** Index	Energy Productivity
1967	100	100	100
1968	102	102	100
1969	104	102	99
1970	104	101	97
1971	105	110	104
1972	105	110	105
1973	107	112	105
1974	113	106	94
1975	122	114	93
1976	134	117	84
1977	146	119	82
1978	154	122	82
1979	161	129	82
1980	151	122	82

* Based on energy (rather than dollar) values to avoid the effects of energy price increases.

** From *Agricultural Statistics 1981*.

tion push. Look at it this way: Suppose U.S. agriculture had maintained the peak energy efficiency level it had *before* the export boom. In 1980, this difference in efficiency would have meant a savings of $4.3 billion in farm energy costs—the equivalent of 126 million barrels of imported oil, at average prices for that year.[12]

If we add this $4.3 billion to the $11.2 billion worth of energy consumed to produce U.S. farm exports, the total energy bill is over $15.5 billion—a figure that erases almost *70 percent* of the $23.2 billion agricultural trade surplus.

Put another way, when we value energy based on its equivalent in imported oil (and consider both lost productivity and energy used to produce farm exports), the total export energy costs amount to almost forty cents for each dollar we earn from farm exports.

Why Declining Efficiency?

How can we explain the decline in American agriculture's energy productivity during the decade of expansion for export?

First, the best agricultural land was already in production before the export push began. Much of the new land pulled into production required more fertilizer and irrigation. Second, the shift to row-crops, monoculture, and more frequent continuous plantings to grow export crops reduced the natural regenerative capacities of the soil, leading to more fertilizer and pesticide applications. The productivity of each acre increased, but the energy cost of producing each unit also increased. In chapter 7 we document how production for export has directly increased the loss of our nation's topsoil—translating the wheat-for-oil strategy into "soil for oil."

In 1976, David Pimentel of Cornell estimated that U.S. farmers used 2.1 billion gallons of fuel equivalent to overcome the cumulative effect of soil erosion—2.5 percent of net energy imports for that year. Each year, however, the application of additional fertilizer and pesticides returns a smaller yield.[13]

Furthermore, the mining of water from underground sources, examined in chapter 8, contributes to energy intensity. As groundwater tables have declined appreciably in some states, it takes more energy to pump the same amount of water.

A more speculative link between rising exports and more intensive energy use is suggested in the preceding chapter. There we document how production for export has contributed to the growing concentration of farms into larger units. A recent study by agricultural economists Frederick Buttel and O. W. Larson III demonstrates that farms with sales over $100,000 have much higher levels of energy use per dollar of output than smaller operations.[14] They give two main reasons. First, larger farms are more mechanized than their smaller neighbors. Second, crop monoculture increasingly prevails as farm size grows. Both practices increase energy use per harvested bushel, and both are employed in the crop specialization associated with production for export.

Still More Hidden Costs from Exports

Secondary energy expenses raise actual costs further. Many of these are not borne directly by the farmer, but by the taxpaying public, either through subsidies to farmers or in the energy costs of environmental cleanups necessitated by agricultural pollution.

The federal government, through the Bureau of Reclamation, provides a large share of the water for irrigated farming. In addition, many western states, including California, have built sizable water systems for supplying irrigation. A full account of hidden energy costs for irrigation would have to include energy for building dams and canals to support the expanded irrigation for export production.

Getting water to farms is only part of the irrigation subsidy. Intensive irrigation creates water runoff problems— salt infusion, silt runoff, and contamination of water supplies by soil nutrients, organic matter, and pesticides. Dealing with these by-products is often enormously expensive.

Salinization in the Grand Valley area of Colorado provides an extreme example. There, on 71,000 farmed acres, irrigation water absorbs half a million tons of salt each year from underlying saline layers and dumps it into the Colorado River. Because a treaty with Mexico stipulates the river's maximum permissible salinity, the Bureau of Reclamation is building a desalinization plant downriver from Grand Valley. This plant is not specifically meant to treat the salinity generated in Grand Valley, but its capacity is similar to the salt added by Grand Valley, which makes them easily comparable.[15] The energy requirements for the plant (including construction, operation, and maintenance) are equal to nearly ten barrels of oil per acre each year. Compare this to the average annual U.S. farm energy needs of only three barrels of oil per acre for *all* production.[16]

Soil erosion also causes costly ecological damage. About three billion tons of sediment collect each year in the nation's waterways, lakes, and reservoirs. Pimentel has estimated that sediment damage costs the nation about a half billion dollars annually, including cleanup in some cases and the loss of economic use of the water in other cases.[17]

Wheat for Oil: A Lousy Bargain?

In this chapter we've examined the wheat-for-oil rationale for farm export expansion, asking: Is it an energy bargain? Does trading wheat for oil make sense as a way to pay for imported fuel?

Even if we ignore other costs and focus only on energy accounting, the United States may have already reached a point where the wheat-for-oil trade is a losing proposition. The dearth of essential data makes a definitive calculation impossible, but we believe the evidence presented here should stimulate a national inquiry into this rationale for farm export expansion.

We have shown that the direct on-farm energy costs of production for export have been seriously underestimated. Estimated conservatively, they must now be over $11 billion annually. We have also shown that this estimate must be added to the higher energy costs for production for domestic use resulting from overall decreased energy efficiency. These costs, which have been neglected altogether, may be over $4 billion. To this $15.5 billion total must be added additional billions for hidden costs, including government outlays, especially for irrigation. Thus, our grand total—for energy costs alone—comes to 40 percent of the earnings of agricultural exports, and possibly a good deal more.[18]

The shortsighted production strategy reflected in the export boom and justified by the wheat-for-oil argument must be judged on more than the calculable energy costs of farm production versus the cost of energy imports. These costs are just one factor among the many far-reaching consequences—human and environmental—that we assess throughout this book.

5 The Free Market in Grain and Other Myths*

A roadside stand selling ripe tomatoes, string beans, and corn on the cob is as close as many Americans ever get to farming. Yet grains—not vegetables or meat—provide most calories and protein for the majority of humankind. Therefore, the farm export boom mainly involves increased exports of grains, mainly feedgrains intended for cattle, chickens, and pigs, rather than grain to be directly consumed by people. Grain traders are its major participants and its greatest single beneficiaries. (See figure 5–1.)

The grain trade involves thousands of individuals and businesses—privately and cooperatively owned county elevators, small, medium, and large brokers and handlers, speculators on the commodity exchanges, and others. But about 85 percent of the world's trade in grain is handled by just six companies. While their names are hardly household words—Cargill, Continental, Louis Dreyfus, Bunge and Born, Mitsui/Cook, and Andre/Garnac—they have enormous impact on the world food trade.[1]

These six "big league" firms, as they are known in the business, handle an incredible 96 percent of U.S. wheat exports, 95 percent of corn, and 80 percent of oats and sorghum. Cargill alone routinely captures 25 to 35 percent of the entire U.S. farm export market.[2]

In this chapter we will look at how the grain companies have profited from the export boom. We will focus on how they have used these profits to expand, obeying the same ground rules that push farmers to expand—but with very different results. And we will look at the largest trader, Car-

*With Frances Moore Lappé.

Figure 5–1
Volume of U.S. Exports of Wheat, Corn, and Soybeans, 1966–1980

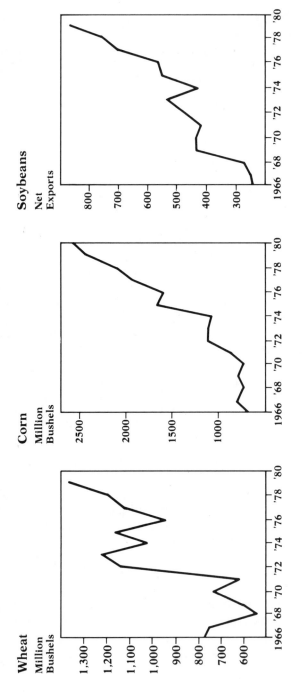

Data from USDA, *Agricultural Statistics, 1981*, tables 5, 40 and 180.

gill, as a prime example of how that growth affects the rest of us and is likely to affect the future of our food system.

There have been few accurate accounts written about the grain trade. As a vestige of pre–twentieth-century private family empires, it can easily be glamorized. International wheeling and dealing, as well as multimillion-dollar scandals, are part of the grain trade's history. So are violations of the law involving the welfare of farmers and consumers.

But these are not our main concern. We want to describe how grain traders benefit unfairly when they do play by the rules, because the rules themselves are at fault. Looking for villains in the boardroom will not bring us a step closer to the real solution to our problems.

The Big-League Traders

Don't be surprised if you've never heard of any of the big-league traders. In his 1979 book *Merchants of Grain*, *Washington Post* reporter Dan Morgan observed, "It is difficult to understand how the international grain companies could have slipped through history as inconspicuously as they have."[3]

Only one of these companies, Mitsui/Cook, the latest entrant, is publicly held. The rest are privately owned "family" businesses. Thus only Mitsui/Cook is required to make the yearly financial disclosures required by the U.S. Securities and Exchange Commission.

The fact that the big grain companies are privately held is not accidental. Secrecy is a key to success in the grain trade.

Commodity Markets

Commodity markets are a mystery to most people. Even farmers, though they must sell their produce, rarely participate in the trading process. Even more than the stock market, trading in agricultural commodities is a complex and unpredictable business, usually left to "experts" or those foolish enough to gamble. Yet what occurs there is decisive, both to consumers and to the winners and losers throughout the food system.

Historically, commodity markets developed to reduce uncertainty and risk for the farmer. The seasonal nature of agricultural production means that without a mediating mechanism there is a glut of produce at harvest time and a scarcity the rest of the year. An established commodity market provides a mechanism—the futures contract—to spread sales commitments throughout the year and to smooth the otherwise sharp fluctuations in supply and demand that would occur as a natural result of the production cycle. Buyer and seller agree to pay for and deliver a given amount of farm produce at a set price on some future date, say, three months from now. The farmer is guaranteed a price for the harvest when it arrives, and the buyer is guaranteed an available supply at a fixed cost. If the delivery date is between harvest cycles, the buyer knows the grain will be put in storage until due rather than sold. In theory, both parties are shielded from the cyclical nature of agricultural production and marketing.

That's the theory. But in practice few farmers actually enter into futures contracts. Only a fraction of trading in agricultural commodities involves the producer and the end user. Instead, the market is largely made up of professional traders, other middlemen, and speculators.

These professional traders have no intention of actually taking delivery on tens of thousands of bushels of wheat or corn or soybeans. They seek to profit from their mere knowledge of prices, rather than through producing or handling the commodities. Their business is to correctly predict either price spreads (the difference in price between the same or substitutable commodities in different markets) or price movements up or down.

Many factors determine prices in both the "spot" (current cash) and futures markets. The need to know about these factors as soon as possible and to be able to evaluate them in light of all other variables makes good market information availability crucial to the trader's success. Transport costs, the size of future harvests and the demand for them, storage availability, and even political developments all enter into price determination in the commodity markets. As markets expand to global dimensions, the variables that can have an impact on prices grow in number and complexity and make it more difficult to predict market movements with accuracy. In addition, global markets are inherently less stable than local ones precisely because these numerous variables can have an influence and set off wider price fluctuations than would normally occur in smaller markets.

These greater uncertainties encourage yet another source of potential instability: speculation. With more variables unknown or difficult to predict, more traders are tempted to gamble on the frailties of the market and on the hope that prices may not really reflect "true" market conditions for the future. Buying and selling by speculators, who work merely on hunches, can create artificial supply or demand for foods. This creates additional opportunities for profit or loss as traders attempt to predict the impact speculation itself will have on price spreads. In effect, heavy speculation turns the trading process into a "floating crap game" in which prices bear little or no resemblance to actual costs of production or market demand. Fortunes are made and lost largely on the bandwagon movements of buyers and sellers divorced from economic realities and highly susceptible to rumor and fluctuations in the market itself.

Given these elements of market operation, the textbook version of commodity trading, wherein risk and uncertainty are minimized by futures contracts, can easily become the reverse. Big grain companies are among the few positioned to navigate this minefield successfully. Their market intelligence and scale of operations permit them not only to outguess the market more often than others, but to actually influence the market to their own advantage.

The grain company advantages result partly from their internal structure and partly from the global structure of the commodity markets in which they operate. Taken together, these elements give the grain companies superior control over market information, the ability to manipulate markets, and the ability to circumvent what little market regulation exists. In each of these three areas rising exports

have increased opportunities for grain company dominance and further tightened their control over the entire
food system.

Knowledge Is Power (and Profits!)

The major grain companies are able to gather, digest,
and act quickly on the information needed to track increasingly complex market developments. All six of the
major grain exporters maintain a global market intelligence network. According to a soybean trader for one of
the largest grain companies, the most urgent messages can
be flashed to headquarters from anywhere in the world in
less than four seconds![4]

These companies alone have the resources to maintain
an army of information specialists, who assemble and process data from every corner of the globe, as well as the computers and telexes to support this effort. As a result, information available in theory to all can in practice be put
to immediate and profitable use by only a few large firms.
For example, satellite technology has made it possible to
substantially improve the quantity and quality of global
crop forecasting. But, while this data is in the public do-
main (available through NASA or the USDA), the major
grain companies are best equipped to use this information
quickly. Even the U.S. and Canadian governments, which
receive the same data, cannot compete: The Canadian government official in charge of a joint Canadian-U.S. effort to
utilize this data admitted that his country simply could not
digest all the data it had access to.[5] By contrast, according
to *Business Week*, one major firm's information network is
so effective that agents of the CIA "often wine and dine the
company's traders to pick their brains."[6]

But if the big traders have an advantage in utilizing publicly available market information, they have an even
greater advantage in the realm of "inside information." In
this sense they *are* the information. Each of the big six
firms handles transactions of sufficient volume to influence
the market. Advance knowledge of these transactions is
closely held within each firm and can be invaluable in an-
ticipating future movements in the market when these

transactions become known. By taking positions in the futures market based on these secret anticipations, the firm is able to translate its inside information into cold cash when the market reacts. While the extreme secrecy that prevails in the grain trade makes it impossible to know how often this occurs and how much money is made, that the opportunity exists is clear.

In early April 1979, for instance, a few of the large grain companies made corn sales amounting to 170 million bushels (at least 110 million of which were to foreign buyers). A congressional investigation later revealed that these sales were accompanied by corn purchases in the spot and futures markets that more than covered the reduction in supplies. Word of the new sales did not reach the market until late April, *after* the grain companies had been able to accumulate corn stocks in excess of what was needed to meet their commitments. When news of the corn demand finally hit the market, prices rose 4 to 10 cents a bushel and the grain companies were able to sell off their supplies at a handsome profit. Thus, by keeping the new sales a secret, the companies involved were able to use inside information to advantage simply by waiting for the "natural" laws of supply and demand to take effect.[7]

According to Representative Neal Smith (D-Iowa), who chaired a recent investigation of grain company operations in the commodity markets, similar sales are common. "The grain companies make substantial fixed price sales. They then purchase more than enough in the cash and futures markets before U.S. sellers of grain know of the new demand and before prices move up on news of the increased export demand. The grain exporters then wait for the news to come out and for the market to move up. They then take profits on the excess long futures."[8]

But the grain companies need not rely on upward price movements to make big money. Price declines will do just as well, as long as inside information enables them to accurately predict how the market will behave.

In 1976 Canada had a bumper harvest of 20 million tons of wheat. The Canadian Wheat Board estimated it could find customers for only 12 to 13 million tons of the 17 million it needed to sell abroad. The chief strategist for the board, a former grain company official, called in representatives from several of the big firms and made them an offer they couldn't refuse. With American spring wheat comparable to the Canadian harvest selling for $148 a ton on the Minneapolis wheat exchange, the board offered to sell its excess harvest at $135 a ton. The big grain companies snapped up the cheap wheat and, by keeping the purchase a secret, were able to locate buyers abroad and cover themselves in the American market for wheat futures on what they could not sell.

Minnesota farmers were the first to feel the effects of this deal when the Minneapolis exchange price for wheat suddenly and mysteriously collapsed as the big grain companies stopped buying the more expensive American wheat. Canada itself contributed to the collapse by unloading 60 million bushels on the Minneapolis futures exchange, driving prices down sixty cents a bushel. The finishing touch was added when news of the big private sale to the grain companies in September was announced in October. Prices fell another forty cents a bushel. The big grain companies sold the cheap grain abroad at a substantial profit, liquidated their futures contracts at their higher price before the news broke in October, and then rebuilt supplies at the new, far lower prices.[9]

In theory, the rules of the game in commodities trading prohibit such maneuvers by making it illegal to purchase more of a commodity than is needed to cover sales commitments. But in practice, this rule is virtually impossible to enforce, especially for the largest traders who maintain a bewildering array of trading activities on both the buy and sell sides. The Commodity Futures Trading Commission (CFTC) simply does not have the resources to regularly detect such abuses. A recent GAO study reported that since its inception the commission had undertaken only *six* trade practice investigations to identify abuses involving the reconstruction of trading activity and that it "does not have responsibility for and does not perform self-initiated trade practice investigations." In other words, unless someone blows the whistle, there is *no* chance an investigation will catch any abuses.[10]

The GAO study concluded: "Without a vigorous and

comprehensive trade practice investigation program, the CFTC cannot protect the trading public from abusive trading and effectively detect and punish violators of the act or regulations."[11]

The big traders' knowledge monopoly, so critical to their profit edge, also derives from their abilities to ensure that grain sales reporting requirements established by the federal government are kept lax and, where they might stand in the way of profit, to legally sidestep these requirements.

Grain trade analyst Richard Gilmore reminds us why sales reporting is crucial: "A concealed foreign sale of any magnitude means that the prices received by local producers' sales are not likely to reflect increases normally associated with such news."[12] In other words, the big traders' power to circumvent reporting rules directly penalizes farmers whose livelihood depends on world demand for grain being quickly registered in the market.

The Russian grain deal of 1972 was a bitter lesson for farmers in precisely this regard. A few of the largest grain companies had secretly arranged huge sales to the Soviet Union, then bought enough grain to cover these sales before farmers were aware of the new demand and before prices went up. In an effort to prevent reoccurrences, in 1973 the federal government began requiring that all large domestic grain sales to the U.S.S.R. be reported to the USDA within twenty-four hours.

But the global structure of the trading process left a gaping hole in this requirement. Since the U.S. government has no jurisdiction over foreign transactions, sales of U.S. grain handled by foreign subsidiaries of U.S. firms are not subject to mandatory disclosure until the foreign buyer is identified, which is not required until time of delivery. As the export boom has intensified, major traders have used this loophole to increasing advantage, routing larger portions of their total sales through foreign subsidiaries. For example, in 1976–77, 65 percent of wheat and corn sold to the Soviet Union was handled directly by U.S. firms. But the following year this figure dropped to only 8 percent, and by 1979 virtually all sales to the Soviets were handled by foreign firms.[13] As a result, domestic reporting requirements have become increasingly meaningless.

The foreign firms handling these trades with the Soviets may be subsidiaries of U.S. firms, and export sales do not need to be reported until the price is set. This allows the multinational traders to privately have their subsidiaries make a foreign sale and to contract with that subsidiary to supply the grain. The U.S. parent can then buy the grain on American markets *before* the sale is reported and before the market can respond to the news of a major sale. After the parent has covered its position, the price can be fixed and the sale is then reported and made public.

Another means of circumventing reporting requirements is called the "optional origins" contract. Such a contract can be fulfilled with grain from unspecified and multiple sources, allowing the firm to juggle sales commitments among affiliates to maximize profits. Since with this type of contract there is no obligation to deliver grain from a specific source, the company's far-flung network can be used to great advantage by shifting grain purchases and destinations in response to new market developments only it is in a position to react to.

Like any contract, international grain sales transactions can be canceled at any time by "mutual consent." This rule allows the major grain traders, with affiliates around the world, to enter into essentially paper transactions with themselves.

This makes it virtually impossible for the federal government or anyone other than the majors to determine the real situation in exports. This inability can confound the commodity markets and has been identified as the major cause of the soybean embargo of 1973. As Gilmore states, "If there is one thing that is now clear about the soybean embargo of 1973, it is that it was enacted in response to a shortage that never existed. The rapid surge in spot soybean prices in early 1973 was the result of a rash of overselling by American grain giants to their overseas affiliates." [14]

To calls for more extensive and timely reporting of grain sales, the major grain firms argue that such requirements would unfairly disadvantage domestic firms. And they threaten that stricter requirements would drive them to use overseas exchanges where there are no requirements.

Indeed, without universal disclosure requirements (a move requiring information exchange among all major markets), a tightening of domestic reporting regulations could still leave large loopholes in the price discovery function that is supposed to put all traders on an equal footing.

As a result, even farmers, who bear the brunt of inadequate sales reporting, seem resigned to swallowing the current economic loss rather than risking a greater loss if tighter reporting requirements forced customers into foreign commodity markets.[15] But how real is this risk? Attempts to accurately judge it are hampered by the problem itself—lack of information. So little is known about the impact of current reporting requirements that when the Inspector General of the USDA was asked to evaluate the possible loss of sales if tighter requirements were imposed, his office replied that "at best, testimony in this area has been unspecific, uncorroborated and unverifiable."[16]

The Phantom Food Weapon

In January 1980, when the Soviet Union invaded Afghanistan, President Carter broke a campaign pledge to never selectively cut off agricultural exports for "political reasons," as his predecessors had done. To make the Soviet Union pay for its aggression, Carter fought back with food—imposing a grain embargo on food sales to the U.S.S.R.

Could such a tactic work, given the realities of a global food trade dominated by a handful of giant grain corporations? The answer is a resounding no. Not even the American government can prevail in its foreign policy objectives, questionable as they are, against the grain trade's twin advantages of information monopoly and trading flexibility.

In deciding how to respond to the Soviet offensive in Afghanistan, presidential advisors depended on an accurate assessment of the potential impact of various U.S. moves. They turned to the CIA's impact analysis of the grain embargo option, which concluded that a grain embargo would substantially damage the Soviet's long-term plan to increase domestic meat production. The CIA predicted a 12 percent loss in meat availability if U.S. grain supplies were cut off.[17] The report presented the embargo as a powerful weapon to ensure the Soviets paid dearly for their misconduct.

But for all their intelligence gathering savvy, the CIA goofed. Its predictions were based on numerous invalid assumptions, including the belief that it had sufficient information on which to evaluate the impacts. But, as we have seen, the U.S. government's data gathering on grain movements is full of gaps. "There was and could have been no certainty about how much grain had already been sold to the Russians and who was holding the contracts," according to Gilmore.[18]

But the greatest weakness in the CIA's analysis was its apparent belief that the major traders would pass up an opportunity to profit. As the embargo wore on, breaches began to appear. "U.S.S.R. Beats the Food Blockade,"[19] and "Soviets Use Back Door to Skirt U.S. Embargo"[20] were prominent headlines. In the words of one leading shipping corporation, the embargo had been "leaking like a sieve."[21]

USDA figures published in 1981 indicate that the Soviet Union suffered only a 2 percent cut in feedgrains and that the embargo had no perceptible impact on meat consumption. The Soviets had made major purchases in the U.S. in anticipation of the embargo. They made up much of their shortfall with higher priced Argentine grain, and they continued to receive grain from Canada under previously negotiated agreements. Finally, the U.S. government had no means for ensuring that U.S. grain wasn't reshipped from its declared destination to the Soviet Union; so the Soviets may have received U.S. grain during the embargo.

That such a process would occur should not have been beyond the planning purview of the U.S. government. A little-known study by the USDA of an earlier embargo in 1977 had reported:

> The Department cannot rely on export reporting destinations. In our review we could not determine the final destinations of commodities because of (1) the vast network of resellers; (2) commodities may change hands many times before they reach their final destination; and (3) U.S. grain is often comingled with foreign grain, and it would be im-

possible to distinguish U.S. grain from foreign grain from reseller records.[22]

The USDA recommended a number of reforms in 1977, but none were undertaken. So it remained business as usual for the grain trade when the later embargo went into effect. The major grain companies' foreign subsidiaries, plus the "confidentiality" needed for "effective functioning of the market," provided an impenetrable smokescreen for foreign transactions.

The embargo was disastrous for U.S. farmers. But were the major grain traders hurt?

As a result of the embargo, the Argentine price for corn rose from $162 per ton in December 1979 to $202 in February 1980. Meanwhile, the U.S. price dropped to $132. Companies that had contracted to buy Argentine corn could now ship that grain to the Soviets and replace it with much cheaper corn bought in the U.S. Those companies made huge profits.[23]

At the same time, the Carter administration created a program to offset any losses traders might have suffered from the embargo. Although they promised not to give the grain companies windfall profits, the federal government lacked the information needed to meet that pledge. In the month prior to the embargo, the traders had changed the declared destinations of 30 percent of their orders from "unknown" to the Soviet Union. The USDA had no way of knowing whether or not those orders were ever intended to be shipped to the Soviet Union, but the government was committed to reimbursement for them anyway.[24]

But by May of 1980, the grain trade's fortune and the farmers' losses were just too obvious. The GAO blew the whistle, and the *Des Moines Register* headlined, "Embargo Compensation Payments Seen Giving Grain Firms a Profit." Members of Congress became alarmed, and Representative Glenn English, after conferring with the GAO auditors, exclaimed: "The situation smells to high heaven. The grain companies have really taken them [the USDA] for a ride." One government official who had studied the USDA's agreements with exporting companies said privately, "Deep down in my gut I feel they [some companies] are making a killing." [25] Despite the outcry, efforts to gain fuller disclosure of grain company contracts over this period were stymied by Agriculture Secretary Bob Bergland, who argued that information revealing which firms held what contracts was "market sensitive" and could unfairly compromise their trading positions.

The Cargill Empire: A Case Study in Grain Company Riches from Exports

The power of the major grain traders is only partly evident from an examination of their role in the commodity markets. The profits garnered from the export boom have not only helped them expand their global trading network but have fueled their expansion into a wide range of other economic activities as well. A look at Cargill, the largest grain company, provides a glimpse of the phenomenal wealth and power held by these giants and how it has been used to tighten the firm's grip throughout the food economy.

In 1979 only six nonoil companies had worldwide annual sales in excess of Cargill's $12.6 billion. If Cargill were to take its place in the ranks of publicly held U.S. corporations, it would be sixteenth in sales on the list of the Fortune 500 industrial firms, ahead of such giants as Du Pont and Tenneco. (Publicly held corporations sell their stock to anyone through the stock exchange; in privately held corporations stock ownership is confined to a small group.) Because Cargill is privately held, and therefore exempt from federal disclosure requirements, only information it chooses to announce is available to the public. But from the business press and from subpoenaed congressional testimony, rough estimates can be pieced together.

However sketchy the details, Cargill's phenomenal growth and power are beyond dispute. While net farm income in constant dollars dropped by one third during the seventies, Cargill's net income in constant dollars grew by a whopping 450 percent. Cargill's annual profits, which averaged $14 million in the late 1960s, rose to an estimated $150 million eight years later, while its net worth mushroomed over tenfold between 1965 and 1977 (from $100 million to $1.1 billion). [26]

Cargill is not only privately held, it is closely held. Thirty-three members of the Cargill and MacMillan families and a few senior executives own virtually all the stock. The firm's international subsidiary, Tradax (reputed to be as large as its parent) is referred to as "independent" by Cargill, but 70 percent of its stock is owned by Cargill directly while the remaining 30 percent is owned by the Salevia Foundation. The foundation is a Swiss-chartered trust whose beneficiaries are thirty-three members of the Cargill and MacMillan families. When asked by a U.S. Senate committee if these were the same thirty-three owners of Cargill, Cargill's senior executives responded that they didn't know! Tradax is legally registered as a Panamanian corporation, but its Panamanian "office" is a letter box. Its real headquarters is in Geneva.

Cargill's Geneva-based Tradax network of "independent" foreign subsidiaries gives it maximum flexibility in arranging global transactions. As export markets have opened up around the globe, Tradax branches have expanded into thirteen countries. Sales routed through the Panama "letter box" operation of the Tradax arm allow the firm to shelter billions: By Cargill's own account, from 1972 to 1974, when gross sales of the Panamanian subsidiary jumped from $775 million to over $2 billion, it paid a total of only $3.5 million in U.S. federal income taxes—thanks to a special exemption in corporate taxes for foreign subsidiaries engaged primarily in the export of U.S. agricultural commodities.[27]

According to a former grain merchant for Cargill, Tradax "was founded to protect the company; if there were ever a national emergency, Cargill would just shift all its assets from the United States to Switzerland."[28]

Closely held, private ownership has several advantages over public ownership. It facilitates secrecy about company operations and gives Cargill flexibility in reinvesting profits. Dividends remain low since pressure from the stock market is eliminated, and the family owners/directors control the direction and pace of expansion.

According to their Senate testimony in 1976, Cargill's worldwide after-tax income leapt from $41 million in fiscal 1972 to $131 million in fiscal 1973 to $231 million in fiscal

1974—an increase of nearly 500 percent in just two years.

By 1980 Cargill's annual profits exceeded *a quarter of a billion dollars*. But Cargill isn't totally insulated from the problems facing the food industry in the last two years. In 1981, Cargill's profits fell, as did farm income. But while farmers were facing bankruptcy in the bust, Cargill's profits, though lower, were still nearly $207 million!

In the export boom years from 1973 to 1981, Cargill's profits totaled over $1.5 billion.[29] And very little of this has been paid out as dividends, since, as a closely held, private company, Cargill has no need to please the stock market or any public shareholders.

These profits have accumulated within Cargill itself. As a result, the equity of Cargills' stockholders (those thirty-three members of the Cargill and MacMillan families) has grown from $353 million in 1973 to just under $1.8 billion in 1981.[30] The company's total assets exceeded $5 billion in 1981.

These profits have been used for Cargill's expansion inside the grain business as well as in other areas. According to a 1979 *Business Week* article, at that time Cargill was seeking to expand its share of U.S. grain exports to 35 percent and was spending $150 million per year toward that end. The same article reported that Cargill controlled 350 grain elevators, 500 barges, 5,000 rail cars, and 14 ocean-going vessels. New export terminals were being built at Burns Harbor, Indiana, and at Toledo, Ohio. And Cargill's export terminals at Duluth, Houston, Chicago, and Norfolk were being expanded.[31]

One interesting sidelight is that the Burns Harbor terminal was built not by Cargill, but by the Indiana Port Commission, using $18 million raised by issuing tax-exempt bonds.[32] Similarly, the Toledo terminal was financed by the Toledo-Lucas County Port Authority,[33] and Cargill's Duluth terminal was jointly financed by the Duluth Seaway Port Authority and a grant from the U.S. Economic Development Administration.[34]

As surging exports stretched America's rail network to the limits in the 1970s, Cargill made breakthroughs in grain shipping with big profit payoffs. Cargill led the way with grain-company-owned fleets of hopper cars. As the export boom intensified, the portion of covered hopper-car equipment in private (nonrailroad) hands almost doubled—from 23 to 40 percent between 1971 and 1980[35]—and Cargill has led the pack with a fleet of at least 1,500 cars now under its own ownership or controlled through leases.

Cargill also pioneered the "unit train"—a train of up to 125 uniform covered hopper cars, all owned by or under contract to a single grain handler. With such big volume, Cargill and other large grain handlers receive preferential freight rates from the major rail lines. These new trains are much easier to load and service than the old boxcars and are particularly well suited to loading grain from the giant elevators used by the major grain companies.[36] The large capital investment and high trading volume required to sustain unit trains have restricted their use to the largest grain companies.

With privately owned fleets of rail cars and unit trains, the major firms have tightened their control over the rail transport link and gained an even greater advantage over farmers dependent on their transport services. This situation has invited abuse, especially during times of rail car shortages. The Interstate Commerce Commission documented how, during the grain transport backup of 1972–74, large firms charged exorbitant freight rates to farmers who were anxious to get their grain to market before prices fell even further.[37]

County grain elevators have been hurt by unit trains as well. They lack enough track space to accommodate the much longer trains, so they can't get the special discount rates. This means they lose farmers' business to the Cargill-controlled subterminals (large inland elevators).

In addition to its growing muscle in rail shipments, Cargill owns or controls several hundred river barges, the plant to build them, over eight hundred trucks, and two Great Lakes bulk cargo ships.

Once out of the farmer's hands and onto a Cargill truck, hopper car, or river barge, grain for export is probably headed for a Cargill-owned or -controlled port elevator. Cargill and Continental (the world's second-largest grain trader) together account for fully *half* of the 86 major port terminals (large elevators with facilities for loading ocean freighters) in the continental United States. Cargill began as a small inland elevator firm in 1865. Since World War II, its increasingly international emphasis has led to heavy investment in port facilities, but it has maintained its strong foothold in inland elevators.

Vertical Integration—Cargill Is Its Own Best Customer

Outside the grain business itself, much of Cargill's expansion has been concentrated in those businesses which are major *users* of grain: flour milling, feed processing, soybean crushing, and wet corn milling. As a result of expansion in these areas, Cargill is not only the leading handler of grains, it is also its leading consumer.

By 1981 Cargill was already the eighth-largest flour miller in the U.S. Then, in January 1982, the company bought Seaboard Allied Milling Corporation for $44 million. Suddenly Cargill had leapt into the number two spot in that business.[38]

By 1969, before the start of the export boom, Cargill was already the number two producer of animal feeds in the world, with thirty-five plants in the U.S. and twenty overseas.[39] During the 1970s Cargill steadily expanded its feed processing operations, and it is now the largest soybean crusher in the world. (Soybeans are crushed to produce animal feeds and soy oil.) For example, Cargill is a major investor in Brazil, developing soybean processing capacity in direct competition with U.S. sources.

But Cargill isn't only one of the largest feed producers, it is also one of the largest feed users. Cargill owns Caprock Industries, the largest feedlot operation in the U.S. It also ranks fourth in table egg production (chickens) and is tied for third place in turkey production. Its feedlot operations alone were estimated to use nearly a billion tons of feed in 1979.[40]

Cargill has also expanded into the next step of the chain. Its 1978 purchase of Missouri Beef (MBPXL) made it the number two beef packer in the United States.

As Cargill has grown by garnering the lion's share of

world traffic in grain, it has diversified to a point where it can effectively generate its own demand for grain. Cargill, for example, can buy its own corn, process it into feed at its own plant, use the feed in its own feedlot to fatten cattle, and then slaughter and process the beef in its own packing house. This "vertical integration" permits the firm to pick up additional profits at each stage of the production process that would otherwise go to unrelated firms. The end result is greater economic power held in fewer hands—a process continually at work in our economic system and one that, in this case, has clearly been underwritten by the phenomenon of rising exports.

This kind of expansion is self-reinforcing and can have severe implications for the future of our food system. Let's take a hypothetical example. Suppose that due to over-capacity and competition, the prices for poultry drop. Cargill, with its massive holdings in grain and feed, can then decide to forego some profit in its feed mills and supply chicken feed to its chicken-growing division at well below market prices. Cargill's competitors, who are not part of a large, vertically integrated company, cannot buy feed so cheaply; so their production costs are higher than Cargill's. Cargill can then undersell the competition and drive them out of the chicken business. The result is a less competitive business, higher long-term profits for Cargill, and higher chicken prices for the rest of us.

Who Really Wins?

The grain trade has profited massively from the export boom, which it helped to promote. These profits have helped consolidate control of the trade into the hands of a few major traders and have allowed these traders to expand their operations into other phases of the food system.

The grain traders claim that their expansion promotes an efficiency that benefits everyone in society. Yet, as we see throughout this book, those benefits have not been distributed throughout society. While the grain traders have continued to accumulate wealth, the rest of us, particularly farmers and consumers, have reaped *no* benefits from the export boom.

Our brief look at the grain traders allows us to draw some lessons about how and why that has happened.

Grain Traders versus Farmers. The grain traders are fond of saying that their prosperity is tied to that of farmers. We know from the effects of the export push, which has so benefited the grain traders while leaving most farmers worse off than before, how untrue this is. *While farmers want timely, accurate market information on which to base production decisions, the big traders thrive on secrecy.* Delays in news of sales can mean millions to them.

Farmers need stable prices, but traders profit from market instability. The export market boom has exaggerated price fluctuations. The resulting dips and peaks wreak havoc on farmers and consumers. But from the trader's point of view, greater price fluctuations mean greater profit opportunities. Grain companies make money by betting on price differences between countries and price changes over time. Commodity price fluctuations are the very lifeblood of the grain trade. An official of the Chicago Board of Trade summed it up nicely when he told agribusiness executives, "Stability, gentlemen, is the only thing we can't deal with."[41] For this reason, the grain trade uses all its lobbying muscle to prevent the government from introducing an international grain reserve system that might reduce commodity price fluctuations.

Farmers want the highest possible price for their commodities, whereas the grain trade cares mainly about volume. In 1980–83 the price of grain has been less than its overall cost of production so that most farmers lost money on every bushel they produced.

But the grain trade gets its margin on every bushel, regardless of price. "The grain trade doesn't care about price," declared a Cargill trader.[42] In fact, the interest of the grain trade would oppose increasing the world price of grain if it led more countries to develop domestic capacity and reduce imports.

Grain Traders Versus Consumers. Farmers tend to identify the grain traders with consumers' interests, but those interests are hardly similar. Consumers, like farmers, require price stability. While the grain trade profited from export growth and rising prices in the early seventies, consumers were saddled with rising inflation.

In the long term, consumers benefit from increased food self-reliance while the grain trade thrives on increased food dependency. No nation wants its basic food needs to be vulnerable to the political manipulations of food exports by other governments. No people wants the supply of its daily bread to depend on whether its government has enough foreign exchange and the inclination to import adequate food. The poor majority in the rural third world do not want its food supply to depend on the policies of better-off urban groups who control food imports.

But national food self-reliance directly threatens the interests of the grain trade. So Cargill preaches that an increase in food imports will do more than self-sufficiency strategies to overcome hunger. It claims that "food self-sufficiency increases a country's vulnerability to its own periodic poor crops,"[43] conveniently ignoring the potential for domestic reserves and the many uncertainties of import dependency.

Cargill likes to be American in America (and, presumably, Swiss in Switzerland), but its interests are not identical to the interests of the American people.

Even though the major grain traders are largely dependent on U.S. farmers and U.S. resources, they are virtually unaccountable to either. The grain traders operate in an arcane and secretive world that makes them immune to many U.S. laws. Since most trade companies are privately held, even basic information on their size and profits is difficult to obtain. Use of foreign subsidiaries allows them to slip through tax and reporting loopholes.

The enormous wealth of the major grain trading firms gives them power to influence U.S. government policy in their interests and to gain access to tax support.

Through its lobbying arms, the grain trade uses its wealth to influence both congressional actions and public opinion on international issues such as the export push itself, and how it taps government largess to help finance its overseas expansion. Lax regulatory oversight of commodity markets is yet another mark of the trade's influence.

The grain trade has achieved significant tax breaks, especially for its foreign subsidiaries. The big traders take advantage of special legal entities called Domestic International Sales Corporations under which only half their export income is subject to U.S. taxes.

At certain periods, the trade has been able to cash in on huge government export subsidies. In order to encourage farm exports in the early 1970s, the government paid the grain exporting companies the difference between the domestic price at which they bought the grain and the lower price for which they sold it abroad. These subsidies rose to forty-seven cents a bushel during the substantial sales to the Soviet Union in 1972. Over a mere seven-week period that year taxpayers handed the six grain exporting companies $300 million in subsidies. (And many analysts agree that the Soviet Union needed no low price incentives to buy in the first place!)[44]

Moreover, the grain traders have achieved access to government bonds to help build port grain elevators which they control. And, of course, the grain trade is aided indirectly by other taxpayer subsidies such as the Corps of Engineers' work to maintain inland waterways, essential to the low barge rates which benefit the trade.

Under the existing ground rules, the process of economic growth guarantees the bulk of the benefits to companies like Cargill. And these very same ground rules determine that Cargill's interests will be at odds with our own.

6 The Food Dollar and the Export Boom: Who Gains and Who Loses?

We've seen how most farmers have suffered while the grain trade has realized a bonanza during the boom and bust of the export decade. But to understand fully who benefits and who is hurt by the forces driving our food system, we must ask where our *entire* food dollar goes and who is best positioned to protect and expand their share. In answering this question, the growing dominance of the corporate giants in the food economy, whose emergence we sketched in chapter 2, becomes clear. As these corporations have further consolidated their hold on the entire food economy, they have elbowed both the farmer and the consumer aside.

Thirty-five years ago the farmer received about half the consumer's dollar. Today the farmer gets considerably less. By 1979, about 69 cents of every dollar spent on food went to firms that transport, process, or retail domestically grown food commodities. Wholesalers and transporters took 18 cents, processing and packing firms took 21 cents, retail food stores received 20 cents, and eating places or vending machines 9 cents.[1] (See figure 6-1.)

Thus, in 1979 the remaining 31 cents went to the farmer for the crop. But with that 31 cents the farmer had to pay the farm supply industries about 17 cents, while other farm expenses, such as rent, interest, capital depreciation, and taxes, claimed an additional 10 cents. This left the farmer with about 4 cents to pocket.[2] Recall the unstable income situation farmers face at the hands of our economic ground rules, as we described in chapters 2 and 3. For example, while the *overall* distribution of the food dollar for 1979 stayed roughly the same in 1980, the sharp drop in farmers' fortunes that year cut their small sliver of the domestic food dollar by nearly 40 percent—from about 4 cents to only 2.5 cents—while consumers paid about 8 per-

Figure 6–1
Components of the U.S. Food Dollar, 1979

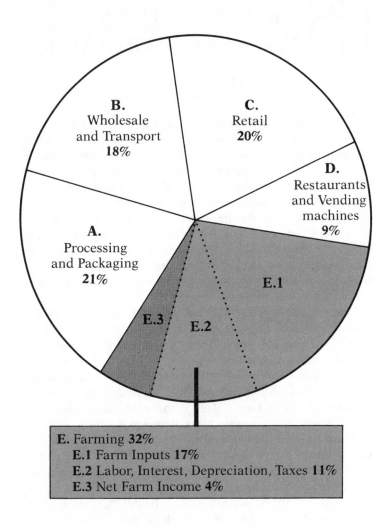

Data from E. Phillip LeVeen, *Towards A New Food Policy: A Dissenting Perspective.*

cent *more* for food in the supermarket. Both farmers and consumers were worse off. To understand why, we must take a closer look at how the farm supply industry and food processing and retailing sectors of the food economy have fared over the past decade.[3]

"We Suffer When They Suffer"

"We do well when our farmers prosper, but we suffer when they suffer," stated Edwin Wheeler, president of the Fertilizer Institute, which represents the fertilizer industry, in 1982.[4] Indeed, as the farm supply industry slumped in the early eighties, industry spokespeople made many such "we're all in the same boat" pronouncements. But *are* farmers and the farm supply industry in the same boat?

Let's go back to 1973, the beginning of the export boom. Farmers were already caught on a production treadmill that depended on labor-saving technology when the export push drew them into even greater dependence on industrial inputs. And the price they pay for this dependence has been high.

Overall farm production expenses, which had risen only 17 percent in the eight years prior to the export push, more than doubled in the seven years of export expansion. This rise reflected both increased purchases and rising prices.[5] As demand for tractors and combines outstripped manufacturing capacity, prices for farm machinery went up. The price of a new tractor increased 27 percent in the 1974 calendar year. Combine prices went up 29 percent, harrows over 32 percent, and hay balers 35 percent.[6]

Industry would probably claim their price increases simply reflected higher costs, mainly higher energy costs. But increases in their profit margins make this single explanation hard to swallow. Before taxes, profit margins for the above four products increased from 65 to 225 percent during this period—far in excess of the percentage increases in price.[7]

These huge profit margins abated after the initial surge in demand for farm machinery, but prices and total profits continued to climb throughout the seventies, rather than settling back to their pre-export-boom levels. While farm commodity prices fluctuated because of the greater market instability of exports, farm machinery prices climbed steadily.

Market Power

In striking contrast to the farmer, the farm supply industry is positioned to protect its profits because it is a highly concentrated industry—a few giant firms dominate production in each product line. While the farm supply industry had narrowed to relative few firms early in this century, economic concentration has continued apace:

- The tractor attachments industry: In 1977 the four largest companies accounted for 80 percent of all industry sales—up from 72 percent in 1958.[8]
- Harvesting machinery: The top four firms had 79 percent of total sales in 1977, a significant increase from 66 percent in 1954.[9]
- Nitrogenous and phosphatic fertilizers: The eight major companies controlled over half of all farm sales in 1977. In agricultural chemical sales, the eight largest firms had 64 percent of the total—up from 57 percent as recently as 1972.[10]
- Pesticides: The market share of the top four firms nearly doubled from 33 percent in 1966 to almost 60 percent in 1976.[11]

These statistics help explain the supply industry's huge profit margins during the 1973–75 boom period. The oligopolistic structure of the farm input industry protects its profits in both the up and down swings of the commodity price cycle. During a boom, the industry reaps windfall profits as demand surpasses supply and prices shoot up far beyond the costs of production. On the downswing, profit margins are protected by cooperation among firms to keep prices static while total output is reduced to meet the lower demand.

Of course, its privileged position protects the farm supply industry only so far. If most farmers can't afford new equipment and are cutting back on costly chemicals, the farm supply industry is squeezed, too. This is precisely what happened by the early eighties. The depression that began for farmers in 1980 hit the farm supply industry hard by 1981. In 1982, tractor sales fell 40 percent in a single year, and International Harvester was on the verge of bankruptcy.

Like depression on the farm, recession in the farm supply industry only accelerates the tightening control within the industry. One firm, John Deere, weathered the slump better than its competitors and is expected to increase its market share from its present 35 or 40 percent to around 50 or 60 percent over the next few years. In April of 1982, John Deere chairperson William Hewitt predicted that "the current chaos in its industry could eventually make the company as dominant in farm equipment as General Motors is in autos."[12] Financial analysts attribute Deere's relative success to its decision to "trim inventories rather than prices."[13] In other words, because it controls such a huge market share, Deere can keep prices up, even when demand drops drastically.

Farmers have neither option; they control neither prices nor supply. The differing abilities of farmers and the farm supply industry to protect their interests is illustrated by comparing the rising costs of farm production to prices farmers receive. From 1965 to 1973 farm commodity prices grew about one fifth faster than the costs of producing them. But from 1973 to 1980, during the export boom years, this ratio reversed itself: the cost of production outpaced the price increases farmers received by over 40 percent.[14]

Monopoly Profits

The monopoly profits resulting from concentration in the farm supply industry are difficult to accurately measure. But a 1972 Federal Trade Commission study does give some indication of the extent to which the farm supply industry gains at the expense of the farmer. The commission analyzed one hundred major U.S. industries, including those of two of the largest farm supply categories—farm machinery and prepared feeds. It calculated a monopoly profit margin based on the opportunity cost of capital, and it estimated inefficiencies and waste due to lack of competition.

The FTC found monopoly overcharges of 5.84 percent for farm machinery and 4.20 percent for the feed industry. If these percentages are applied to sales revenues in these industries, farmers were overcharged $827 million for farm machinery and $775 million for feeds in 1980. Taken together, the overcharges accounted for over 8 percent of net farm income that year. If similar rates of overcharge existed in the other major farm supply industries that year, the total loss to farmers amounted to at least $2.8 billion, or *one seventh of their total net income*.[15]

These overcharges contribute to the cost side of the farmers' cost/price squeeze. They clearly illustrate how our economic ground rules selectively reward concentrated economic power—in this case, the oligopolistic farm supply industry, which has the power to take advantage of the boom and bust cycles that are devastating to most farmers.

Exports and Food Price Inflation

Finally, let's turn to that aspect of our food system with which all Americans have some familiarity—the price of food. Boosters of farm export expansion claim that all of us—even consumers—benefit. One group of export promoters claims that "the relationship between food and fiber exports and consumer food prices is much more complex—and beneficial—than [the] common perception suggests."[16]

To understand the impact of rising exports on our food dollar we must first understand how the structure of the food industry has evolved in recent years. At first glance, the sheer numbers of food processing and retailing firms suggest a high degree of competition. While we have lost half of all our food companies in the last three decades, still about twenty thousand remain. But of these, a mere fifty of the largest firms, or 0.25 percent, now control two thirds of the industry's assets.[17]

This figure for the industry's general economic concentration actually understates the economic power held by a few. Within key product groups, such as canned soups, baked goods, or grainmill products, only four firms account for over half the sales in a majority of the nearly sixty major product categories. And *within* these categories, among the specific product types where producers compete directly for sales, the dominance of a few firms increases further. In 1980, the leading brand *alone* claimed over half the market in more than a third of the 425 supermarket items surveyed by Nielson.[18]

We miss these facts partly because what the industry calls "product differentiation" obscures the large number of food items manufactured by a single company. For example, while we see an incredibly large number of dry cereal brands on the market—everything from Corn Kix to Captain Crunch—few of us realize that only four firms make most of them and capture over 80 percent of the sales.[19]

We also fail to see that the market control exercised by a few giant enterprises has steadily tightened over recent decades. Our top fifty superfirms have nearly *doubled* their share of industry assets since 1950, and if present trends continue, food economist John M. Connor projects they will have claimed virtually *all* of industry assets by the year 2000.[20]

The pattern of growth underlying these trends is neither new nor unusual given our economic ground rules. In fact, it reflects a continuation of the industry's earlier consolidation into ever fewer firms, which goes back to the last century (as we traced in chapter 2). But this process of big fish eating smaller ones has become particularly ferocious in recent years. In his March 1980 article entitled "The Food Monsters: How They Gobble Up Each Other—and Us," Daniel Zwerdling observed that "takeovers have become the single most important strategy for building market power" in the food industry.[21] Indeed, Connor showed that between 1950 and 1975 at least 40 percent of the total assets of the 100 largest food-processing companies were due to mergers rather than internal growth, as the "takeover wars" of the late sixties and seventies set records for their scale and intensity.[22]

As control over markets and assets by a few firms has increased, so has industry profitability. Average after-tax profits as a percentage of equity has risen steadily from 8.4 in the early 1950s to 11.4 in the late 1960s, and stood at 15.1 in the late 1970s.[23] By 1980 many major food companies had rates of profit as high as those of the big oil companies—26 percent at Kellogg, 19 percent at Iowa Beef, 21 percent at General Foods, and more than 27 percent at Lucky Stores. Even during the early 1980s, in the face of the worst recession since World War II, some food giants were able to sustain and even expand high profits. In a mid-1982 article reporting on the "recession beaters," *Forbes* magazine pointed to the food industry as particularly well insulated from the ups and downs of the general economy since "after all, people have to eat." Of the 106 major corporations *Forbes* listed as substantially increasing their profits as the economy moved into a deep trough, more than 1 in 9 were food related.[24]

The key to understanding how this concentration within the food industry and its resulting higher profits have affected our food dollar lies in the way "shared monopoly" market power translates into higher food prices. The relationship between market power and high prices has been well documented. Twenty-seven of twenty-eight econometric studies have found a significant correlation between the two, and an internal FTC report noted that "if highly concentrated industries were deconcentrated to a point where the four largest firms control 40 percent or less of an industry's sales, prices would fall by 25 percent or more."[25] This estimate suggests what industry concentration currently costs consumers. To see how the relationship between size and prices has affected our food dollar, let's look at how rising exports have worked with the food industry's concentrated structure over the past decade.

In the two years from 1972 to 1974, food prices leapt almost 30 percent. With the exception of 1976, food price inflation remained at rates ranging from 6.6 percent to almost 11 percent for the rest of the decade. (See figure 6–2.) E. Phillip LeVeen, agricultural economist and director of Public Interest Economics West, argues that the export

Figure 6–2
Ratio of Food and Non-Food Prices, 1951–1980

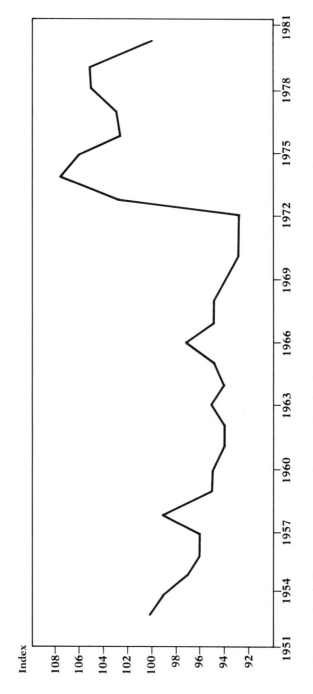

Source: E. Phillip LeVeen, *Towards A New Food Policy: A Dissenting Perspective.*

boom has been the primary reason food prices began rising faster than overall inflation after 1972.[26]

LeVeen explains that during both the 1953–1972 and post-1972 periods, food processing and distribution costs rose only slightly faster than the percentage rate increase in nonfood prices. "There was no sudden shift in the behavior of processing and marketing prices that would account for the sudden shift in retail food prices."[27] Rather, the intense rounds of food price inflation since the early seventies are the result of severe price fluctuations in farm commodities, characteristic of the pre-1950 period. Greater exposure to the vagaries of the world market has increasingly destabilized farm gate prices, and as these price fluctuations register in the processing and retailing sectors, consumers discover that "what goes up does not come down."

LeVeen illustrates how this works by describing the impact of the grain cycle of 1972–1975 on food prices.

Between 1972 and 1974 grain prices *tripled* in reaction to the increased global demand for U.S. grain and soybeans. Devaluation of the dollar, detente with the Soviet Union, and poor grain harvests outside the U.S. combined with a limited domestic supply of grain to create this increased demand. Food processors and retailers, who price according to cost-plus-profit markup formulas, quickly passed on their higher costs through higher consumer prices.

A lag, however short, in passing on these price increases may have meant that the processing/retailing sectors absorbed some of the impact of rising farm prices during the initial phase of the boom. But not for long. The widening spread between farm and retail prices during 1974 and 1975 indicates that firms were able to more than compensate for any losses at the beginning of the cycle.

But what happened to food prices on the downswing of the commodity cycle?

Food price inflation continued its upward spiral, even as grain prices plummeted. Food prices rose an average of 6 percent a year in the three years after 1974, while food grain prices fell by an average of 24 percent and feedgrains dropped by an average of 10 percent.

Why this discrepancy? Something in the food processing and retailing links of the distribution chain turned raw commodity price *decreases* into food price *increases*. The rapid increase in oil prices was one factor. So was the market power and markup pricing strategies of food processors and retailers, which allowed them to keep prices rigid when the costs of farm commodities fell, as well as to pass on these costs to consumers when they rose. But LeVeen also credits the impact of what economists call the "second round effects" of inflation. The second round effects work something like this:

The initial boom in farm commodity prices and the resultant price surge are felt quickly at the retail level. We consumers immediately see our food dollar buy less at the supermarket and feel the pinch on our budgets. We have learned that inflation is a fact of economic life in the post-Vietnam era, so we expect prices to go up and don't expect them to come down again. In addition, as consumers we feel powerless to combat inflation. The best we can do is press for higher wages, trying to recover some of our lost purchasing power.

When wages go up in response to higher food prices, the second round effect is set in motion. Wage increases cause labor costs to rise throughout the economy, including the food processing and retailing sectors. Wage increases, unlike the pass-through of farm price increases, are not automatic and generally take some time to achieve. Thus, their effect on food prices does not fully take hold until farm prices begin to peak and then decline. These increased labor costs then provide middlemen with the excuse that prices cannot be lowered because labor costs have risen. In this way, industry protects its profits and simply passes the higher labor costs on to the consumer. This helps fuel yet another round of inflation.

Through this process, the commodity cycle resulting from rising exports actually creates an opportunity for increased profits. As costs rise, the markup formulas used by the middlemen result in greater absolute profits even if their profit margin is held constant. Initial commodity price increases pass through each stage of the distribution chain and fail to shrink even when costs fall. Thus, the food processing and retailing industries come out on top.

Cheap Food?

The impact of these mechanisms has been obscured by "cheap food" rhetoric from those who would have us believe all is well, despite the intense rounds of food-price inflation characteristic of the past decade. From the secretary of agriculture to the food manufacturers, leaders of the American farm and food economy tell us that we spend less for food than the citizens of any other industrialized country. By 1980, however, the facts began to call this into question. In that year Americans spent 20.6 percent of after-tax income for food, while the French spent 18 percent, the English 16.5 percent, and the West Germans 22.4.[28]

But even those statistics are drastically distorted by the high incomes of a very small number of families. In fact, all but the wealthiest families in the United States actually spend much more than 20 percent of their income on food. While data on the actual food expenditures of families according to income and size are simply not available, LeVeen, using USDA data for 1978, has calculated that families with incomes of less than $15,000 a year spent substantially more than the USDA figure. And since food is a necessity, the poorer the family (or individual), the larger the percentage of income spent on food.

While the typical family spends more on food than is generally recognized, the average percent of after-tax income spent on food continued to drop in the 1970s, even though the real cost of food was rising faster than most other items consumers buy. When compared to average weekly earnings, food prices fell throughout the 1950s and 1960s, and Americans as a whole spent a decreasing percentage of their after-tax income for food.

But after 1972, for the reasons we have just described, average weekly earnings did not rise as fast as the cost of food during the 1970s, meaning that a family with a single breadwinner was forced to spend more and more of its income on food. The catch is that during this decade, the number of wage earners in the average family grew, especially because so many women began to take jobs. In addition, consumers have partially offset the impact of rising food prices by choosing less expensive foods, eating less meat, or substituting chicken and pork for higher priced beef.

"The reality is that the individual worker must work ever harder to afford the same level of food consumption," concludes LeVeen. "This reality is disguised by the conventional spending measure; it is starkly visible in the comparison of food prices and average weekly earnings."[29] Young, well-educated professional couples with no or few children are doing better than ever, while retired couples, single-parent families, and those without marketable skills cannot buy as much food as they used to.

When we compare the relative positions of farmers, consumers, and the food industry in light of these issues affecting our food dollar, the true picture emerges. The food processing and retailing industries have gained disproportionately. Their after-tax profits shot up by two thirds in real terms between 1970 and 1980, while real farm income actually declined by over one third and the real purchasing power of an average worker dropped by 8 percent.[30] The winners and losers are clear. The way concentrated industrial blocks are able to protect themselves from inflation, unlike farmers and consumers, demonstrates how the forces driving our economy distribute power unevenly throughout our society.

Now let us turn to other hidden costs—the environmental costs that were overlooked in the rush to expand farm markets abroad.

7 Soil for Oil: The Invisible Threat to Our Food Security

"At current rates of soil erosion, we could lose every single acre of topsoil in America within a hundred years!"

Such dire predictions suggest that in a century America will be unable to grow food. Yet it is difficult to take them seriously when our biggest farm problem continues to be periodic overproduction.

Exaggeration doesn't help us understand the *real* problem of soil erosion. If erosion were threatening the survival of American agriculture within the next few years, we might be frightened enough to face the root economic causes of the problem. We make the case that it is precisely *because* soil erosion in America is not an immediate threat to our food supply that it is a serious problem. Because it is invisible, because it is not accounted for in the price of food, because its impact takes centuries—not decades—to assess, soil erosion has ominous potential to destroy our agricultural land. Soil erosion's significance spans more than our lifetimes—and *we have no effective mechanism for addressing a problem of this nature.*

We must first assess the threat that soil erosion poses, grasp what is causing it, and uncover what—in our economic ground rules and in our culture—stands in the way of solving it.

"A Million Acres a Year. . ."

In the last five years, three major government-initiated studies have examined erosion rates. But their estimates of topsoil loss must be considered along with the rate at which nature builds topsoil from underlying layers.

The U.S. Soil Conservation Service has accepted the rule of thumb that cropland can lose up to five tons of top soil an acre each year and still suffer no net loss. But in recent years the scientific basis for this five-ton guideline has been widely challenged by soil scientists.[1] They argue that under the best conditions nature can build topsoil at a rate no faster than 1.5 tons per acre each year, and under some conditions, the rate is only 0.5 ton per acre per year.

Using the government guidelines, about one quarter of U.S. cropland is losing its race with nature, losing topsoil faster than new soil is formed. While even this estimate is alarming, it is grossly understated. If we use 1.5 tons per acre per year as an average acceptable limit, *about two thirds of U.S. cropland is experiencing a net loss of topsoil.*[2]

On average, each acre of U.S. cropland is losing about seven tons of topsoil yearly. This includes loss from water-caused erosion nationwide and wind erosion on the Great Plains.[3] So, on average, we are losing topsoil five times faster than nature can build it, even under the best conditions.

Soil conservationist Neil Sampson explains the problem in his 1981 book *Farmland or Wasteland.* He suggests that we think in terms of the acre-equivalents of farmland productivity we lose each year through erosion. Losing a thousand tons of topsoil on one acre—equivalent to six inches of soil—would destroy the productivity of most cropland. So, how many times over are we losing the equivalent of six inches of topsoil per acre each year? His answer is that well over one million acre-equivalents of farmland productivity are lost each year. Over fifty years, this could amount to 62 million acre-equivalents or about 15 percent of our current cropland base.[4]

Good News/Bad News

These figures *are* alarming. They reveal that soil erosion is worse today than it has ever been in our nation's agricultural history—even worse, in average yearly losses, than during the Dust Bowl era.[5]

Why is the loss not more visible? Soil erosion is highly concentrated: almost half of water-caused erosion is occurring on less than 7 percent of our cropland. So the crisis is not as widespread as averages indicate. But this concentrated erosion—with losses of ten to even fifty tons per acre—is occurring on some of our *best* cropland, including the Corn Belt states, the southern Mississippi Valley, the Palouse Basin in Washington and Idaho, and east central Texas.[6]

Washington's Palouse Basin, for example, produces abundant harvests of wheat and other crops, primarily for export. With soil losses of fourteen tons per acre annually on about a million acres, it is "noted for some of the highest grain production in the world . . . [and] for some of the worst erosion in the country," according to a 1980 USDA study.[7] Applying Sampson's guideline that a loss of six inches of topsoil kills the soil's productivity, this area's fertility could be destroyed in less than a century at current erosion rates.

That some of our nation's worst soil erosion is concentrated in some of its best agricultural regions is a double curse. Not only are prime farmlands most affected, but because the soil is fertile and in some cases relatively deep, damage from even severe erosion does not appreciably diminish the soil's productivity in the short run. It shows up later. So it's hard for farmers and others to believe that erosion is a serious problem.

Equally important, our nation's topsoil erosion is not visible because of a national "cover-up." We're not referring to government efforts to downplay erosion but to the fact that farmers can use chemical fertilizers on eroded cropland to maintain high yields in the short run. Once inexpensive, fertilizer prices rose by nearly 140 percent between 1973 and 1980. Farmers are becoming less able to afford this means of overcoming soil depletion and thus of masking the soil's declining fertility.

Soil for Oil?

Increased farm exports, purportedly intended to pay for imported oil, are not the fundamental cause of our soil erosion problem. But the boom and bust decade of expansion for export has indisputably accelerated our soil losses.

First, government programs encouraging acreage reductions were discarded during much of the last decade. Farmers surmised that only by an all-out push for maximum production, planting fence row to fence row, could they maintain their incomes.

Second, as discussed in chapter 3, the boom and busts of the export decade have tightened the cost/price squeeze into which farmers are locked. Soil conservation adds to out-of-pocket costs. Terraces, for example, are expensive to build. Almost every conservation decision—such as planting oats or clover to hold the soil—involves forgoing income in the short term that might be earned by continuous planting of the most profitable, but more erosive crop. Windbreaks take land away from crops. As costs of production have continued to rise faster than commodity prices, farmers have increasingly felt they couldn't afford to lose their immediate income by investing in such soil conservation methods.

Soil erosion has immediate costs, too. It washes away expensive agricultural chemicals, at an annual rate conservatively estimated at $1.00 to $3.50 per acre. Naturally occurring nitrogen, phosphorus, and potassium carried away in the eroding soil are estimated to be worth about $20 per acre annually at the average rate of soil loss nationwide.[8] But the farmer cannot easily see, much less measure, these losses. Therefore, it is easier to ignore them, especially when yields remain high. Where soils are thick, as in much of the north central states, erosion has little or no *immediate* effect on yields;[9] so there's no economic motive for preventing it.

Plowing Fragile Soils

Because the best land was already in use, much expansion has taken place on land with thin or fragile topsoil, which is prone to erosion or rapid loss of fertility. The government estimates that 43 percent of land planted in row-crops in the Corn Belt is highly susceptible to erosion.[10] This practice of plowing up fragile soils that should have remained pasture and will only produce a few harvests has been labeled "a modern version of slash-and-burn jungle agriculture," by conservationist Neil Sampson.[11]

Harvested acreage grew by 63 million acres, or 22 percent, between 1969 and 1980.[12] Corn, soybeans, cotton, and wheat have been favored because they've brought the best price in the export markets. Nearly three fourths of the growth in harvested acreage was in just two crops, corn and soybeans. Unfortunately, these two are linked to the highest rates of soil erosion. Planted in rows, they leave part of the soil exposed, unlike grasses or clover which cover the ground entirely. Soybean's shallow roots also leave soil more susceptible to erosion.

Small grains, such as oats and barley, and hay such as alfalfa have been progressively eliminated from crop rotations because of their relatively meager cash value. Yet these crops are grown close together, which reduces surface water runoff.

In response to the export markets, which have opened up primarily for a narrow band of crops, farmers began planting the same crops each year instead of rotating them or allowing the earth to lie fallow. They have thus reduced the opportunity for soil to rebuild itself and have further accelerated erosion.

During the early seventies farmers invested in bigger cultivating machines that are not compatible with conserving topsoil. When farmers push for huge yields using such machinery,

> windbreaks [rows of trees protecting the soil from wind] become a real pain, so thousands of miles of them have been torn out to enlarge fields so that big tractors or center-pivot sprinkler systems can have free travel. Terraces—particularly those that wander around on the contour—can't be tolerated. . . . [W]ith six- or eight-row equipment, an operator can't even get to the ends of some of the rows without jamming the other end of the machine in the terrace bank! So the old terraces have had to go, victims of technological obsolescence. Harvesting equipment imposes the same kinds of limits.[13]

Moreover, bigger machines are heavier machines. They

compact the soil, leading to poor drainage, greater surface water runoff, and thus more soil erosion.[14]

Absentee Conservation?

Another indirect consequence of the export boom and bust has been the increase in farm tenancy discussed in chapter 3. Today about half of our farmland is operated by renters. Farmers rent from absentee owners who have little concern for the long-term productivity of the land. The trend toward absentee ownership in itself works against conservation. Agricultural economist John Timmons points out that "rental arrangements usually do not encourage soil conservation investments with a long-term payoff. . . . landlords who are interested in short run returns on investment usually are not motivated to make long-term soil conservation investments."[15]

Iowa: One Hundred Years in a Single Spring's Rain

Americans have a big stake in the state of Iowa where 10 percent of our food supply grows.

Yet, throughout Iowa, the heart of the Corn Belt, an average of *half* the topsoil has been lost since the land was put to plow.[16] The soil erosion rate is 50 percent higher than the national average. Iowa's average topsoil depth has dropped from sixteen to eight inches.[17] Much of Iowa farmland has become so vulnerable to erosion that, during heavy rains in the spring of 1982, Gary Walters, soil conservationist at Anthon, Iowa, reported half of his county lost at least twenty tons an acre and that about fifteen thousand acres had losses approaching one hundred to one hundred and fifty tons![18]

In other words, what took nature a hundred or more years to build was lost in a single spring's rain.

Some of the most reliable long-term data on soil erosion has been gathered for Iowa, and the destructive influence of export-led expansion in this state can be well documented. Although Iowa produces about 10 percent of the nation's food supply, its contribution to the "export stream" in farm commodities is twice as high—about 20 percent of the national total. Thus, it didn't surprise us to learn that Iowa's soil erosion rate is much higher than the national average. After steady declines in erosion rates during the 1950s and 1960s, the trend reversed itself in the early 1970s; by 1974, soil losses had jumped to 22 percent above 1957 levels.[19] By the late 1970s, hilly Iowa farmland was losing thirteen tons of topsoil per acre annually. (Recall that topsoil, at best, is formed at the rate of 1.5 tons per acre per year.)[20]

"It used to be that we had lots of different crops here, including oats and hay," said George Rankin, a conservation technician for the Soil Conservation Service stationed in Story County, Iowa, in 1978. "But now we just have corn and soybeans in intensive cultivation, and we have more erosion."[21] From 1969 to 1980, acres planted in corn and soybeans in Iowa grew one third faster than the total expansion in cropped acreage. They grew at the expense of pastureland and less-erosion-prone small grains and grasses.

With the rush to plant more acreage in corn and soybeans, "a lot of the conservation practices have gone out the back door," said Howard P. Johnson, a professor of agricultural engineering. "Terraces have been plowed out, and contouring has stopped because it's a nuisance to the big new cultivating machines."[22]

Marilyn Fedelchak, an Iowa farmer during the midseventies, saw smoke rising from fence rows and shelterbelts as farmers burned them in an anxious drive to clear every available bit of land for unobstructed row cropping. She recalls watching her neighbor try to harvest a field so steep, "he had to lower the harvesting equipment down the hillside from a tractor parked at the top," she said. "It was just too steep to drive on."[23] And certainly too steep to be row-cropped without massive soil loss.

Iowa as a state exemplifies the problem: the worst erosion is happening on the best land, where its consequences are less immediately evident. On the fragile soils of western Iowa, erosion averages twenty-five tons per acre annually. But because the secondary soil is deep, the resultant loss of an inch of topsoil every six years appears *less* of a problem than lower erosion rates occurring on the very thin soils of southern Iowa. There the topsoil is almost gone; but, because they use big doses of fertilizers, many farmers aren't convinced they need topsoil.[24]

The Corn Belt at Risk

By 1975, only three years into the export boom, the twelve Corn Belt states registered a 39 percent increase in soil erosion. The erosion rates in a third of this region exceeded ten tons per acre annually.[25]

Surely, the implications of the export boom on Corn Belt soil needed to be studied, but no government agency undertook the task. In 1977, Dennis Cory, a doctoral student at Iowa State University, analyzed the relationships among soil erosion, exports, and land utilization throughout the Corn Belt. He predicted soil loss by 1985 using two major scenarios, one assuming a continuation of historical export trends, and the other assuming even higher exports.[26]

Cory's "high export" scenario better fit actual events. He predicted that Iowa's planted acreage would increase by one quarter while soil erosion would double by 1985. Clearly, he expected the new acreage to be more erosive acreage. Cory actually *underestimated* the pace of acreage expansion. As export markets continued to expand, by 1980, Corn Belt acreage had already grown to almost 85 percent of the level Cory forecast for 1985.[27]

No government agency assembles comprehensive land use data.[28] Soil Conservation Service measurements of nationwide erosion rates grossly understate the extent of the problem. For example, the Soil Conservation Service includes only a *portion* of water-induced soil loss, primarily caused by rainfall, in its soil erosion estimates. It ignores erosion by snow and by improper irrigation techniques, and it fails to account for erosion by wind—a serious problem in the Great Plains. In the total cropland base used to estimate soil loss per acre, aggregate Soil Conservation Service data is "watered down" by including hay and pastureland, on which erosion is negligible.[29]

Conservation in Conflict with Economics

"The knee-jerk reflex that tempts American farmers to plow to the barbed wire every time Russian farmers have a crop failure makes a mockery of the conservation ethic we espouse in principle," says Iowa farmer Charles McLaughlin.[30]

In our country's brief history, application of McLaughlin's "conservation ethic" is rare compared to some other cultures. Chinese farmers, for example, have successfully tilled the same land for at least forty centuries. In the United States, the frontier seemed to offer us the alternative of using up resources and then moving on to the next piece of land.

We are not accusing most farmers of wanting to ruin the land; no conservation ethic alone could override the economic forces that work against soil conservation. In the last several decades these forces have gained strength. Historically, farmers wanted to leave their offspring a well-cared-for legacy of land. This motive for conservation has weakened as fewer farm children consider farming a viable option, as more farmers rent rather than own the land they farm, and as some assume their land is just as likely to become a shopping center as to become someone's future farm!

Soil conservation as government policy was born in the late 1920s. The Soil Conservation Service was established in 1934, the year that clouds from the Midwest dust storms blotted out the sun over Washington, D.C. The government has spent tens of billions of dollars on conservation, but the problem is worse today than during those dramatic dust storms. Government conservation efforts have always expressed the proverbial "too little, too late" and consistently play second fiddle to other government priorities.

Neil Sampson writes:

Farm policies that push farmers to plow "fence row to fence row," as were common in the early 1970s, have not really changed despite widespread recognition of the soil damage that is occurring as a result. To meet the calls for more crops, farmers are still encouraged to use marginal land, where productivity is lowest and the cost of conservation treatment the greatest. The government provides financial support for added production through loans, price supports, or crop insurance programs, but these are not in any way related to the use of the land. The farmer who misuses marginal land can qualify for government assistance as readily as the one who does not.[31]

A 1977 study by the Comptroller General found that "the greater part of these [Agricultural Conservation Program] funds was spent for practices which had only temporary erosion control benefits or which were oriented more toward stimulating agricultural production than toward conserving cropland topsoil or practices having the best payoffs for reducing erosion."[32]

Some government policies directly penalize conservation-oriented farmers. The 1977 Farm Bill is one recent example. It legislated that a farmer's benefits from government farm programs would depend on how much land the farmer had diverted to uses other than "normal crop acreage." Because acres already planted to grass as a conservation measure were not counted as "normal crop acreage," the conserving farmer had to set aside additional acres to obtain credit for land diversion. Many farmers did the obvious—they simply plowed up the grass before the deadline for computing their "normal crop acreage." Once plowed up, it could be labeled "cropland" and again diverted to get a government bonus.[33]

While the need for soil conservation practices has steadily increased over the last several decades, government investment has not kept up. By 1975 the total real value of soil conservation improvement had deteriorated over 20 percent from its peak in 1955, according to a USDA study.[34]

This deterioration occurred during a period when good land was needed more than ever, as millions of acres of erodible lands were being plowed.

The problem of soil erosion in America does not result from inadequate government programs. Rather, soil conservation, as it is approached in the United States, is extraneous to the business of farming. The economic forces at work do not reward—cannot reward—soil conservation, at least in the short term. And the short term is the only time available to most farmers as they struggle to survive from year to year. In other words, just as the farm family has no way to pass on the rising costs of fuel or machinery, it cannot pass on costs of terracing or contour plowing. As profits per acre steadily decline and real income is stagnant or falling, these farmers are not likely to invest in conservation.

Ironically, soil conservation also suffers when farm income temporarily rises as it did in the early 1970s. Many farmers rush out to buy new, bigger machinery and plow up more land.

Only a conservation technique that brings immediate savings to farmers can succeed. Conservation tillage—meaning little or no-till farming—is one example. It is "already the fastest growing farming system in history," said Peter Myers, head of Missouri's Soil Conservation Service in 1982.[35] He may be right—by the early 1980s conservation tillage was being used on almost a quarter of our cropland. Farmers choose it primarily because it saved them money rather than because it conserves land. Tenants and part owners also prefer this method. They can view the purchase of conservation equipment as an investment even if they don't own their land. Terraces, on the other hand, can't be moved. But, while conservation tillage reduces erosion, it will not substitute for basic good farming—crop rotation with nonrow crops, contour plowing, and terracing. This is the kind of farming that should pay off for the farmer.

The Vanishing Buffer

A central question yet remains: Why worry about soil erosion if we can simply bring new acres under the plow when the topsoil on our present farmland is gone?

For most of U.S. history, cropland seemed limitless. For the agricultural sector as a whole, as well as for the individual farmer, expansion—first through pushing back the frontier, then through the quest for new markets—has been taken for granted.

In the last five years, however, several major studies have criticized these assumptions.[36] While basically valuable, the studies themselves might contribute to the myth that we have a cushion of "extra" land. The 1980 National Agricultural Lands study, for example, states that some 540 million acres, about one fourth of America's land, make up our cropland base. Of this, roughly three quarters is regularly used as cropland. The rest has moderate to good potential for production.[37]

This suggests we have almost a quarter of the cropland base with which to absorb pressures to expand planted acreage. But do we?

First, this potentially cropped land is *not* idle. It includes almost 40 percent of America's pastureland and substantial amounts of our forest and rangeland. We cannot sacrifice such a significant part of our timber, dairy, and cattle land.

Second, we are rapidly losing this reserve. Only the rate at which it is shrinking is open to question. In 1977, the USDA found that about 700,000 acres of this land was disappearing each year due to urban and suburban construction, water, and highway use.[38]

Neil Sampson draws from government data to present more alarming estimates: Between 1967 and 1977 approximately 45 million acres were lost to our total cropland pool—35 million from cropland itself and an additional 10 million from land with high or medium potential for cropping.[39] This is the *net* loss, reflecting a much larger shift in land use over the 1967–1977 decade. Two of every three acres converted from cropland to other uses were lost to farming forever. This land went either to urbanization, water use, and highways, or was made useless by soil deterioration.

Will there be enough cropland available to meet both domestic and foreign demand in the near future without pushing up the price of food still further? That is the big question.

The congressionally mandated 1980 Resources Conservation Act study published in 1981 estimates that we will need about 450 million acres by the year 2000 to meet both domestic and foreign needs without significantly raising land and food prices. If we subtract this need from the generous 540 million acre current estimate of our total cropland base, we are left with only a 90 million acre cushion. That isn't too reassuring, since most of this is locked into other uses. If we continue to lose cropland at the rate Sampson calculated for the 1970s, by the year 2000 virtually *all* of our cushion will be gone.[40]

In appraising our future cropland needs, the study for the Resources Conservation Act held all variables constant except one—productivity. The study projected that if the average annual rate of productivity growth drops only 1 percent over the next fifty years (from 1.6 to 0.6), future cropland needs will rise from 380 million to 497 million acres.[41]

This projection adds striking evidence that we are close to the margin. The difference between these acreage projections is roughly equal to *all* of our currently available potential cropland reserve. Thus, a *single percentage point shift* in productivity could spell the difference between maintaining our present reserve for expansion and exhausting it altogether!

Left to its own devices, the economic forces at work offer only one "solution" to the problem of a shrinking and overburdened cropland base—higher food prices and greater farmland inflation. Clearly, price increases in both these areas would exacerbate the already painful economic squeeze felt by most farmers and consumers.

The Real Problem

We introduced this chapter by stating that the real issue is not soil erosion itself, or the loss of cropland, but our society's inability to deal with the problem. We can't rely on old techniques—all have proven inadequate against the powerful economic forces that squeeze farm income and push for greater production.

The costs of soil erosion are real costs. They will have to be borne by future generations. For the present, these costs are hidden, not hidden from view but excluded from the economic equations our society chooses to use in making its investment decisions.

The problem of soil erosion cannot and will not be successfully addressed if the production imperative is left in place. That imperative is a direct result of the growth dynamic which is the basis of our food system.

8 The Export Boom and Vanishing Water Resources

Several hundred years ago Adam Smith popularized the comforting notion that the individual pursuit of self-interest would result in the greatest good for the greatest number. Not surprisingly, the idea caught on. But in the last chapter we saw that what makes sense from the point of view of the individual farmer on the production tread-mill does not work for the nation as a whole. Today our long-term agricultural productivity is jeopardized by soil depletion and cropland loss.

Our water problems parallel those of soil degradation because we are mining both essentially nonrenewable resources. Roughly 32 million acres of our farmland are irrigated by groundwater, which is drawn from underground aquifers, water-bearing layers of sand and gravel. The largest of these, the Ogallala Aquifer, is tapped to irrigate 12 to 15 million acres. A 1981 study of groundwater irrigation in eleven western states found that for over half the land irrigated by groundwater, the water table was falling by *more than six inches per year* and was in chronic decline.[1]

Unlike mining topsoil, it is expensive to mine groundwater. Only a minority of farmers can afford the investment. Thus, a national resource—underground water—becomes the source of wealth for a few. As such, it fosters the tightening of farmland ownership with all the ramifications discussed in chapter 3.

After farmers dependent on irrigated farming begin to deplete local water resources, regional economic interests often pressure the government—i.e., the taxpayer—to bail out irrigators through subsidized irrigation schemes that bring water in from other areas.

In all this, the public interest loses out, as do future generations of farmers who will not be able to benefit from these irrigation sources.

"Enough water to float a destroyer"

On a national average, 87 billion of the 106 billion gallons of water used daily in the United States are claimed by farming. It takes almost 15,000 gallons of water to grow a bushel of wheat, 120 gallons to put a single egg on the breakfast table, and to raise a one-thousand-pound steer requires enough water to float a destroyer![2]

Absolute water availability is not the issue. Over forty times the amount needed for total U.S. consumption falls within our national boundaries each year. The real issue is whether the water is where it can be used to farm arid land or increase yields.

The various estimates of the amount of irrigated land in the U.S. are in striking *dis*agreement. For example, the 1978 Census of Agriculture indicates there are less than 51 million acres irrigated, while the 1977 National Resources Inventory, believed to be more reliable, shows nearly 58 million acres.[3]

The National Resources Inventory documents more than a 30 percent increase in farmland irrigation over the last ten years. The percentage of our cropland that is irrigated rose from 8 to 14 between 1958 and 1977. More than a quarter of the value of all crops is now grown on irrigated acreage. But west of the Mississippi irrigation is even more important to agriculture. There, *50 percent of crop value is generated by irrigated farms.*[4]

Increases in irrigation have also meant greater use of groundwater as opposed to surface water. Although most water used by agriculture still comes from federally financed irrigation projects using surface water (rivers, lakes, etc.), the annual amount of water used from federal sources peaked in 1955; it has ranged between 85 and 100 percent of this level since. Use of privately pumped ground-

water for irrigation, however, has increased dramatically.
From 1940 to 1960, while federally irrigated acreage drawing primarily from surface water increased by 131 percent,
irrigation from groundwater grew over threefold.[5] Over the
thirty years since 1945, the rate of groundwater with-
drawal for irrigation has increased more than *fivefold*.[6]

The export boom's impact on irrigation is clear. As foreign demand for corn, wheat, soybeans, rice, and cotton
has increased, acreage devoted to these crops has expanded, too—by 72 million acres. Much of this expansion
has occurred in regions (west of the Mississippi) and for
crops requiring irrigation. In Texas, for example, corn
acreage jumped by over 90 percent in the decade of the
seventies, triple the national average.[7]

Expansion in irrigated acreage has been concentrated in
areas where production of crops for export has been emphasized most—in the northern and central High Plains,
especially in Kansas and Nebraska. Between 1967 and
1977, Kansas and Nebraska together accounted for 40 percent of irrigation expansion for the entire country. Nebraska irrigated less than one million acres in 1959, but
that figure jumped to almost seven million by 1977.[8]

In the late 1960s, before the export boom, groundwater
withdrawals for irrigation in the Texas High Plains had actually decreased, already reflecting a depletion of groundwater, sinking water tables, and the high cost of pumping
from greater depths. But between 1970 and 1975, withdrawals began to increase in spite of the depletion. Data on
acreage expansion in Texas tells us why. During these years
corn acreage doubled, wheat acreage increased 85 percent,
and soybeans increased nearly two and a half times. Meanwhile, acreage devoted to oats, barley, rye, and flaxseed,
crops that seldom require irrigation, dropped nearly by
half.[9]

In areas such as Nebraska and most of Kansas, water
trapped in layers of gravel—aquifers—*could* be a renew-
able, sustainable national resource because rainfall replen-
ishes the aquifer at a rate that allows indefinite pumping.
In other areas, such as north Texas, the aquifer is essentially nonrenewable. There, recharge by rainfall is so insig-
nificant that almost any pumping amounts to mining.

Thus, while part of the aquifer could be a long-term national irrigation resource with prudent use, sources in other areas could last for several decades only if pumped conservatively.

Instead, by pursuing extravagant production strategies, we risk losing one quarter of our groundwater supplies in just four decades, according to the federally commissioned High Plains study. In southern regions, especially in Texas where the aquifer is thinner, predictions are dire: There, *two thirds* of current groundwater supplies are predicted to be used up by the year 2020.[10]

In 1930 the Ogallala was over fifty-eight feet deep in central Kansas; today it is only eight feet deep in that region. Each year, on average, the water table sinks from six inches in some areas to three feet in others.[11]

As a result, nearly half of the 13.2 million acres of irrigated land estimated to overlay the aquifer are expected to revert to dryland farming over the next several decades. Within fifty years, an insufficient groundwater supply is expected to force nearly all of it out of irrigation.[12] If policies that promote more U.S. farm commodity exports continue, five of the six states in the High Plains region would lose irrigated acres as water tables sink over the next forty years. Only Nebraska, where two thirds of the total water stored in the Ogallala lies, would gain irrigated land.[13] But pumping that water under Nebraska involves enormous environmental hazards, as we discuss below.

In other words, much of our irrigation is temporary. Sooner or later millions of irrigated acres that depend on groundwater must return to dryland farming or be taken out of farming altogether when water supplies are depleted.

The Threat of Desertification

Desertification of parts of the Great Plains could result from soil erosion related to mining the Ogallala, warns a 1982 study by the Working Group on the Ogallala, a consortium of midwestern public interest groups.[14]

The commonly used center-pivot irrigation systems cannot operate where shelterbelts have been planted to lessen wind erosion; so the shelterbelts have been removed. Even more serious, irrigation enables farmers to cultivate soil highly susceptible to wind erosion, soil so fragile that its only sustainable use is as grazing land.

In the Great Plains almost all the irrigated cotton, half the irrigated corn, and two thirds of the irrigated soybeans and sorghum are grown on land that is rapidly losing top-soil—five tons or more per acre annually—*just from wind erosion.* Most of this land loses more than ten tons annually.

Irrigation drawing on the Arkansas River and excessive groundwater mining is creating one desertification danger zone—the Sand Sage Prairie in southwest Kansas. A second danger zone is the much larger region of the Nebraska Sandhills. Nebraska's water wealth may be its agricultural curse. Since most of the water stored in the entire Ogallala lies under Nebraska, it is a great temptation to those who can afford the irrigation investment, even though the soils over much of this water become highly susceptible to wind erosion once they are cultivated.

Vicious Circle I: Exports, Irrigation, and the Cost/ Price Squeeze

From 1973 to 1975, when farmers invested heavily in yield-increasing technology to produce exports, irrigation was a favored technique.

Irrigation has been attractive because water for agriculture has always been cheap. Through federal irrigation projects, mostly using surface water, government subsidies have allowed farmers to pay little more than 3 percent of the real costs.[15] Irrigators still don't pay the full social cost of even privately financed groundwater pumping. Ground-water itself is free, and investors often benefit from federal tax breaks. In Nebraska, for example, federal tax write-offs for investing in irrigation can amount to as much as one third the purchase price of irrigable land. According to a recent Internal Revenue Service ruling, overuse of ground-water makes farmers or investors eligible for a depletion allowance![16]

When land values soared, irrigation allowed farmers to take advantage of the promised boom by expanding production without buying (or buying very little) expensive land. In fact, most of the recent growth in Ogallala irrigation has been on land not previously farmed—that is, less desirable and therefore less expensive land. Water, in a sense, is a "land substitute."

Water is relatively inexpensive; irrigation technology is not. Irrigation equipment prices were relatively stable during the fifties and sixties, but climbed three to four times faster when farmer demand increased in the 1970s. Thus the shift from dryland to irrigated farming requires a substantial capital investment. In the 1970s, center-pivot sprinkler systems and the associated well to pump the water cost as much as $60,000 to install. By 1979, it cost $513 to install irrigation for one acre this way, compared to $103 in 1950.[17]

The farmer hopes, of course, that increased yields from irrigation will raise overall volume enough to offset the heavy investment costs. This heavy investment motivates the farmer to pump as much groundwater as possible to increase yields that will pay for the greater overhead. The irrigator thus becomes even more tightly bound to the production treadmill than are other farmers.

The Energy Squeeze. Costly irrigation technology makes farming more energy dependent. For example, one study found that growing corn with center-pivot irrigation systems in Nebraska used 50 percent more energy than dryland techniques in Iowa and Illinois. The Nebraska farmer, as a result, was far more vulnerable to energy price hikes.

Even more energy is needed to pull water from lower depths as water tables fall. Costs rise accordingly. One federal study showed the cost to pump an acre-foot of water in the Texas High Plains has risen from $1.60 to $60 in a single decade. Another study looked at pumping costs to produce grain sorghum in Arizona. At $35 in 1973, costs by 1980 were predicted to hit $186![18]

Locked In. By 1976, when grain prices began to plummet, irrigation and other production costs continued to rise. The experience of a hypothetical Nebraska irrigator illustrates how a farmer locked into climbing production costs tries to ride the roller coaster of boom and bust cycles that have been intensified by expansion for export.

From 1965 to 1970, corn prices in Nebraska averaged only $1.16 per bushel. But in the early seventies, prices jumped. In 1974 they averaged $3.02 and were $2.54 in 1975. To take advantage of these higher prices by producing higher yields, Farmer Jones invested in irrigation and grew more corn on the same acreage and planted additional acreage to spread his investment over more acres of production. So did Farmer Jones' neighbors, at least those big enough to get loans to invest in irrigation. So did outside investors.

As a result, corn supplies rose rapidly, jumping over 7 percent from 1975 to 1976. Then, without markets to absorb all that additional corn, prices dropped sharply—down to $2.15 in 1976 and to barely $2.00 the next year.

One might imagine that Farmer Jones would give up on expensive irrigation, at least for the time being. If farmers could cut back production and reduce the oversupply, prices would recover. But, as we've noted before, such collective action, possible in industries dominated by a few giants, is not possible for farmers competing against each other for sales. In part because of the high fixed cost of irrigation, Farmer Jones felt compelled to *continue* producing record harvests.

So, instead of less corn there was more. Between 1976 and 1979 corn acreage decreased only slightly, but yields increased substantially, in part because of irrigation practices. Almost 24 percent more corn was produced in 1979 than in 1976, despite stagnant prices. The boom developed into an even bigger bust.[19]

Consider Farmer Jones' choices. In 1978, producing corn in north central Nebraska cost $268 per acre, including the $41 annual fixed cost of irrigation equipment. The corn crop, however, could be sold for an average of only $251 per acre, at a loss of $17. A dryland farmer, on the other hand, could expect to do a bit better, losing only $16 per acre, while producing about 40 percent as much corn.

But Farmer Jones' choice was not between a $16 or $17 loss. He had to choose between a $17 loss and a $58 loss, because, whether he used it or not, Farmer Jones had to cover the $41 cost of his irrigation equipment. So he decided to continue irrigating until prices recovered, or he went broke.[20]

With these forces operating at the farm level, it is not hard to see why water use continues to rise. Once undertaken, irrigation is no longer an option but a necessity.

Heavy investments and fortunes staked on rising land values make continuing expansion of export markets a necessity, too. "In short, we no longer export because we *can*; we export because we *must* to keep American agriculture financially afloat," concluded the Working Group on the Ogallala Aquifer. Challenging a government-sponsored irrigation study based on high future exports, this public interest research team suggested that "export policy becomes the tail that wags the dog."[21]

Vicious Circle II: Exports, Irrigation, and the Demise of the Family Farm

Because only some farmers can afford the heavy investment, expensive irrigation has helped accelerate the trend to fewer and larger farms. Not only are irrigated farms bigger than their dryland counterparts, but they are growing more rapidly.

In 1974, when the average U.S. farm size was four hundred and seventy acres, the average irrigated farm was over twice as large, or about one thousand acres. Where irrigation expanded most rapidly, this gap steadily widened. For example, between 1969 and 1974, irrigated farms in Nebraska grew nearly three times as fast as those using dryland techniques.

The few largest irrigated farms now claim a disproportionate share of our water resources. Nationwide, the largest irrigators (those using over one thousand acre-feet annually) make up less than 9 percent of all irrigated farms but account for over 45 percent of all irrigated land and use *61 percent* of all agricultural water.[22]

More Waste. The big irrigators use over one third more water *per acre* than smaller farms.[26] Clearly the trend toward farm concentration is accompanied by more profligate water use, further aggravating water depletion problems.

The Shakeout. Because of its cost, irrigation speeds the steady shift toward fewer and bigger producers. Ironically, the demise of irrigation will have the same effect. Over 80 percent of the irrigated acres in Texas already have serious groundwater depletion problems.[23] Experts predict that more than half of the available groundwater in the Texas High Plains will be gone in less than forty years.[24]

A 1970 study by the Texas Agricultural Experiment Station looked at how this will affect control of almost 7 million acres in the High Plains. This study concluded that only 14 to 30 percent of the farms could survive a shift from irrigated to dryland farming. The majority would simply disappear, their land either absorbed into the few remaining farms or taken out of production altogether.[25] By the mid- to late-1970s, this scenario had already begun to unfold.

Absentee Irrigators

Expansion for the promising export markets, accompanied by accelerated inflation in land values, has brought speculative investment in farmland, especially in irrigated land. Nebraska provides a striking example. In 1975, the Center for Rural Affairs in Nebraska studied absentee investment in groundwater irrigation in six counties in north central Nebraska. The center found that concentration of ownership was much higher within the outside investor group than among owner-operators. On average, non-family farm corporations owned about three times as much irrigated land as owner-operated farms. In Dundy County, for example, four firms accounted for 88 percent of all investor-owned irrigation.[27]

Why are the largest tracts investor owned? Perhaps the most important reason is that most of the economic benefits derive from *owning* the land, not from farming it.

Investor-owners, who don't have to depend on farm income, can more easily bear the financial burden and associated risks of center-pivot sprinkler installation and take fuller advantage of the benefits. Tax breaks, such as investment tax credits and accelerated depreciation allowances for installation of the irrigation equipment, reduce the real cost. Moreover, outside investors are more often able to forego current income, wait for the land to appreciate, and then profit from the increase in land values when they sell out. And the profits are handsome, because of the capital gains tax provision which makes 20 percent the maximum effective tax rate.

Concentrated ownership by outside investors also aggravates soil erosion problems. The Center for Rural Affairs discovered that natural resource abuse was more prevalent among investor-owned irrigation operations. The Sandhills area in Nebraska overlying the Ogallala is extremely sandy and subject to severe wind erosion if tilled. As a result, the USDA has classified much of it as "Class VI," land with severe limitations that make it generally unsuitable for cultivation.

Over half the land in Dundy County, where irrigation has grown most rapidly, is Class VI. The study found that almost *three quarters of the irrigated Class VI soils were investor owned*, a figure all the more striking because farmers outnumbered investors by almost eight to one among center-pivot irrigators in the county. The future looks even more disturbing. Almost 84 percent of the acreage planned for irrigation is Class VI. Of that, *almost all* is investor owned.[28]

America's Water Future

In this chapter we document how, as nonfarm investors and better-off farm families pursue their own short-term interests, a national resource—groundwater—is mined. Profit for a minority in this generation is stolen from future generations. In the process, topsoil that cannot be replaced during our lifetime is also lost.

The taxpayer is caught, too. So far, as water tables sink and pumping becomes unprofitable, the economic interests involved have been powerful enough to secure a taxpayer bailout.

The Central Arizona Project is designed to carry water

from the Colorado River in northern Arizona to the central and southern parts of the state. The Central Valley Project is designed to carry water from northern California to the arid south. The costs of these massive, federally funded schemes exceed the economic gain. Agricultural economist E. Philip LeVeen estimates that government-financed water costs about two dollars for every dollar in economic returns. The General Accounting Office estimated in 1981 that users of six federally subsidized irrigation projects it studied were paying only about 8 percent of the cost of delivering the water. If the irrigators had to carry the full cost, the GAO admitted, irrigation would not pay.[29]

In 1976, the Congress authorized $6 million to study a bailout for states over the Ogallala. Because it assumed U.S. agriculture's export role, the study did not seek alternatives to mining the Ogallala. Instead, it suggested ways to keep land in irrigated production, including massive river water transfers across states, which would cost from $33 billion to $81 billion![30] At such a price, these schemes are unlikely to be adopted. Nevertheless, they are instructive. They reveal that so far we as a people have been unable to challenge the conventional wisdom. We have not questioned the underlying economic forces that drive farmers to greater production, even at the price of depleting essentially nonrenewable resources. We have not questioned the individual's right to privately gain from a national resource without corresponding social obligation, even when it speeds the concentration of farmland ownership. We have not questioned the propriety of taxpayers shouldering much of these costs.

Yet these are the very questions we must ask if we want to pass on to the next generation's offspring a resource base that will sustain their physical needs and an example of the fair distribution of benefits from our natural resources.

9 The Global Economic Crisis and Rising Agricultural Exports

Policymakers usually point to OPEC-induced trade deficits as the reason behind the farm export push. The wheat-for-oil swap, they have told us, will keep the U.S. economy afloat in the international trade arena. Yet exports had been considered as a remedy for farm surpluses long *before* the first OPEC oil price hike. And the balance of trade crisis was apparent as early as 1971, the year of the first trade deficit of this century.

The OPEC rationale hides the true origin of the export push and blinds us to the energy costs of our export policy. In this chapter we want to probe the real roots of the export push.

The United States Emerges as the World's "Breadbasket"

Chronic overproduction and low farm income plagued U.S. agriculture throughout the nineteenth century. In the twentieth century, World War I and World War II created temporary respites by generating more demand for food throughout the world. Our farm production grew steadily as U.S. agriculture adopted more technologically intensive methods to feed the Allied countries.

The United States emerged from World War II as the only major Allied nation with its industrial plant intact. It therefore became the linchpin of the new global economy and the source of capital and aid to rebuild war-torn Europe. The American dollar became the new international currency. The United States replaced Britain as the leader in world trade. At the same time, the domestic economy underwent an unprecedented period of growth. Business took advantage of postwar demand at home, and, as foreign economies began to recover in the late fifties and sixties, U.S. business expanded into markets abroad.

The configuration of world trade in food commodities also changed. In the immediate postwar years, the Marshall Plan temporarily "solved" the problem of agricultural surplus at home by providing food aid to a hungry and devastated Europe. In the late forties and early fifties, the Korean War absorbed our surplus agricultural production just as World War II had. Whereas only 10 percent of total U.S. exports came from agriculture in 1940, the figure nearly quadrupled to 37 percent by 1945. The U.S. grabbed a growing share of world trade in food. During the 1930s, America contributed an average of 5.8 percent of all wheat moving in international channels; by 1947, it claimed almost half. The figures for corn exports moved from almost nothing in 1930–37 to more than half of world trade in 1947.[1]

Pump Priming: Food Aid as the "Foot in the Door"

As farm exports rose during World War II, so did net farm income. But the postwar years saw the return of boom and bust. Farm income began a jagged decline that by the mid-fifties had erased most of U.S. agriculture's gains in real terms. After the Korean War, foreign demand for U.S. grain dropped sharply, and exports fell from $4 billion to $3 billion in the single year from 1952 to 1953.

So agricultural surpluses hadn't gone away—indeed they'd increased as a result of war-induced productivity gains. By the 1950s, dumping U.S. grain in Europe was no longer viewed as aid, but as threatening competition to European farmers. Food aid to rebuild other industrial economies provoked opposition from two major exporters friendly to U.S. interests—Canada and Australia. But withdrawing exports and replacing that income with higher government subsidies to U.S. farmers hardly seemed like the answer; it would just encourage overproduction.

American agribusiness and farm interests hit on an ingenious plan at the 1952 American Farm Bureau conference. In 1954, the plan became Public Law 480—PL–480, or "food aid." Under PL–480 the U.S. continued to ship farm surpluses abroad but directed them primarily to underdeveloped countries that could not afford to pay with dollars. This allowed the U.S. to maintain its friendly relationships with the industrialized nations and yet keep open for itself the possibility of raising U.S. farm prices through exports to countries where international competition was not viewed as a threat. With local currency received as payments from recipient governments, the U.S. government covered expenses for military security, embassy costs, and the purchase of strategic materials for national defense. It also used this money to make loans for industrial development favorable to U.S. corporate interests.[2]

The program had the immediate strategic advantage of tying developing nations more closely to U.S. interests, which suited U.S. foreign policy objectives in the new "Cold War" era.

From our perspective in the early eighties, the link between government food aid during the fifties and sixties and current levels of commercial exports to key countries is striking. (See figure 9–1.) "Graduates" of PL–480 became big commercial customers for U.S. grain. As Richard Gilmore explains,

> The transition from aid recipient to commercial buyer was not, however, merely a natural ontogenetic process whereby developing countries went off the food dole as they grew more prosperous. Rather, inducements to conversion were written into PL–480 contracts from the beginning. Eventual commercial purchases were, therefore, in many cases a *precondition* for the receipt of aid.[3]

PL–480 enabled big private grain traders to gain a toehold in new foreign markets. In the 1950s and 1960s when food aid amounted to as much as 56 percent of U.S. agricultural exports in wheat and feedgrains, PL–480 was essential to trading company profits. In addition, through special programs funded by PL–480 proceeds, the U.S. government further subsidized expansion of the grain

Figure 9-1
Government and Commercial Agricultural Exports
to Developing Countries
Fiscal Years*

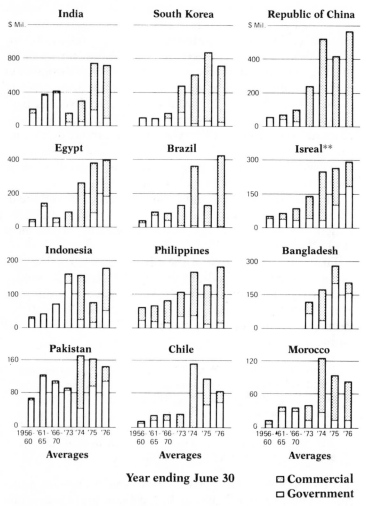

*Government includes PL 480 and mutual security/aid programs
**Until the last few years was considered developing

Source: Richard Gilmore, *A Poor Harvest.*

trade in aid-recipient countries. Many foreign embassies, awash in local currency from the sale of food aid and unable to spend it elsewhere, set up programs with U.S. producers' trade associations to promote U.S. agricultural commodities, thus paving the way for the private grain companies to establish subsidiaries and expand commercial trade.

The U.S. government used funds from the sale of food aid to make loans on attractive terms to agribusiness firms for storage and processing facilities in aid-recipient countries. Nearly half a billion dollars was made available for this purpose over a twenty-year period, 90 percent of which went to U.S. multinational corporations.[4] Another special program used PL–480 funds to facilitate joint ventures between local companies and their American counterparts to build U.S. export sales.

As surpluses mounted through the fifties and sixties, food aid shipments grew apace. By 1964 they accounted for 78 percent of U.S. wheat exports—up from 33 percent when shipments began in 1954. As late as 1978, when PL–480 was almost eclipsed by independent commercial sales abroad, a blue ribbon panel reviewing the program reaffirmed it as "an integral part of U.S. efforts to promote exports and expand markets for its agricultural products."[5]

Economic Origins of the Export Push

In spite of the growth in PL–480 shipments, by the mid-sixties it became painfully evident that food aid was not absorbing enough of agriculture's surplus. As we noted in chapter 2, in response to the limited success of food aid and the mounting costs of domestic farm programs, the Berg Commission in 1966 suggested pushing commercial farm sales abroad as a solution to overproduction.

But it remained for larger global events to set the stage for the export boom in the early 1970s: 1) the serious erosion of the U.S. position in the world economy, 2) the expansion of U.S. agribusiness abroad, and 3) the growing dependency of third world countries on food imports. These developments were not the results of historical accidents or problems originating in OPEC's pricing strategies. They reflected the most basic dynamics in our economic system. The export push has masked these underlying causes and has actually contributed to a deepening of the global economic crisis we are experiencing in the 1980s.

No Longer King of the Mountain

The conditions of *growth* that gave the U.S. a position of global economic dominance in the post–World War II years became the conditions of *crisis* by the late 1960s. Those of us who remember international developments during the sixties can recall the manifestation of this crisis: the growing weakness of the dollar abroad; shrinking trade surpluses as the U.S. began to lose its competitive edge in world trade; our deepening involvement in the "quagmire" of Vietnam; and growing federal deficits, domestic inflation, and productivity losses at home. As the sixties drew to a close, the United States was beset by domestic and international problems that seriously challenged its preeminence as an economic and political power of the post–World War II era.

These problems reflected an erosion in U.S. global economic performance over the last two decades. Why did this erosion begin and how has it triggered the push to export ever more U.S. farm commodities?

Capital Flight: Changes in the Postwar Global Economy

In the immediate post–World War II era, the United States experienced extraordinary economic expansion, both because of the release of pent-up domestic demand and as the dominant force in world trade. But within about fifteen years the basis of that expansion began to shift.

First, the reconstructed economies of Europe and Japan emerged as strong competitors in international trade. With newer plants, cheaper labor, and more effective management, they were able to capture a larger share of world markets. The United States began to lose its unchallenged dominance. The U.S. share of global trade in manufactured goods dropped from 21 percent in 1960 to 15 percent in 1976, while U.S. imports of these same items increased from 44 percent of world imports to 67 percent in 1971. Japanese goods—everything from cars to color television sets—flooded U.S. markets and threatened domestic producers.[6]

Second, as domestic markets became saturated, U.S. corporations moved abroad in search of new markets and more profitable investment opportunities. At first the outflow of U.S. capital was hailed as a great boon to the national economy and regarded as merely an extension of domestic expansion. Corporate leaders assured the public that they would use their profits for domestic investment and to help modernize U.S. industry.

But the newly emerging multinational corporations did not act with the American people in mind. They sought cheaper labor outside U.S. borders, particularly in third world countries, such as Brazil, Taiwan, and South Korea. Multinational profits soared in the sixties, while the domestic economy began to falter.

Productivity in the domestic industrial sector stagnated, reducing the annual rate of profit. Corporations made even more investments abroad as profits on U.S. corporate assets sank from an average of 8.1 percent between 1951 and 1959 to 5.7 percent between 1970 and 1976.

All these trends made the U.S. more dependent on imports, and this import dependency is what has ultimately made us so export dependent. In *The Poverty of Power,* Barry Commoner describes how investment priorities in this earlier period were a "setup" for our OPEC oil dependence in the 1970s.[7] In the quest for short-term profits, U.S. oil companies neglected domestic exploration to develop and exploit foreign oil sources instead. Artificially cheap energy, together with the failure of U.S. automakers to manufacture fuel-efficient cars, created energy consumption patterns that further weakened the self-sufficiency of the domestic economy and made it more vulnerable to the global shocks of later OPEC policies.

Export Markets and the Rise of Transnational Agribusiness

The development of a global food system was reinforced by the expansion of U.S. agribusiness operations abroad in the sixties and seventies—a move which helped to reshape foreign diets and create new commercial demand for major U.S. agricultural exports. Developments in the food processing and retailing industries at home, from 1945 to about 1965, laid the foundation for this foreign expansion.

Most important, grain surpluses at home led to falling real prices for grain, as we have already seen. Grain became so cheap that it was more profitable as livestock feed than as products sold directly to consumers. Before 1950 few cattle were fed significant amounts of grain; by the early 1970s, three fourths were primarily grain fed, and half of the harvested acreage in the United States produced feed for livestock.

As meat became relatively inexpensive, Americans ate more of it. By 1965 we were eating 30 percent more meat than in 1935, and meat had come to account for a quarter of the American food bill.[8] A meat-centered diet became synonymous with good health and the "the American way of life."

Feeding livestock was an effective way of absorbing millions of tons of surplus grain each year, since on average it takes seven pounds of grain and soybean to produce one pound of meat. In a sense, then, America turned meat into a form of processed food—processed grain.

Other processed foods began to take hold, too. The food industry learned that "the biggest growth and profit potential lies in prepared foods," according to *Forbes*. Food processors increased their share of the retail food dollar from fifty cents in 1947 to sixty-three cents in 1964.[9] By the 1960s, processed food accounted for one third of all the food Americans ate.

Flagging domestic economic growth and market saturation, however, began to limit food company profits, and U.S. agribusiness took a harder look at growing consumer markets abroad. By the 1960s, the top 10 to 20 percent of the population in underdeveloped countries constituted an emerging consumer class—and one often lacking the servants that had before made "convenience foods" unnecessary. So, while manufacturing corporations went abroad during this period in search of cheap labor, U.S. food companies developed foreign markets for high-profit processed products. From 1955 to 1968 U.S. corporations nearly tripled the number of food processing operations abroad. The increase in farm-export-related operations (i.e., food and feedgrains) was even more striking—the number of U.S. grain milling subsidiaries abroad increased fivefold during this same period.[10]

The link between these strategies and the growth of U.S. agricultural export commodities was made clear by Eldridge Haynes, president of Business International, as early as 1957: "We are not exporting bread, we are exporting wheat. Somebody has to convert it into bread. If they do not, if there are not more facilities to make bread, it will not be consumed."[11] It has been no coincidence that the countries experiencing the greatest growth in U.S. food processing and retailing subsidiaries are the same countries that received the bulk of U.S. farm exports in the two decades prior to the export boom of the 1970s.

U.S. marketing and promotional strategies were transplanted abroad as well, helping to create new consumer demand for a "global supermarket" on the American model—one that emphasized a highly processed grain and meat-centered diet, for those who could afford it.

The evolving global food system, particularly in less developed countries, was hardly based on an interest in "feeding the hungry." The hungry were not developing a taste for Ritz crackers, Hellman's mayonnaise, or Skippy peanut butter. But the profit goals of corporations were well served by their new strategy. A survey of eleven U.S. parent food processing firms in the 1960s revealed a profit rate of 14 percent per year on overseas operations, compared to a domestic rate of only 8 percent.[12] *Business International* surveyed a similar group of nineteen food transnationals over this same period and uncovered average overseas profit rates of 16.7 percent versus 11.5 percent at home, with many major U.S. food firms recording foreign profits in excess of 25 percent.[13] The surveys show that by

1970 U.S. food companies were making one fourth of their total sales abroad, and in many areas foreign sales were increasing at the phenomenal rate of 50 percent a year!

Monetary Crisis and a New Financial Order

By the close of the 1960s it was clear that what was good for U.S.-based multinationals was not necessarily good for the U.S. economy as a whole. As more U.S. firms placed their investment bets abroad rather than at home, the domestic economy was less able to compete in foreign trade. The war in Vietnam created federal budget deficits that worsened global inflation. A crisis was brewing. How the U.S. government coped with it provides key answers to the origins of the export push as formal government policy.

Developments in the late sixties and early seventies introduced the American public to the terms "balance-of-payments crisis" and "devaluation of the dollar." As the U.S. bought more and sold less abroad during the sixties and as domestic economic problems mounted, it became increasingly difficult to convince foreigners to hold American dollars—dollars that had been the basis for all international exchange since World War II. Many commercial interests abroad began to shift from dollars to gold and put pressure on foreign governments to do the same. By 1968 nervous foreign governments had drawn down U.S. gold reserves to $10 billion—the minimum regarded necessary to meet emergency requirements. The heavy outflow of capital from the U.S.—nearly $4 billion a year by the early 1960s—added decisively to these pressures.

In early 1968 President Johnson placed restrictions on foreign investment and cut down on government spending abroad. But throughout 1968 and into 1969, gold markets were rocked by speculative buying. The price of gold moved to record levels with each new crisis of confidence in the international monetary system.

Meanwhile, the domestic economy continued to weaken, further undermining the strength of the dollar abroad. Federal fiscal and monetary policies designed to remedy the high inflation and interest rates succeeded only in provoking a national recession.

European governments tried to defend their currencies. In May 1971, four European countries revalued their money upward in relation to the dollar. In early August the French central bank announced measures to stem the speculative flow of dollars into France, an action which set off panic selling of dollars in Zurich, Frankfurt, and London.

By July, U.S. monetary reserves had fallen to their lowest level since 1938, and the Secretary of Commerce warned of the first U.S. trade deficit in a century. Finally, on August 15, 1971, amidst chaotic trading in the international money markets, Nixon announced his "New Economy Policy." The president unilaterally suspended dollar convertibility into gold, effectively devaluing it, and instituted a wage freeze, a tax surcharge on imports, and a series of measures to improve U.S. export performance— with increased *agricultural* exports the center of this strategy.

In December the major Western economies worked out a new set of agreements governing the global monetary system, including a general realignment of currencies in relation to the devaluation of the dollar. The gold standard was formally abolished. The dollar, however, continued to fall to record lows, creating fresh anxieties over the strength of the new agreements.

After more months of chaos and further devaluations, the Western economies agreed in 1973 to cut all foreign currencies loose from fixed exchange rates, letting them "float" in the international money markets. This solution, however, fundamentally altered monetary relations in the global economy and created new possibilities for international instability. The floating exchange rates made national economies—particularly the U.S.—even more vulnerable to external shocks and ushered in a new era of global economic interdependence. Foreign trade performance became an even more crucial variable in national economic well-being. Many economists argued that expansion of exports was imperative for the U.S. to salvage any semblance of its post–World War II global hegemony.

In this precarious economic environment, it was particularly easy to adopt a "quick fix" approach and refuse to address fundamental causes. The strategy of pushing commercial agricultural exports emerged as the perfect way out of the crunch.[14]

The Berg Solution Warmed Over

Nixon's New Economic Policy in 1971 did not emerge from a popular call to "do something" about the international monetary crisis. Rather, it reflected key economic interests that wanted to maintain a global economic environment friendly to their expansion overseas. These interests were represented in a special commission appointed by President Nixon in 1970 to study the crisis. Called the Williams Commission after its chairman Albert M. Williams, chief of finance for IBM, the group was comprised of executives from major U.S. corporations and their lawyers.

In its 1979 report, the commission advocated what it termed a "new realism" regarding government intervention in trade. From its members' point of view, the worldwide "economic integration" resulting from stepped-up multinational corporate investment strategies and the havoc they had created in the international economy had to be reconciled. In its summary remarks, the commission's report stated, "The ultimate goal should be to achieve for all people the benefit of an open world in which capital and goods can move freely." But to achieve this goal—one that, in effect, would give corporate interests an even freer hand in international expansion—it was clearly necessary to patch up the damage already done to the U.S. economy. To do this the the Williams Commission advocated short-term government policies to contain the current crisis—exchange rate adjustments, import surcharges, and export subsidies—that would open the way to longer-term policy objectives of "progressive reduction and eventual elimination of barriers to trade and investment."[15]

Their plan's success depended on locating and promoting the key areas of U.S. strength in global trade that would keep the U.S. afloat in the stormy seas of the global economy. The Williams Commission found two potential areas of U.S. trading strength: items that were manufactured using high technology, such as capital equipment, armaments, and computers; and agricultural commodities, especially food and feedgrains. "Our primary interest is to maximize, on a continuing basis, the contribution of international trade and investment to the well-being of the United States."[16]

Thus the agricultural export push was born of a need to make the world safe for continued corporate expansion by propping up one of the victims of this very quest for private profits—the U.S. economy. Agricultural exports became a key element of Nixon's New Economic Policy and of U.S. farm policy throughout the balance of the 1970s.

The Berg proposals in 1966 had advocated essentially the same strategy, and that export push had fallen flat because markets failed to materialize. What could make it work now, in the early 1970s?

The Nixon administration pursued a three-pronged strategy to sweeten export markets for farm commodities and overcome resistance at home. First, the hook for foreign buyers was baited with low prices and liberal credit terms. In 1972, for instance, the Commodity Credit Corporation arranged a massive loan to the Soviet Union to entice it to buy American grain. The devaluation of the dollar also helped lower the price of U.S. farm products abroad.

Second, other countries were persuaded to lower their tariffs against U.S. grain exports in exchange for U.S. measures to abolish domestic price supports. This all fit neatly under the banner of free trade. U.S. legislators were eager to cut the cost of farm programs, while farmers were promised burgeoning export markets as a better solution to low farm income.

Finally, after paving the way for expanded markets abroad and creating increasing foreign dependence on U.S. farm output, farm prices were boosted by reintroducing acreage controls. Beginning in September 1972, U.S. farmers took 62 million acres of farmland out of production. With the Soviets on-line as a big customer, the dollar devalued, and acute worldwide weather problems, the acreage cutbacks guaranteed shortages that caused booming sales at booming prices. It was a spectacular send-off for the export strategy. Between 1970 and 1974 the volume of American wheat exports alone jumped 90 percent, and domestic prices skyrocketed by almost 400 percent.[17]

To sustain the export push, however, new markets had to be carefully tended and others needed to be located. Based on its experience from the PL–480 effort, the Foreign Agricultural Service (or FAS, an arm of the USDA) worked hand in hand with the food processing industries and the major grain companies to expand its "cooperator" programs, which linked U.S. grain producers' trade associations with foreign markets. It sponsored exhibits all over the world that introduced foreign consumers to the American diet. Schools were set up to teach people how to cook with wheat in areas where wheat was not traditionally eaten. Agricultural attachés were sent abroad to assist American food companies and grain exporters.

The result was the successful partnership between corporate food interests and the U.S. government to mold the eating habits of a narrow strata of middle- and upper-class people abroad—making them dependent on products they had never before wanted—in an effort to boost the U.S. position in the global economy. The "success" of this strategy has been illusory. Even as it expanded farm exports, it failed to address the underlying problems of the U.S. economy. As we documented in chapter 3, the strategy has only intensified the problems of most farmers. It has not addressed the problems that led the government to seek farm exports in the first place—not only chronic overproduction in agriculture, but declining productivity in industry, mounting international competition, and the unaccountability of corporate and financial institutions whose investment decisions have accelerated our economic decline. Nor has this strategy been good for most people in the third world, as we will see in the following chapter.

The Export Push: A False Solution that Hides the Real Problem

This overview of global developments that precipitated the export push permits us to see that it did not arise in response to the isolated shocks of OPEC to the national economy, as policymakers often suggest, but was the outgrowth of much deeper problems. Agricultural exports were sought not only to relieve the problems of domestic farm surpluses, but to salvage the eroding position of the United States in the global economy of the seventies. The same quest for profits and corporate expansion that had fueled domestic growth, crossed over national boundaries in the post–World War II period in a way that finally undercut the domestic economy itself. Rather than confront the investment priorities of multinational expansion that lie at the roots of the problem, the government pursued policies that did not challenge these growth dynamics, and, in fact, by boosting exports, U.S. policy gave corporations even more latitude, which further deepened the global and domestic problems they had created.

As we view the 1970s from the vantage point of another global economic crisis of the early 1980s, it is easy to see that the damage done by this pattern of growth, both here and abroad, cannot be repaired by "quick fixes" that address only the trade aspects of the problem. The massive growth in agricultural exports over the past decade has failed to alter the instability in global economic relations or the structural imbalances of increasing export and import dependence that giant corporate enterprises create as they pursue their growth imperative in the international arena. The export push has, in fact, contributed to these problems by disproportionately benefiting these enterprises and fueling their expansion.

Moreover, focusing only on repairing the trade deficits from this expansion has not only given the narrow corporate interests that are responsible for our economic plight a stronger hand, but has diverted our attention from the real source of the problems exports are intended to address. Just as the export solution has sought only to absorb farm surplus at home, rather than intervene in the growth dynamics that create squeezes and cause farmers to overproduce, it has also masked how the same growth dynamics underlie corporate power in the international economy where they serve the interests of profit rather than the welfare of the majority.

10 The Export Boom and Its Impact Abroad

We've explored how the push for agricultural exports was generated by our chronic agricultural oversupply and the drive by U.S.-based multinational firms to expand their sales abroad. But to get the full story, we must also grasp the "pull side" of the equation: Just what forces have created the markets abroad that U.S. policymakers and agribusiness leaders have been so eager to seize?

By the 1950s, food production in many third world economies began to stagnate, and countries that before World War II had been food exporters gradually became dependent on food imports. By the early 1980s, underdeveloped countries as a group imported the equivalent of 15 percent of their total domestic production; while in some countries—Egypt, for example—imports had come to supply over half of the people's basic staple foods.[1]

While it is easy to blame rapid population growth for this turnabout, a host of factors are responsible. To avoid competition for their own industries, U.S. and Japanese policies limited competitive imports from the less developed countries. This reduced the export markets open to underdeveloped countries while the reconstructed Western industrial economies reasserted their dominance in world trade. More important, with the end of formal colonialism came the development of capitalist agriculture. Land, which under feudal structures had been primarily a source of family wealth and status, became the new growth industry. Those with capital, literacy, and political pull bought up land or expanded their holdings. Governments and international lending and aid institutions fueled this "agricultural development" with new lines of credit and new technology.

Why didn't this aid help the third world become *more* self-reliant in food? Because producing food was not the goal of this new capitalist agriculture in the third world; its goal was maximum return on investment. The way to achieve the highest return is to produce for the highest-paying customer. And this customer was not a poor person in the third world but a relatively well-fed person in one of the industrialized countries.

As the minority of affluent, landed farmers expanded, they did so at the expense of tenants and small farmers. In many countries the number of people made landless by this process increased faster than the natural rate of population growth. With these additional people competing in the job market, real wages for day laborers began to fall, and the gap between the rich and poor continued to widen. As the income of the majority declined in real terms, they became less powerful in making demands in the marketplace for the basic foods—largely grains and beans— they needed to survive. Those in control of the best land and seeking the most lucrative markets turned to luxury crops—coffee, cotton, beef, bananas, vegetables, and feed-grains—for the small local elite and, increasingly, for export markets.

International lending agencies and third world governments funneled agricultural credit toward export crops, thus reinforcing the neglect of basic food crop development. Agriculture as a whole was neglected for urban priorities: Of seventy-one underdeveloped countries studied in the mid-1970s, three quarters allocated less than 10 percent of their central government expenditures to agriculture.[2]

These are the underlying reasons why third world nations have become major food importers. While population growth is blamed for their dependency, the truth is that their potential to produce sufficient food staples has been thwarted—thwarted by increasingly unequal control of the land and the siphoning off of credit and other resources for the export production goals of an affluent minority.

As third world countries began to industrialize, often with multinational corporate investment, cheap food for urban workers became a top priority. But third world governments found that it better served their interests to accept food aid and commercial food imports than to undertake the redistribution of farmland and resources necessary to significantly increase food production. The massive influx of food aid—over $30 billion worth since 1950—became yet another blow to the small peasant producer and sharecropper in the third world. Food aid and commercial food imports undercut the prices they received for their crops. "These cheap food policies are a major reason for the grinding poverty that grips rural families in many low-income countries," concludes agricultural economists Dale Adams and Donald Larson of Ohio State University.[3]

As a result of these many forces, all over the world food has increasingly been produced for foreign markets. Yet hunger has increased and food production per person has stagnated in many third world countries. And in our own country, the problems driving many efficient U.S. farmers from the land have only worsened.

Let's look at two examples of how U.S. grain exports have become linked to the underdevelopment of domestic agriculture in the third world.

"Jomo's Getting a Taste for Bread"

So reads an advertisement by Continental Grain—the second largest U.S. grain trader. The ad continues:

> There's a big change in what Jomo's eating these days. And market development teams from America's grain industry are largely responsible. They introduced wheat into local diets. They helped the Africans create better bread. This new taste has excited African palates.[4]

This ad captures much of the story of wheat in Nigeria. Until the late 1960s, Nigeria imported little food. But when Nigeria's oil boom generated unprecedented foreign exchange in the early 1970s, the government decided it was more politic to escalate wheat imports for a relatively small urban class than to develop the indigenous foodstuffs on which its malnourished majority must survive. Throughout the 1970s wheat imports increased 20 percent each year. By the 1981–82 season, Nigeria was importing 1.2 million tons of wheat a year from the United States.[5]

A recent study by social scientists Gunilla Andrae and Bjorn Beckman of the University of Stockholm concludes that "Nigeria is plunging headlong into a reliance on a food crop essentially alien to its environment."[6] By 1980, domestic production of wheat amounted to less than 1 percent of total consumption and no significant increase in domestic production is expected.[7] Because of Nigeria's "poor physical conditions for growing wheat," Andrae and Beckman argue that producing wheat there requires huge capital costs, diverting funds needed for development of indigenous foodstuffs and resulting in production costs several times the world market price.

Even more alarming, while total Nigerian food production increased about 4 percent over the 1977–81 period, per capita production dropped 18 percent over the same period.[8]

When the "market development teams" encouraged Nigerians to develop a "taste" for wheat bread, they also encouraged Nigeria to become dependent on a food staple it would have to import, given its climate, unsuitable for growing wheat. Nigeria could easily produce all the food it needs, but the Nigerian government is investing money that should go for agricultural development into the importation of wheat from the United States. Dependence on food imports is sure to grow—just as Continental Grain planned.

South Korea: An Economic Miracle?

Over the decade of the export boom, most U.S. farm exports have gone, in addition to Japan, the Soviet Union, and Western Europe, to a select group of third world nations. These have been primarily oil-exporting countries such as Mexico, Venezuela, and Nigeria, and a handful of Asian countries, particularly China, Taiwan, and South Korea.

South Korea is typical of those countries the USDA congratulates for having "graduated" from the status of food aid recipient to that of major commercial buyer of U.S. food. Beginning in 1945, this relatively small nation received more U.S. food aid than any other country in the world, except India and Pakistan.[9] By 1980, virtually all of its agricultural imports from the United States were on commercial terms, and South Korea ranked seventh in the world among importers of U.S. farm commodities.

This dependence on imports is seen by our government as a sign of South Korea's development success. "In a growth spurt reminiscent of that experienced in Japan, South Korea is generating an 'economic miracle' that promises to boost U.S. farm exports there," according to a 1980 article in the USDA's *Foreign Agriculture*. The article outlines the promotional efforts that encouraged food imports from America. It quotes the U.S. agricultural attaché stationed in Seoul, Gerald W. Sheldon, as saying, "As Koreans increase their incomes, they want to eat more and better. They want more animal protein but don't have the grains to feed livestock, so they're importing—fortunately, from us." The article notes that in just one year, 1977–78, Korean beef consumption soared 41 percent per capita; pork consumption rose 30 percent; and poultry consumption, 22 percent. Annual consumption of these three animal foods amounted to about ten kilograms per person.[10]

But these are statistical averages, divorced from the day-to-day reality of South Korea's development. They don't mean that most Koreans now regularly eat meat in small quantities. As Lutheran missionary Shirley Dorow wrote to us, "Average beef consumption has risen. . . . This means, of course, that some people never eat beef and a few are eating it regularly, for it is a status food."[11]

The shift from traditional diets based on rice or corn and beans to diets of meat and wheat is often described as a welcome "upgrading" of nutritionally poor indigenous cuisine. But most poor people in the third world cannot afford meat, certainly not meat produced from imported grain. Half the increase in grain fed to livestock abroad during the 1970s depended on imported grain, mainly from the United States.[12]

Moreover, the meat-centered diet that Americans, and now much of the world, have come to associate with the "good life" is increasingly viewed by medical authorities as a health threat. According to the World Health Organization, coronary heart disease is on the rise in precisely those countries—such as South Korea, Sri Lanka, Malaysia, and the Philippines—where better-off urbanites are forsaking traditional foods for the status of meat and processed foods.[13] Increasingly, traditional third world plant-centered diets are recognized as nutritionally sound. The problem is not of quality, but of quantity in the diets of many third world people. The poor majority just can't afford to buy enough of the traditional foods.

Cheap Food and the Decline of Korean Agriculture

South Korea's impressive growth in GNP—a 160 percent increase from 1967 to 1977—has made the country an internationally acclaimed model of economic development.[14] That model—pushed by U.S. advisors in South Korea for thirty years and adopted by the Korean government—has emphasized rapid urban industrialization. The model does not feature developing heavy industry, which could someday free the country from its dependence on industrial imports, but the manufacturing—or often simply the assembly—of consumer goods for export. Rather than an independent industrial base, this model of development has turned South Korea into an "export platform," dependent on foreign-based multinational corporations for capital, raw material, and semifinished goods.

This "economic miracle" has been achieved by a repressive dictatorship which Amnesty International has cited for "the arrest and detention of prisoners of conscience, frequent and serious irregularities in the judicial process, the ill treatment and torture of political prisoners and the use of the death penalty for political and criminal offenses."[15]

By outlawing free trade unions and turning a blind eye to pollution and industrial safety, production costs are kept low to attract multinational investors. But equally important to maintaining cheap labor is the role of cheap food.

Food makes up about one fifth of South Korea's urban

consumer price index. Keeping food cheap has been essential to maintaining an urban industrial work force on wages low enough to attract foreign investment. Cheap food might have been supplied by developing local agriculture. Instead, the South Korean government has relied on over $2 billion in food aid and on commercial food imports.[16]

This import strategy has had a double advantage. First, it has been easier to import food, especially since the United States offered easy terms in exchange for the political allegiance of the dictatorship, including military bases. Second, food imports allowed the South Korean government to set prices for domestically produced grain very low, undercutting local producers' incomes and driving as many as 7 million rural people into the cities between 1962 and 1977.[17] This rural exodus was a godsend to the budding export industries, as rural emigrants competed for jobs in factories.

The import strategy has also been self-reinforcing—the more food imported, the more domestic agriculture suffered, and the more imports were needed. In 1960 South Korea produced virtually 100 percent of its food needs. But by 1968 this figure had fallen to 68 percent, and by 1975 South Korea was able to meet only 60 percent of its overall food requirements from domestic production.[18]

The shift to imports was devastating in the countryside. Although its rhetoric stressed "food self-sufficiency," the South Korean government had no reason to protect its farmers' incomes, given cheap food imports from the U.S. So it set low prices for farmers' crops. As a result, tenancy, outlawed by the early fifties "land reform," began to rise in the sixties as farm income was hit by low prices for crops combined with the rising costs of farm supplies. Many farmers incurred heavy debts and to pay them off, they sold their land. Renting was the only way they could continue in agriculture. Others fled rural poverty for factory jobs in the cities, but rented out their plots to supplement their low factory wages. By 1977, almost a fifth of the cultivated land was worked by tenants or through other nonownership arrangements.[19]

In 1981, agricultural researcher John Sayer of the Hong

Kong–based Asia Monitor Resource Center studied South Korean agriculture for the Institute for Food and Development Policy. His study concludes that "on top of increasing inequality of incomes within the countryside lies the long-standing imbalance between rural and urban income levels. More than any other fact, this discrepancy is tangible evidence of the lopsided effects of South Korea's export-oriented development policies."[20]

Of course, the other side of exports was imports. While multinational manufacturing firms were turning South Korea into a platform for assembling consumer goods for export, U.S. producers and multinational grain traders were engaged in shaping new dietary preferences to better fit the foodstuffs that could be most profitably supplied by the United States. They had on their side the full support of the U.S. government.

Wheat is a classic example. Before the 1960s, South Koreans ate virtually no Western-style bread. Wheat played a relatively small part in the diet, compared to rice. Then, between 1966 and 1977, while domestically produced wheat fell by 86 percent, imports of wheat leapt over four-fold, much of it financed with U.S. government help.[21]

In 1967, Western Wheat Associates, representing U.S. wheat producers, came to South Korea. In cooperation with the USDA, Wheat Associates spearheaded an eat-wheat campaign that included demonstrations, technical advice to new bakeries, and efforts to make wheat rolls a mainstay of school lunches. Western Wheat Associates also served as a liaison between South Korean entrepreneurs and the multinational grain companies. In 1972 the first automatic biscuit and cracker equipment was installed in three South Korean plants, and wheat utilization rose dramatically. By 1979 over twenty-one thousand housewives in more than one hundred cities were attending special sandwich-making schools.[22]

The strategy worked beautifully. By 1975 over seven thousand bakeries had sprung up while almost no wheat was being grown in the country.[23] And in 1978, South Korea joined what the USDA calls the "billion dollar club"— those countries importing more than $1 billion worth of U.S. farm commodities, much of it wheat.[24]

Two consequences were the erosion of the traditional rice-centered diet and the loss of rice self-sufficiency in the former "rice bowl" of the southeast peninsula. The South Korean government keeps the prices farmers receive for rice so low that they cannot even cover their costs of production. In 1977 the government price for 80 kilos of rice was set at only $65, while the farmers' costs exceeded $95. Moreover, throughout the 1970s, the South Korean government coerced farmers to plant less popular but higher yielding varieties of rice, only to discover that these varieties were less resistant to pests and flood damage.[25] Farmers became more dependent on the fertilizers and pesticides supplied by multinational chemical firms, while the country as a whole became more dependent on rice imports. Rice purchases from abroad shot up from virtually nothing in calendar year 1978 to about 241,000 metric tons the following year. These purchases more than tripled in 1980 to 900,000 metric tons.[26]

More wheat and less rice has not been the only change in the Korean diet. With the help of $12 million in U.S. government credits derived from sales of food aid, in 1975 three U.S.-based grain corporations, including Cargill, set up poultry and animal feed operations in South Korea. According to Mitchell Wallerstein of M.I.T., when U.S. aid officials extended loans to the grain corporations, they obtained guarantees from the South Korean government that no restrictions would be placed on exports of feedgrains from the United States to South Korea for at least three years.[27]

To create local demand for meat and poultry, the Korean government, again with the backing of U.S. advisors, promoted domestic livestock production, generating increased demand for imported feed. Before 1960 there were fewer than one hundred families in South Korea raising beef cattle; by 1977 there were almost four thousand.[28]

This strategy was also a success from the point of view of U.S. export interests. Almost 100 percent of South Korea's feedgrains are now imported. In 1978 imported beef accounted for over 40 percent of local consumption. In addition, almost 40 percent of South Korean beef cattle were imported.[29]

Many economists would justify, and in fact celebrate, South Korea's dependency on exporting consumer goods and importing food as a classic example of how nations benefit from "comparative advantage." The theory of comparative advantage is that each nation should export what it can produce most cheaply, and import goods that are more inexpensively produced by others. Everyone wins. Indeed, the giant grain trader Cargill says that "policies aimed at more open agricultural trade along lines of comparative advantage will do more than self-sufficiency strategies to overcome . . . hunger." [30]

In the Institute's book, *Food First: Beyond the Myth of Scarcity*, we look critically at this simplistic formula. Its primary flaw is in viewing nations as undifferentiated units, never asking who *within* each country benefits from trade. Moreover, the comparative advantage approach does not address the fact that it is multi-national firms, whose interests are not those of *any* national population, which increasingly determine trade patterns.

For example, while there is no question that South Korea can produce cheap electronic and textile goods, *who* benefits? It would be difficult to demonstrate that the majority of South Koreans benefit when the *minimum* cost of living for an average family in 1978 was *twice* the average wage, according to the government's own figures. Textile workers, employed in one of the key export sectors of the Korean economy, earned on average only 16 percent of the minimum cost of living for the average family in 1978. [31]

Poverty doesn't tell the whole story. Along with low wages, South Korean workers must survive hazardous working conditions, including exposure to chemicals, dangerously fast assembly lines, high industrial accident rates, poor ventilation, and high levels of noise. Air pollution in Seoul is so serious that concentration of particulates in the air is more than ten times what is officially judged the safe maximum.

Moreover, South Korea's comparative advantage in consumer goods exports is achieved at the cost of the majority's welfare, by maintenance of a U.S.-supported dictatorship which restricts workers' efforts to organize for their own protection.

Throughout the 1970s, the Park government attempted to prevent union organizing and to maintain the low wages that attracted such foreign investors as General Motors, IBM, Monsanto, and General Electric. Workers were prohibited from forming unions in foreign firms without permission from the government's labor office, and existing unions were required to seek the same office's permission before entering into disputes with employers.[32] According to Amnesty International's 1982 annual report, more than fifty trade unionists and students were charged under South Korea's "National Security Law" in 1981.[33]

Those primarily benefiting from South Korea's export boom are, first, the multinational firms which profit significantly more on such foreign investments than on investments at home. Second are the affluent in South Korea, the top 20 percent whose share of the nation's income is growing. Only they can afford to buy locally assembled consumer products and the meat produced from imported feed.

U.S. food exports have directly undercut South Korean food production and have created a demand for foods that are both expensive and nutritionally unnecessary. Even a 1982 World Bank report concluded that the benefits of "developed country disposal of agricultural surplus . . . tend[s] to accrue largely to a relatively affluent urban minority of consumers, while adverse effects are felt by the poor rural majority."[34]

Is Our Security Increased?

For decades U.S. policymakers have suggested that U.S. security is increased by making other countries dependent on us. "If you are looking for a way to get people to lean on you and to be dependent on you, in terms of their cooperation with you," Hubert Humphrey said in 1957, "it seems to me that food dependence would be terrific."[35]

But isn't this perspective incredibly shortsighted? Encouraging an elite class to become accustomed to a diet that cannot be sustained by their local resources and cannot be enjoyed by the entire population is a setup for eventual confrontation. Protests by South Korean farmers and factory workers hurt by this strategy will only increase, and the small elite locked into dependence on the export/import model will struggle to maintain its privileges. Ultimately, U.S. security will be threatened as more South Koreans see the integral link between U.S. interests and their own oppressive development model.

The view that South Korea's dependence on our farm exports is an unalloyed good for the United States also overlooks the other side: South Korea's capacity to import our food in part hinges on its production of consumer goods that used to be produced here. This point returns us to a basic issue discussed in the preceding chapter: U.S. policymakers push farm exports because *we* have become increasingly dependent on imports, under the direction of multinational corporations unaccountable to the vast majority of Americans.

11 Lessons from the Export Decade

Farm exports make us all winners, Americans were told in the early 1970s. Mounting grain exports will save our farmers, help feed the hungry world, and pay for essential oil imports. Instead, the massive export boom helped precipitate the second greatest farm depression of the twentieth century; its bounty bypassed the hungry abroad, while increased agricultural production generated enormous hidden costs that may well outweigh any gain from foreign exchange earnings.

Why has this economic strategy hurt the very people its proponents claimed would be served?

To understand, we have had to probe the most basic forces driving our economy. The economy, we have seen, is not separate from our daily lives. It is continually formed by the myriad decisions we make each day. But it is based on underlying rules that determine the way in which those decisions are made—and who benefits. Thus, these ground rules are neither impenetrable nor immutable. We as a people should be able to examine them regularly to assess whether or not they are leading us in a direction that benefits the majority and is consistent with our most widely shared values about how we want to live. We should recognize our right to change these rules if they don't measure up. Above all, this understanding is what we hope you will take from this book.

As the dreams of millions of Americans are being destroyed by poverty and joblessness in the 1980s, and as even many with work find themselves increasingly insecure, many sense that something is profoundly wrong with our economy. After inflation had subsided in 1983 and the

Reagan administration predicted recovery from a deep recession, the majority of Americans still remained pessimistic about our economic future. Nevertheless, we as a people find it hard to penetrate to the core of our economy's problems. Economic issues have become emotionally charged, for to look critically at how capitalism works in the United States, and in whose interest, is seen by some as almost treasonous! Capitalism is believed by many to be synonymous with democracy, and democracy is believed to encompass all that is good about the American way of life. To these people, pointing out fundamental flaws in our system automatically means advocating what they perceive as the only other alternative—Soviet-style, top-down economic planning.

This book is a call to let go of such black-and-white thinking and to look with fresh eyes at one aspect, a most basic aspect of our economy—farming and food. We chose to consider one instructive phenomenon—the origins and impact of the farm export boom of the last decade—because it represents the intensification of a process that has been transforming the American farm and food system since that system's beginnings.

Through the export boom, we have seen how our fundamental rules of the game define success and failure in business enterprise and determine the distribution of rewards for all who participate—farmers, workers, consumers, and corporations alike. Economic ground rules at the core of our economy's growth process have shaped the fundamental features of our food system—the economic relationships among its various sectors and their relative positions of power. Ultimately they determine who gets to farm, how fast our land loses its fertility, the price of our food, and our nation's impact on producers and consumers abroad.

Contradictions in the Food Economy

Inherent in this process of growth are basic contradictions between production for profit and production for human need. These conflicts take many forms, but all arise from the way our ground rules mandate that the individual ownership of productive resources and the quest by these

owners for the highest returns to capital through expanding production lead to a concentration of wealth and capital, at the expense of the majority. The increasing dominance of giant food corporations, the trend toward fewer
and larger farms, and the tragic paradox of hunger in the
midst of plenty all reflect those contradictions at work
in our food economy. Severe imbalances follow, not only
within economic sectors and among them, but among entire nations as well—creating winners and losers in an increasingly inequitable fashion.

The export boom has only exacerbated the problems
built into this dynamic of growth. The rush to plant fence
row to fence row for export quickened the farmer's pace on
the production treadmill and increased agriculture's dependence on industry for farm supplies and technology. Increased exports heightened farmers' vulnerability to unstable, highly competitive global markets for their harvests.
As the export decade wore on, boom and bust intensified
and the cost/price squeeze tightened its grip on farmers,
accelerating the trend toward concentration of farms and
culminating in a severe depression for agriculture.

Within agriculture the growth imperative became a survival imperative that kept short-term gain ahead of long-
term environmental protection. Thus, over the past decade, soil erosion rates and water depletion problems have
escalated dangerously under the pressure of all-out production for export. Yet our economy's ground rules include
no mechanism for addressing problems that threaten our
very food-producing capability.

Chapter 2 described how our ground rules have given
the giant industrial enterprises that emerged in the late
nineteenth century a degree of market control foreclosed to
farmers. These enterprises have used their market power to
further their own growth at farmers' expense. Our comparison of the fate of farmers during the export decade
with that of the farm supply industry and food processors
and retailers graphically illustrates how this uneven development operates in the food economy of today.

Further, this same uneven power allows more of the consumer's food dollar to be siphoned into the hands of the
fifty giant firms that dominate the food industry. The in-

tense merger activity in the late 1960s and 1970s further tightened their control over industrial assets and markets, allowing food companies to pass on their costs to consumers through administered pricing. Thus, the impact of the export boom on food prices only magnified the profits these shared monopolies had already ensured for themselves.

Moreover, as markets for U.S. grain mushroomed abroad, the few big-league firms that dominate the international grain trade have been able to reap a bonanza, using their vast global network and special trading advantages. These profits garnered from the export boom helped fuel the expansion of firms such as Cargill into other branches of the food economy, increasing concentration in those sectors as well.

The export boom also calls attention to how uneven development that characterizes growth in our domestic farm and food economy has achieved global dimensions since World War II. Rising agricultural trade was integral to imbalances that grew in the international economy during this period. Reduced domestic opportunities for profit accumulation in the 1950s and 1960s led U.S. food corporations to expand operations abroad, seeking new markets for the lucrative meat-centered and highly processed diet that had helped underwrite their growth at home in earlier decades. The dietary shift they promoted among foreign elites increased demand for U.S. grains and feedgrains abroad—providing both a commercial outlet to absorb mounting U.S. farm surpluses and a new source of profits to sustain corporate expansion.

These developments occurred within a larger context of multinational corporate growth that reshaped the global economy and eroded U.S. dominance within it. In their quest for greater profits, corporate giants deemphasized investment in new U.S. plants and equipment in favor of establishing "export platforms" in third world countries that offered cheaper labor and less government regulation. American industries were left increasingly unable to compete in the international arena. And the entire global economy became more export and import dependent.

Cheap U.S. grain flowing into third world countries also undercut local producers and served the interests of the multinationals and their local elite partners. As we described in the case of South Korea's "economic miracle," the peasants driven out of farming provided the cheap labor needed in urban sweatshops. Such "developing" countries mirror in more extreme form the way the ground rules of profit accumulation and growth disproportionately benefit a few here at home and abroad.

Finally, we have seen how the export push illustrates the government's role in the economy. Government attempts to cope with the contradictions in our food system have dealt only with their manifestations in the market and have failed to address the ground rules of profit accumulation and growth that caused them. Thus, policies pursuing solutions through greater markets abroad have only backfired. As overproduction, low farm income, environmental damage, food price inflation, and general economic instability worsen with the "success" of the export boom, government has been more deeply drawn into the affairs of domestic agriculture and the international economy. The government escalates its farm program outlays in response to the weakening agricultural economy at home—outlays that go hand-in-hand with promoting investments by multinational corporations in the international arena. Meanwhile, the increased global instability that accompanies growing export and import dependence only increases the importance of trade issues on the public agenda. These lessons from the export decade direct us to address even more fundamental issues.

The Myth of Basic Fairness

Strategies to save the family farm by expanding markets are accepted by farmers and nonfarmers alike because they assume that our economic ground rules reward hard work, efficiency, and aggressive entrepreneurship. Those who fail to take advantage of expansion are seen as just "not willing to change or not wanting to compete," in the words of past Secretary of Agriculture Earl Butz.[1] This belief in the basic fairness of our economic ground rules is crucial: for if we believe that our economic ground rules are fair, then it is easy to justify the success of the few at the expense of the many as the proper reward for efforts and skills.

Efficiency and work are necessary for success in our economy, but they are not sufficient. While our economic ideology says that our system rewards all those who are efficient entrepreneurs, in fact it rewards only those who can continuously expand production. As we've seen, they are a minority, and a shrinking minority at that. But not a randomly selected one. Control over productive assets and the economic power that goes with it, more than anything else, determine the winners. The greater the wealth and volume of sales, the more easily businesses weather slumps, expand production, and pass on costs, ensuring their profits. As wealth begets wealth, economic growth becomes synonymous with the increasing concentration of productive assets as economic power falls into ever fewer hands.

This process is necessarily a rocky one. For the very system that determines the winners makes their existence more precarious. Those corporations who rise to the top must themselves scramble to expand profits, in part by keeping labor costs as low as possible. But workers and farmers are also consumers. And, as the economic power (job opportunities and real wages) of this majority is reduced, they are less able to purchase goods produced by the shrinking numbers of farm and industrial owners. This unequal development between the producing and consuming sectors creates periodic recessions. Then, these same producers call for government to step in and "stimulate" the economy.

Bigger Is Always Better?

We cannot look objectively at our country's economic development until we examine in more depth our own notions of efficiency, especially the notion that the bigger the scale of the operation, the more efficient. This assumption is another justification for the development process we've just described.

The myth that bigger is always better grew in part from

the accurate observation that each unit can generally be produced more cheaply if fixed costs are spread over a large number of units. The problem with the bigger-is-always-better credo is that it suggests an absolute, when in reality economies of scale are not absolute; they have an upper limit. In other words, in every type of production a size can be reached at which the cost to produce each unit can no longer be reduced by increasing the output. In farming that size turns out to be relatively small. At roughly $50,000 to $100,000 in gross sales, most economies of scale are captured on most types of farms.[2] Yet farms larger than this now produce most of our food.[3]

The bigger-is-always-better credo also reflects the imperative in our ground rules for greater production, the cost of which is measured only in terms of the enterprise, rather than in full social costs. Chapter 4 provides evidence of the energy costs of farm exports, and chapters 7 and 8 weigh the hidden soil and water costs of mounting production, which will ultimately accrue to future generations. Subsidies, the cost of public works, and human costs, such as unemployment and the loss of a way of life, do not enter into the calculations of efficiency based on production for profit.

Big Is Bad?

One reaction to the simplistic notion that bigger is always better is that bigness itself is the enemy. A potential misreading of this book could be that what's wrong with our economy is simply a question of scale and that the multinational grain traders or the farm supply industry should simply be carved down to competitive size.

Such a diagnosis misses several key points.

First and foremost, focusing on size overlooks the economic forces that generate greater size to begin with: production made by and in the interests of the minority who own productive property; the necessity to expand production and lower costs to survive; the relative ability of those with greater wealth to undercut competitors and grow; and the differing rates of concentration that result among economic sectors, giving the more concentrated industries (the grain trade or farm supply manufacturers) advantages over the more competitive ones (farming). These are our economy's givens. Unless we address them, breaking up monopolies is illusory reform and simply allows the exploitative basis on which growth occurs to continue.

Thus, the strategy of breaking up the monopolies, a battle cry of social reformers for more than a century, leaves unaddressed the basic contradiction between profit and human need in our system. True, more competitive industries might be more responsive to market demand than the oligopolies predominant today, and we *do* pay a higher price for their extra profits in the marketplace. But the more basic question is, Can human needs be met if our ground rules are left in place—to dictate the *only* basis for citizen participation in the economic system that determines so much of our lives? With our "vote" in the marketplace, for example, we cannot demand the protection of our natural resource base, nor can we promote the dispersed ownership of farmland. Market demand alone will not give Americans any say in whether our nation's wealth is invested here or abroad, or whether it supports productive, job-creating enterprise or goes into real estate speculation or corporate mergers.

But . . . We're Feeding the Hungry

Another reason Americans seldom consider the roots of our current farm problems is that on the surface our agriculture appears so successful. Not only are we repeatedly reminded that the price of food in the United States is among the lowest in the world, but we are told that our nation's breadbasket feeds a hungry world.

However, the marketing strategies of the multinationals direct most expansion of U.S. grain exports into *feedgrains for livestock*, not the basic foods of the hungry. While hunger increases around the world, almost half of world grain production now goes to feed livestock, up from one third a decade ago.[4]

This expansion of world food trade is powerful evidence that the question of human need is incidental to our economic ground rules. More than half of our grain exports go to other relatively well-off industrial countries. As for the underdeveloped countries that import our grain, most are locked into the same development process we are—in many cases, within the constraints of more inequitable social and political structures. As a result, the beneficiaries of our exports to underdeveloped countries are those wealthy enough to buy meat fattened by imported U.S. grain. By relying on our relatively cheap imported grain, their governments continue to avoid the redistribution of control over agricultural resources, which is the necessary first step in developing agricultural capacity to meet local needs.

Attention to food imports by underdeveloped countries distracts us from one crucial fact, documented in *Food First: Beyond the Myth of Scarcity*.[5] There is *no physical* reason why more third world countries have become increasingly dependent on food imports just to meet survival needs. Virtually every country in the world has the physical resources necessary to meet the basic food needs of every citizen. Indeed, in most of the countries where millions go hungry today—the Philippines or India, for example—enough grain is *already* being produced to satisfy the nutritional needs of the people. Scarcity is not the cause of hunger; the increasingly narrow control over food-producing resources is.

Rather than contributing toward long-term food security, our agricultural exports often help create demand for foods that could never be supplied for the majority of the population from local resources—for example, wheat in climates unsuited to its production. Our exports set the stage for heightened conflict. The majority who are now disenfranchised in the third world are demanding rightful access to life's necessities—food being the first. Once made dependent on an expensive imported consumption style, however, the better off will resist even more strongly these just demands for change.

A Basis for Change

Although this book offers a fundamental critique of our economy, we are not blind to the material abundance it has brought most Americans. Nor can we ignore our relative political freedom, which allows us to write and publish a book that questions the very basis of our economic organization.

But those factors, material abundance and freedom of expression, should not be allowed to mask the need to come to grips with what is wrong. For this, we need to have criteria by which we can evaluate any system—criteria that help us judge how well the system meets human needs and upon which we can establish a basis to work for change.

Is It Truly Democratic? Do people have a say over decisions that affect them in an essential way? We have seen how the ground rules that govern our economic system concentrate economic power in ever fewer hands. The few who own and control productive assets in our society alone have decision-making power over how those resources are used. The investment policies of major corporations largely determine our job opportunities and income; yet most of us cast not one single vote in setting these priorities. In 1981 and 1982, for example, these corporations alone decided to tie up over $136 billion in mergers, fueling inflation and tying up credit in activities that only tightened their grip on the economy.[6] By relegating the concept of democracy only to the political sphere, we fail to see that such decisions taken in the economic sphere often have an even more fundamental impact on our lives than laws passed by Congress.

Moreover, the concentration of economic power, which flows inevitably from our economy's dynamic of growth, itself threatens our goal of political democracy. A relatively minor, but telling, case in point was mentioned in chapter 3. Throughout this century, mammoth agribusiness operations made millions annually by skirting the law directing publicly subsidized irrigation water only to small farms. After years of protest by small farmers, the big farming interests got the law changed in 1982, finally making legal what they had been doing illegally for decades.[7]

A more personal example was provided by a high government official we interviewed in Washington who was skeptical of the benefits of pushing agricultural exports. He told us with remarkable candor, "If I don't toe the line on exports, the major grain companies would have me out of a job tomorrow."

Does the System Foster Personal Freedom? Freedom must be defined in both the negative—freedom from interference from others or the state—and in the positive—freedom to achieve that which makes life worth living, including a satisfying job and basic security for one's self and one's family. Essential to this positive definition of freedom is the opportunity to choose among varied options and to receive full reward for the fruits of one's labor.

Yet the ground rules that drive our economy end up denying more and more people such positive freedom. The transformation of American farming we outlined in chapters 2 and 3 provides a vivid example. The livelihood of farmers is increasingly insecure, and they are subject to economic forces beyond their control that systematically rob them of the full returns from their work. By the late 1970s most analysts of farm economics agreed that only those who inherit land or who are already considerably wealthy can afford to choose farming.

Does the System Safeguard General Economic Welfare and That of Future Generations? We have seen how the growth dynamic that concentrates productive assets also directly undermines the very assets upon which further production depend—soil and water, for example. Perhaps most alarming, this mining of our resources is all but invisible. Our ground rules give owners the right to destroy the resources they control. Those who do not own these resources—the vast majority of Americans—have little ability to control this destruction. Future generations, who will suffer most from resource destruction, will pay the price.

More important, the failure of government attempts to step in and "manage the economy" reflects the way our ground rules, left unaddressed, do more than generate economic crises. They also prevent smooth growth—a balance between production and consumption or between investment and its returns to society as a whole—balances that are necessary to avoid inefficiency and waste, as well as to meet human needs. "Overproduction" of farm commodities in the face of growing hunger and deprivation and multinational investment priorities that create dislocations and unemployment among factory workers at home and peasant farmers abroad are only two examples of how the instability built into our system fails to serve the general welfare.

A Fresh Look at Old "Givens"

Having sketched the criteria for evaluating whether any economic system is meeting our needs, let's consider some basic facets of our own economy and examine how well they measure up.

The Market. In theory, the market acts as an efficient "clearing device" to allow buyers and sellers to come together on an equal footing and exchange goods for money. Freely operating forces of supply and demand determine a market price, and goods are distributed throughout the economy on the basis of the dollar votes we cast as consumers. But we have seen how reality differs form this theory. The imbalances in economic power inherent in how our economy grows make a mockery of the equal footing both buyers and sellers are supposed to have in the marketplace to make it function as an accurate reflection of consumer needs and preferences.

For example, the contrast of sixty thousand new food items hitting the market over the past decade—including junk food such as "Pop Rocks" and "Pringles"—while infant mortality rates, a prime measure of malnutrition, remain high in some of our inner cities illustrates how market demand, left to its own devices, funnels resources toward luxury items in the face of growing deprivation. Thus, as long as there are major inequalities in the distribution of purchasing power, the market alone cannot be relied on to wisely allocate resources.

More important, to fully understand the failure of the market we must see how our ground rules make its very mechanisms—supply and demand—captive to the economic power of large producers. The market power that farm supply industries achieve over farmers and that the food industry exercises over consumers are graphic examples of how this happens. In each case, our ground rules mandate a growth process that leaves a few giant firms in a position to influence supply and demand itself—by cooperating to hold prices rigid and cut back on production when demand falls and by market promotion strategies to stimulate demand for products consumers never wanted before, "Pop Rocks" here at home and wheat in Nigeria and South Korea. Further, the administered pricing strategies these firms are able to pursue (because of their combined share of the market) undercut the competitive pricing mechanism that is supposed to operate in theory and allows them to accumulate higher profits at both farmer and consumer expense. In this way, the market becomes not a mechanism for registering true buyer preferences, but a conduit through which the minority who own productive assets can exercise—and reinforce—their disproportionate economic power.

Private Ownership of Productive Resources. The right to private property is what protects us from the concentration of state power—without it, we would lose our freedom, we have been taught to believe. While this view reflects legitimate fears, it fails to acknowledge a crucial distinction. The right to control our personal property—a house or car, for example—is not at all the same as the right of relatively few individuals, given our ground rules, to effectively control most of our productive assets. Not when these assets are resources upon which we *all* depend and to whose productivity we *all* contribute—in the factory, office, or farm. The first right may enhance our well-being, while the second may *threaten* the welfare of society as a whole and the majority who work within it.

Moreover, ownership of productive assets by a shrinking minority not only has profound implications for control over their use, but for the distribution of rewards from production itself. How our economic system distributes economic power directly affects wealth and income prospects for everyone—determining who can travel first class and who cannot even afford a ticket, who can buy a house and who cannot.

This is the context within which we must ask whether the right to unlimited private ownership of productive assets in our system is a guarantee of freedom or an obstacle to it. The ownership of farmland provides one clear example. Every time a big farm expands, another farmer loses land. Because the supply of farmland is limited, the right of Southern Pacific Railroad to control 4 million acres—as it now does in the western United States[8]—directly undercuts the opportunities of thousands of farm families to own any farmland in this region at all.

Putting investment decisions in private hands is often thought to ensure our freedom from the kind of top-down planning that occurs in state-controlled economies. But it is essential that we realize how our own system results in top-down planning as well.

We saw, for example, in our tour of the origins of the export strategy in chapter 9 that our government *chose* to vastly expand farm exports—a choice that favored multinational corporate interests. This was not the only option for dealing with the deep structural problems that led to mounting import dependency. The trade deficit that agricultural exports were promoted to counter could have been an opportunity to fundamentally reevaluate our economic situation in the world. But such an approach would have required that the government confront the forces that drive multinational corporations to move abroad or use scarce capital for mergers and speculative investments rather than respond to majority needs. Since, under the logic of our economic structure, these giant firms are simply doing what they must, to attack the roots of our mounting import/export dependence would have required addressing the way our economy's ground rules turn private ownership of productive assets into a tool that benefits a few at the expense of the many.

Our point is simply that we have economic planning, too. It is largely carried out by powerful private concerns. Our government claims that our well-being is served by corporate free reign, when, in fact, corporate interests and those of the majority are often in direct conflict. Recall, for example, the growing power of the big-league grain firms described in chapter 5. Producers and consumers want stable, predictable prices, while the grain trade thrives on market instability. Producers and consumers throughout most of the world would benefit from self-sufficiency in basic foods, whereas the more dependent countries become on food imports, the more the grain trade profits.

Conclusion and Commencement

"I can think of no one who would not benefit from the expansion of export sales," the executive director of the North American Export Grain Association, Joseph Halow, said in 1978.[9] By promising everyone progress through ever larger markets, promoters of the farm export strategy have tried to conveniently bury the contradictions inherent in the growth of our food economy. But wishing these contradictions away resolves nothing; it only ensures that they will remain hidden from public scrutiny, which benefits only the powerful minority.

Certainly few would argue that economic expansion, per se, is harmful to human welfare. Historically, in fact, growth has clearly been necessary for attaining many of society's most basic goals—for example, adequate food and shelter and liberation from backbreaking work. The real question, as we have seen throughout this book, is on what basis does economic expansion occur? And how consistently does it deliver benefits to the majority of people?

Throughout human history, people have lived in fear of food shortages. Indeed, much of the world still lives not only with this fear, but with this reality. Yet we tolerate an economic system whose ground rules make food surpluses a liability rather than an asset. While the United States sits on one of the largest grain gluts in history, there are more hungry people in the world than ever before. And our secretary of agriculture is left hoping for a surge in doughnut popularity in China as part of his solution to the problem of surplus. The absurdity becomes rational only if we fail to question the basic priorities of our system.

Clearly there is a need for an alternative better suited to

human needs and aspirations—one in which the democratic process is extended into the economic sphere and in which the quest for profits at the expense of the general welfare is eliminated. Yet, quite deliberately, this book does not propose solutions. To propose solutions would contradict the basic assumption that has motivated this book: We as a people must reach a widely shared agreement on what are the real problems in our society before lasting solutions can be effectively formulated and successfully implemented. Blueprints for a new society and programs to solve the basic problems outlined in this book that bypass this crucial step are both premature and doomed to failure.

Our purpose has been to clarify the underlying forces at the root of our farm and food problems—forces that are central to many other aspects of our economy as well. With such an understanding we can no longer be misled by false promises; we can no longer be made fearful of change. Freed from the myths that keep us locked on a destructive path, we can work for economic structures truly worthy of the human potential.

We hope this book will help make the 1980s an era in which more and more Americans come to such realizations and engage in such a quest. Knowing that history is in our hands, we need no longer live in a society that is trading the future.

Notes

Chapter 1

1. Constructed from data in *Economic Indicators of the Farm Sector, 1981* (Washington, D.C.: U.S. Department of Agriculture, 1981).

2. *New York Times*, November 29, 1981.

3. John M. Connors, "Structural Adjustment of the Food Industries of the United States," Staff Report of the National Economics Division, Economic Research Service (Washington, D.C.: U.S. Department of Agriculture, July 1982), table 21, p. 76.

4. *Wall Street Journal*, May 12, 1982.

5. U.S. Department of Agriculture, *Foreign Agricultural Trade Statistical Report, Fiscal Year 1981*, (Washington, D.C.: U.S. Department of Agriculture, 1981), p. 1.

6. *Business Week*, March 21, 1983, p. 106.

Chapter 2

1. Wayne D. Rasmussen, "American Agriculture: A Short History," based on W. D. Rasmussen, ed., *A Documentary History of American Agriculture*, 4 vols. (New York: Random House, 1975), p. 26.

2. Paul Gates, *The Farmers Age: Agriculture 1815–1860* (New York: Holt, Rinehart and Winston, 1960), pp. 70–72.

3. Rasmussen, pp. 26–30.

4. Harvey Wasserman, *History of the United States* (New York: Harper, 1972), p. 65.

5. Henry John Frundt, "American Agribusiness and U.S. Foreign Agricultural Policy" (Ph.D. diss., Rutgers University, May 1975), p. 23.

6. *Ibid.*, p. 24.

7. Robert Fellmeth, *Interstate Commerce Omission: Ralph Nader's Study Group Report*, (Union of Radical Political Economists, P.E.A.C. Food Project History Section, Part 2) (New York: Grossman, 1970).

8. C. Wright Mills, *White Collar: The American Middle Class* (New York: Oxford University Press, 1956), p. 15.

9. Lawrence Goodwyn, *The Populist Moment* (New York: Oxford University Press, 1978), p. 264.

10. Frundt, pp. 29–43.

11. Mills, pp. 17, 41.

12. Mills, p. 16.

13. Data on farm numbers from U.S. Department of Agriculture, *Economic Indicators of the Farm Sector, 1981*, Statistical Bulletin no. 647 (Washington, D.C.: Department of Agriculture, Economic Research Service, 1981), table 61, p. 85.

14. National Advisory Commission on Food and Fiber, Sherwood O. Berg, chairman, *Food and Fiber for the Future—Report to the President* (Washington, D.C.: July 1967).

15. Fred H. Sanderson, "U.S. Farm Policy in Perspective," *Food Policy*, February 1983, p. 8.

Chapter 3

1. U.S. Department of Agriculture, *Handbook of Agricultural Charts, 1981* (Washington, D.C.: U.S. Department of Agriculture, 1981).

2. U.S. Department of Agriculture, *Handbook of Agricultural Charts, 1975*, p. 65, and *Handbook of Agricultural Charts, 1976*, pp. 30, 33.

3. U.S. Department of Agriculture, *National Food Review, 1978* (Washington, D.C.: U.S. Department of Agriculture, 1978).

4. *New York Times*, April 2, 1982, p. 1.

5. U.S. Department of Agriculture, *Agricultural Prices* (Washington, D.C.: U.S. Department of Agriculture, Crop Reporting Board, Annual Summary, 1978).

6. Schertz, et al., *Another Revolution in U.S. Farming?* (Washington, D.C.: U.S. Department of Agriculture, Agricultural Economic Report no. 441, 1979), p. 48.

7. U.S. Department of Commerce, *Statistical Abstract of the United States, 1980* (Washington, D.C.: U.S. Department of Commerce, 1980), table 609.

8. Marvin Duncan and Ann Laing Adair, "Farm Structure: A Policy Issue for the 1980s," *Economic Review* (Federal Reserve Bank of Kansas City) November 1980, p. 26.

9. U.S. Department of Agriculture, *Economic Indicators of the Farm Sector, 1980* (Washington, D.C.: U.S. Department of Agriculture, 1980), tables B16, B20.

10. *Independent Banker*, December 1982, pp. 11ff.

11. Telephone interview, March 1983.

12. Daniel Levitas, "Crisis of Dignity," unpublished paper, Rural America, 550 - 11th Street, Des Moines, IA 50309.

13. Telephone interview, March 1983.

14. Schertz et al., p. 31.

15. U.S. Department of Agriculture, *Agricultural Outlook* (Washington, D.C.: U.S. Department of Agriculture, September 1982), p. 11.

16. U.S. Department of Agriculture, *Agricultural Statistics, 1981* (Washington, D.C.: U.S. Department of Agriculture, 1981), table 626, and *Economic Indicators of the Farm Sector, 1980*, table 82.

17. U.S. Department of Agriculture, *Economic Indicators of the Farm Sector, 1981*.

18. Ken Meter, "More Grim Statistics," *Prairie Sentinel*, June–July, 1982, p. 7.

19. *Agricultural Record* 12, no. 42 (November 15, 1982).

20. Marty Strange, "The Corn Glut," *Prairie Sentinel*, Feb.–March 1983.

21. Interchange between Iowa Farm Bureau President Dean Kleckner and State Representative Gene Blanshan at hearings before the House and Senate agriculture committees of the Iowa legislature, February 1983.

22. U.S. Department of Agriculture, (UN*Economic Indicators of the Farm Sector, 1981*, tables 46, 54, 56.

23. *New York Times*, February 1, 1983.

24. *Minneapolis Tribune*, March 30, 1982, p. 3–B.

25. National Farmers Union, *Depression in Rural America*, Denver, Colorado 80251, 1982.

26. Personal interview, March 1983.

27. *New York Times*, March 30, 1982.

28. Telephone interview, March 1983.

29. *Ibid.*

30. *Ibid.*

31. *Ibid.*

32. U.S. Department of Agriculture, *Economic Indicators of the Farm Sector, 1981*, tables 46, 54, 56. The average net income for a mid-sized farm is a very rough estimate, since the cutoff point I used was $150,000, which does not correspond to a precise U.S. Department of Agriculture category. In the 1970s $100,000 in gross sales was considered the upper limit for mid-sized farms. To account for inflation I have pushed it up to $150,000.

33. Telephone interview, March 1983. See also: Thomas A. Miller, Gordon E. Rodewald, Robert G. McElroy, *Economies of Size in U.S. Field Crop Farming* (Washington, D.C.: U.S. Department of Agriculture, Economics and Statistics Service, Agricultural Economic Report, no. 472).

34. J. Patrick Madden, *Economies of Size in Farming* (Washington, D.C.: U.S. Department of Agriculture, Economic Research Service, 1967); Bailey, Warren, *The One-Man Farm* (Washington, D.C.: U.S. Department of Agriculture, Economic Research Service, August 1973).

35. U.S. Department of Agriculture, *Structure Issues of American Agriculture*, (Washington, D.C.: U.S. Department of Agriculture, Economics, Statistics and Cooperative Service, Agricultural Economic Research Report no. 438, 1979), p. 112.

36. U.S. Department of Agriculture, *A Time to Choose: Summary Report on the Structure of Agriculture* (Washington D.C.: U.S. Department of Agriculture, January 1981), table 24, p. 58, indicates that 100 percent of the economies of scale are, on average, reached when sales average $133,000. From table 5, p. 43, one can calculate that roughly 50 percent of sales are from farms above this size. Using lower estimates (see note 33) of the point at which all economies of scale are reached, considerably more than half of sales are from farms larger than efficiency justifies.

37. George Patton, Economic Research Service, U.S. Department of Agriculture, interview with research assistant David Ritchie.

38. U.S. Department of Agriculture, *Time to Choose*, p. 75, table 26.

39. U.S. Department of Agriculture, *Status of the Family Farm*, Second Annual Report to Congress, (Washington, D.C.: U.S. Department of Agriculture, Economics, Statistics and Cooperative Service, Agricultural Economic Report no. 438, 1979), p. 3.

40. Duncan and Adair, pp. 22, 23.

41. Philip M. Raup, "Some Questions of Value and Scale in American Agriculture," *American Journal of Agricultural Economics*, May 1978, p. 303.

42. Telephone interview, March 1983.

43. Mel Manternach, National Farmers Organization *Newsletter*, July 1981.

44. U.S. General Accounting Office, *An Assessment of Parity as a Tool for Formulating and Evaluating Agricultural Policy*, Report by the Comptroller General of the U.S., CED 81–11, October 10, 1980, p. 28.

45. William L. Flinn and Frederick H. Buttel, "Sociological Aspects of Farm Size: Ideological and Social Consequences of Scale in Agriculture," *American Journal of Agricultural Economics*, December 1980, p. 950.

46. Myron Magnet, "The Company that Makes Farming Pay," *Fortune*, March 21, 1983, p. 135.

47. *Forbes*, July 5, 1982, p. 188.

48. *San Francisco Chronicle*, January 23, 1983, p. A7.

49. U.S. Department of Agriculture, *Time to Choose*, p. 95.

50. U.S. Department of Agriculture, *Economic Indicators of the Farm Sector, 1981*, tables 61, 80.

51. U.S. Department of Agriculture, *A Time to Choose*, p. 54.

52. *Independent Banker*, December 12, 1982, pp. 11ff.

53. *Iowa Dairy Marketing News*, November 1982.

54. Telephone interview, March 1983.

55. *Small Farm Advocate* 4, no. 2 (Fall 1982): 4.

56. *Food Monitor*, January/February 1983, p. 10.

57. R. Neil Sampson, *Farmland or Wasteland: A Time to Choose* (Emmaus, Penn.: Rodale Press, 1981), p. 34.

58. *Business Week*, February 14, 1983, p. 38.

59. Ronald L. Meekhof, "Implications of Increased Reliance on International Markets," in U.S. Department of Agriculture, *Structure Issues in American Agriculture*, p. 259. See also, U.S. Department of Agriculture, *A Time To Choose*, p. 52, table 16.

60. *The Drovers Journal*, February 25, 1983, p. 40.

61. U.S. Department of Agriculture, *A Time to Choose*, p. 53, calculated from table 18.

62. *Ibid.*, estimated from table 8.

63. "Inflation and Growth Biggest Impacts on Investment," *Commodities*, November 1979, p. 28.

64. *Los Angeles Times*, June 2, 1980.

65. Commodity Futures Trading Commission, *Grain Pricing*, Economic Bulletin no. 1, pp. 23–24.

66. *Des Moines Register*, February 24, 1983.

67. U.S. Congress, House Committee on Small Business, *Export Grain Sales*, 96th Congress, Washington, D.C., June 1979, p. 42.

68. U.S. Congress, Senate Committee on Foreign Relations, Subcommittee on Multinational Corporations, *Hearings on International Grain Companies*, 94th Congress, June 1976, p. 39.

69. U.S. Department of Agriculture, *Status of the Family Farm*, pp. 11, 18.

70. *Ibid.*

71. Pioneer Hi-Bred International, *Attitudes Toward Grain Transportation Among Grain Producers* (Des Moines, Iowa: Pioneer Hi-Bred International, May 1980).

72. U.S. Department of Agriculture, *A Time to Choose*, p. 61.

73. *Des Moines Register*, July 8, 1981.

74. *New York Times*, Nov. 29, 1981.

75. Charles Davenport, Michael Beohlje, David Martin, *The Effects of Tax Policy on American Agriculture* (Washington, D.C.: U.S. Department of Agriculture, Economics and Statistics Service, Agricultural Economic Report no. 480, 1980).

76. U.S. Department of Agriculture, *A Time to Choose*, chapters 6, 8.

77. "Farm Real Estate: Who Buys and How," *Monthly Review of the Federal Reserve Bank of Kansas City*, June 1977, p. 5.

78. *St. Paul Pioneer Press*, January 19, 1983.

79. U.S. Department of Agriculture, *Economic Indicators of the Farm Sector, 1981*, tables 46, 54, 56, 57.

80. *Farmline*, April 1982, p.4; interview with Donn Reimund of U.S. Department of Agriculture's Economic Research Service; *Des Moines Register*, September 17, 1982, p. 1A.

81. *Rural America* 7, nos. 3 and 4 (Fall 1982): 12.

82. Telephone interview, April 1983.

83. Schertz, et al., p. 301.

84. Arthur Daughterty and Robert Otte, *Farmland Ownership in the United States* (Washington, D.C.: U.S. Department of Agriculture, Economic Research Service Staff Report no. AGES 830311, 1983), p. 13.

85. The Kansas Rural Center, "Distribution of Land & Water Ownership in Southwest Kansas" (P. O. Box 133, Whiting, KS, 66552) 1982, p. 8.

86. *Iowa Land Ownership Survey: Preliminary Report on Land Tenure and Ownership in 47 Iowa Counties* (Des Moines, Iowa: Farmers Union, 1982), pp. 3, 10. Order from the Iowa Farmers Union, 6538 University Avenue, Des Moines, IA 50311.

87. Telephone interview with Dan Levitas, research consultant at Rural America, 550–11th, Des Moines, IA 50309, April 1983.

88. Donald Paarlberg, *Farm and Food Policy: Issues of the 1980s* (Lincoln, Nebr.: University of Nebraska Press, 1980), p. 198.

89. *Farmline*, September 1980, pp. 8–9.

90. *Fortune*, March 1983, pp. 140, 145.

91. U.S. Department of Agriculture, *Alternative Futures for U.S. Agriculture*, Part I (Washington, D.C.: Office for Planning and Evaluation for the Committee on Agriculture and Forestry, U.S. Senate, September 1975).

92. William Lin, George Coffman, and J. B. Penn, *U.S. Farm Numbers, Size and Related Structural Dimensions: Projections to the Year 2000* (Washington, D.C.: U.S. Department of Agriculture, Economics, Statistics and Cooperative Service, Technical Bulletin no. 1625, 1980).

93. U.S. Department of Commerce, Bureau of the Census, and U.S. Department of Agriculture, Economic Research Service, *Farm Population of the United States: 1981*, (Washington, D.C.: U.S. Department of Agriculture, Farm Population Series P–27, no.55, 1981), p. 4.

94. *Ibid.*; Lin, Coffman, and Penn, p. iii.

95. For documentation on agribusiness' use of federally subsidized irrigation water, write to National Land for People, 2348 N. Cornelia, Fresno, CA 93711.

96. *Harper's*, October 1982, p. 17.

Chapter 4

1. U.S. Department of Agriculture, *What Farm Exports Mean to You* (Washington, D.C.: Office of Governmental and Public Affairs, May 1981), p. 14.

2. U.S. Department of Agriculture, *U.S. Foreign Agricultural Trade Statistical Report, Fiscal Year 1981*, (Washington, D.C.: U.S. Department of Agriculture, 1981), p. 1; *Basic Petroleum Data Book*, vol. 3, no. 1, January 1983, section VI, table 13.

3. Mort Hantman, "Export Agriculture: An Energy Drain" (San Francisco: Institute for Food and Development Policy, unpublished, 1982).

4. U.S. Department of Agriculture, *Handbook of Agricultural Statistics 1980*, table 630, p. 440; *Economic Indicators of the Farm Sector: Production and Efficiency Statistics, 1979* (Washington, D.C.: U.S. Department of Agriculture, 1979), table 27, p. 47; U.S. Department of Commerce, *Statistical Abstract of the United States, 1980* (Washington, D.C.: U.S. Department of Commerce, 1980), table 1213, p. 695.

5. John Steinhart and Carol Steinhart, "Energy Use in the U.S. Food System," *Science* 184 (1973): 306; Carol Steinhart and John Steinhart, *Energy Sources, Use and Role in Human Affairs* (North Scituate, Mass.: Duxbury Press, 1974); Eric Hirst, "Food Related Energy Requirements," *Science* 184 (1973): 134–38; Eric Hirst, *Energy Use for Food in the United States* (Oak Ridge, Tenn.: Oak Ridge National Laboratory, 1973); U.S. Department of Agriculture, *The U.S. Food and Fiber Sector: Energy Use and Outlook, 1974* (Washington, D.C.: U.S. Department of Agriculture, 1974).

6. Booz-Allen Hamilton, *Energy Consumption in the Food System* (Washington, D.C.: Federal Energy Administration, 1976).

7. Larry J. Connor, "Agricultural Policy Implications of Changing Energy Prices and Supplies," in William Lockeretz, ed., *Agriculture and Energy* (New York: Academic Press, 1977), p. 669; Center for Agricultural Science and Technology (CAST), *Energy Conservation in Agriculture* (CAST Special Publication no. 5, October 1977).

8. Hantman, Appendix B.

9. *Ibid.*, table 5.

10. *Ibid.*, table 4.

11. *Ibid.*

12. *Ibid.*

13. David Pimentel, "Land Degradation: Effects on Food and Energy Resources," *Science* 194 (October 1976): 153.

14. Frederick Buttel and O. W. Larson III, "Farm Size, Structure and Energy Intensity," *Rural Sociology*, 1979, pp. 471–488.

15. S. L. Rawlins, "Irrigation and the Energy Economics of Water Management for Hydrologic Basins," in William Lockeretz, ed., *Agriculture and Energy*, pp. 131–40.

16. Hantman.

17. Pimentel, pp. 149–55.

18. Hantman.

Chapter 5

1. Roger Burbach and Patricia Flynn, *Agribusiness in the Americas* (New York: Monthly Review Press, 1980), p. 221.

2. Richard Gilmore, *Poor Harvest: The Clash of Policies and Interests in the Grain Trade* (New York: Longman, 1982), p. 24.

3. Dan Morgan, *Merchants of Grain* (New York: Viking Press, 1979), p. 13.

4. Confidential interview with soybean trader for major grain company, February 1981.

5. Susan George, *Feeding the Few: Corporate Control of Food* (Washington, D.C.: Institute for Policy Studies, n.d.).

6. *Business Week*, March 11, 1972, p. 84.

7. U.S. Congress, House Committee on Small Business, *Export Grain Sales*, 96th Congress, June 1979.

8. *Ibid.*

9. Morgan, pp. 330–31.

10. U.S. General Accounting Office, *Regulation of Commodity Futures Market—What Needs to Be Done* (Washington, D.C.: U.S. General Accounting Office, May 17, 1978), p. 74.

11. *Ibid.*

12. Gilmore, p. 132.

13. U.S. Congress, *Export Grain Sales*, p. 20.

14. Gilmore, p. 147.

15. U.S. Congress, *Export Grain Sales*, p. 46.

16. *Ibid.*

17. Gilmore, p. 166.

18. *Ibid.*, p. 168.

19. *Latin American Commodities Report*, July 1980.

20. *Los Angeles Times*, May 12, 1980.

21. *Latin American Commodities Report*, July 1980.

22. U.S. Department of Agriculture, Office of Audit, *Export Sales Reporting Program* (Washington, D.C.: U.S. Department of Agriculture, January 1977).

23. Gilmore, p. 166.

24. *Ibid.*, p. 173.

25. *Des Moines Register*, April 29, 1980.

26. *Forbes*, September 18, 1978, p. 2.

27. U.S. Congress, Senate Committee on Foreign Relations, Subcommittee on Multinational Corporations, *Hearings on International Grain Companies*, 94th Congress, June 1976, part 16, pp. 114–17.

28. Confidential interview with Cargill grain trader, March 1983.

29. *Wall Street Journal*, May 7, 1982.

30. 1973 figure from Morgan, p. 168; 1981 figures from *Wall Street Journal*, May 7, 1982.

31. *Business Week*, April 16, 1979.

32. *Wall Street Journal*, March 6, 1979.

33. *Wall Street Journal*, December 21, 1977.

34. *Montana Stockgrower*, August 15, 1973.

35. Association of American Railroads, *1972 Yearbook of Railroad Facts*, p. 51, and *1981 Yearbook of Railroad Facts*, p. 50 (Washington, D.C.: Association of American Railroads, 1972 and 1981).

36. Gilmore, p. 119.

37. Interstate Commerce Commission, Ex Parte no. 307, 1977.

38. *Wall Street Journal*, May 9, 1982.

39. *Feedstuffs*, November 1, 1969.

40. *Feedstuffs*, October 29, 1979.

41. Frances Moore Lappé and Joseph Collins with Cary Fowler, *Food First: Beyond the Myth of Scarcity* (New York: Ballantine Books, 1978), p. 212.

42. Confidential interview with Cargill grain trader, March 1983.

43. *Daily Bread: An Abdication of Power*, The Joseph Project Report on Hunger, Grain, and Transnationals, sponsored by the Senate of Priests of St. Paul and Minneapolis, 1982, p. 92.

44. William Robbins, *The American Food Scandal: Why You Can't Eat Well on What You Earn* (New York: Morrow, 1974), p. 185; A. V. Krebs, "Of the Grain Trade, By the Grain Trade, and For the Grain Trade," in Martha Hamilton, ed., *The Great American Grain Robbery and Other Stories* (Washington, D.C.: Agribusiness Accountability Project, 1972), p. 289; U.S. General Accounting Office, *Exporters' Profits on Sales of U.S. Wheat to Russia* (Washington, D.C.: U.S. General Accounting Office, February 12, 1974), pp. ff.

Chapter 6

1. E. Phillip LeVeen, *Towards a New Food Policy: A Dissenting Perspective* (Berkeley, Calif.: Public Interest Economics West, April 1981), p. 23.

2. *Ibid.*

3. U.S. Department of Agriculture, *Economic Indicators of the Farm Sector, 1980* (Washington, D.C.: U.S. Department of Agriculture, 1980), p. 111.

4. *Agri-Marketing*, April 1982.

5. U.S. Department of Agriculture, *Agricultural Statistics, 1980* (Washington, D.C.: U.S. Department of Agriculture, 1980), table 649.

6. Executive Office of the President, Council on Wage and Price Stability, *Report on Prices for Agricultural Machinery and Equipment May 1976* (Washington, D.C.: Government Printing Office, 1976), table 17, p. 25.

7. *Ibid.*

8. U.S. Department of Commerce, Bureau of the Census, *Census of Manufacturing, 1977* (Washington, D.C.: U.S. Department of Commerce, 1977), table 7, "Concentration Ratios in Manufacturing."

9. *Ibid.*

10. *Ibid.*

11. *Farmline*, March 1981, p. 10.

12. *Forbes*, April 12, 1982.

13. *New York Times*, May 6, 1982.

14. U.S. Department of Agriculture, *Agricultural Statistics, 1981*, table 646.

15. *Antitrust Law and Economics Review* 5, no. 3 (Spring 1972): 33, table 1.

16. Agricultural Council of America, *U.S. Farm Export Strategies for the Eighties* (Washington, D.C.: Agricultural Council of America, February 1981), pp. 41–42.

17. U.S. Congress, Senate Subcommittee on Antitrust, Monopoly, and Business Rights of the Committee on the Judiciary, *Impact of Market Concentration on Rising Food Prices*, 96th Congress, first session, April 6, 1979.

18. John M. Connor, "Structural Adjustment of the Food Industries of the United States," Staff report of the National Economics Division, Economic Research Service (Washington, D.C., U.S. Department of Agriculture, July 1982), p. 43–45, 47.

19. *Ibid.*, table 14.

20. John M. Connors, "U.S. Food and Tobacco Manufacturing Industries: Market Structure, Structural Change and Economic Performance," *Agricultural Economics Report no. 451* (Washington, D.C.:U.S. Department of Agriculture, March 1980), figure 1, p. 12.

21. Daniel Zwerdling, "The Food Monsters: How They Gobble up Each Other and Us," *The Progressive*, March 1980, p. 16.

22. Connors, "U.S. Food and Tobacco . . . ," pp. 10, 13.

23. Connors, "Structural Adjustment . . . ," table 21, p. 76.

24. *Forbes*, July 5, 1982, pp. 103, 106.

25. Mark Green with Beverly C. Moore and Bruce Wasserstein, *The Closed Enterprise System* (New York: Grossman, 1972), p. 14 cites internal report, Antitrust Division of the Federal Trade Commission, by Weiss, "Economic Studies of Industrial Organization."

26. LeVeen.

27. *Ibid.*, p. 24.

28. Data for France, United Kingdom, and West Germany from *O.E.C.D. National Accounts 1983–1980* 2 (1982); U.S. data from *The World Book Almanac and Book of Facts 1983* (New York: Newspaper Enterprise Association), p. 131 cites U.S. Department of Commerce, Bureau of Economic Analysis.

29. LeVeen, p. 13.

30. Data on farm income from, *Economic Indicators of the Farm Sector, 1980*, table 82, p. 111; data on real weekly earnings from *Economic Report of the President, 1980*; data on corporate profits from, U.S. Department of Agriculture, *Handbook of Agricultural Statistics, 1980* (Washington, D.C.: U.S. Department of Agriculture, 1980), table 641, p. 445.

Chapter 7

1. W. E. Larson, "Protecting the Soil Resource Base," *Journal of Soil and Water Conservation* 36, no. 1 (January/February 1981): 13ff.

2. The Office of Technological Assessment claims that one third of U.S. cropland is losing 1 ton of soil or less annually, while half is losing 2 tons or less, and if 1.5 tons is the maximum acceptable loss, we can assume that at least one third is experiencing no net loss. U.S. Congress, Office of Technological Assessment, *Impacts of Technology on U.S. Cropland and Rangeland Productivity* (Washington, D.C.: Government Printing Office, August 1982), table 2, p. 27.

3. *Ibid.*

4. R. Neil Sampson, *Farmland or Wasteland* (Emmaus, Penn.: Rodale Press, 1981), p. 131.

5. Comptroller General of the United States, *To Protect Tomorrow's Food Supply, Soil Conservation Needs Priority Attention— A Report to Congress* (Washington, D.C.: Government Printing Office, February 14, 1977), p. 6.

6. Office of Technological Assessment, p. 33.

7. *Des Moines Register*, April 6, 1980.

8. *California—Arizona Cotton*, April 1982, p. 22.

9. Office of Technological Assessment, p. 34.

10. National Agricultural Lands Study, *Soil Degradation: Effects on Agricultural Productivity*, Interim Report no. 4 (Washington, D.C.: Government Printing Office, 1980), p. 20 cites National Resources Inventory.

11. R. Neil Sampson, *Forbes*, August 31, 1982.

12. *Agricultural Statistics, 1981* (Washington, D.C.: U.S. Department of Agriculture, 1981), table 626, p. 436.

13. Sampson, *Farmland or Wasteland*, p. 57.

14. Office of Technological Assessment, p. 43.

15. John Timmons, "Agriculture's Resource Base: Demand and Supply Interactions, Problems and Remedies," in *Soil Conservation Policies: An Assessment* (Ankeny, Iowa: Soil Conservation Society of America, 1980), p. 56.

16. *Successful Farming Magazine*, January 1982, p. 24.

17. James Risser, "Soil Erosion Creates a Crisis Down on the Farm," *Conservation Foundation Letter*, December 1978.

18. *Des Moines Register*, May 27, 1982.

19. Timmons, p. 55.

20. Risser.

21. *Des Moines Register*, September 11, 1978.

22. *Ibid.*

23. Personal interview with Marilyn Fedelchak of the National Family Farm Coalition, June 1980.

24. Risser.

25. W. E. Larson, "Soils and Soil Conservation: The Natural Resource Base" (University of Minnesota Agricultural Economics Department, unpublished) p. 4; Tom Barlow, "Three Quarters of the Conservation Job Not Being Done," in *Soil Conservation Policies: An Assessment*, p. 129.

26. Dennis Cory, "Estimation of Regional Planted Acreage and Soil Erosion Losses for Alternative Export Demand Projections and Conservation Technologies: A Macro-Economic Approach" (Ph.D. diss., Iowa State University, 1977), pp. 98ff.

27. U.S. Department of Agriculture, *Crop Production, 1980* (Washington, D.C.: Crop Reporting Board, 1980).

28. Phillip M. Raup, *Land Economics*, May 1982, p. 61.

29. Barlow, pp. 128–29.

30. Charles McLaughlin, "Current Soil Conservation Policies and Institutions: A Farmer's Assessment," in *Soil Conservation Policies: An Assessment*, p. 77.

31. Sampson, *Farmland or Wasteland*, p. 59.

32. Comptroller General of the United States, *To Protect Tomorrow's Food Supply*, p. 29.

33. Sampson, *Farmland or Wasteland*, p. 60.

34. Economics, Statistics and Cooperative Service, *Natural Resource Capital in U.S. Agriculture: Irrigation, Drainage and Conservation Investments since 1900*Washington, D.C.: U.S. Department of Agriculture, March 1979).

35. *Economic and Marketing Information* 25, no. 12 (December 1982): 2.

36. U.S. Department of Agriculture and the Council on Environmental Quality, *National Agricultural Lands Study* (Washington, D.C.: U.S. Department of Agriculture, 1981); U.S. Congress, Office of Technological Assessment, *Impacts of Technology on U.S. Cropland and Rangeland Productivity* (Washington, D.C.: Government Printing Office, August 1982); U.S. Department of Agriculture, *Soil and Water Resources Conservation Act* (Washington, D.C.: U.S. Department of Agriculture, 1980).

37. U.S. Department of Agriculture and Council on Environmental Quality, *National Agricultural Lands Study* (Washington, D.C.: U.S. Department of Agriculture, January 17, 1981), p. 10.

38. U.S. Department of Agriculture, *Potential Cropland Study* (Washington, D.C.: U.S. Department of Agriculture, Statistical Bulletin no. 578, Appendix 2a), p. 16.

39. Sampson, *Farmland or Wasteland*, Appendix C, pp. 350–59 cites *National Resources Inventory* and 1975 *Potential Cropland Study*.

40. Sampson estimates 103 million acres will be lost between 1977 and 2000, table C–4, p. 357.

41. U.S. Department of Agriculture, *Soil and Water Resources Conservation Act*, 1980.

Chapter 8

1. Gordon Sloggett, *Prospects for Ground Water Irrigation: Declining Levels and Rising Energy Costs* (Washington, D.C.: U.S. Department of Agriculture, Agricultural Economic Report no. 478).

2. *Newsweek*, February 23, 1981.

3. U.S. Department of Commerce, *Census of Agriculture, 1978* (Washington, D.C.: U.S. Department of Commerce, 1978); Kenneth D. Frederick, *Irrigation and the Future of American Agriculture* (Washington, D.C.: Resources for the Future, 1980), p. 4.

4. U.S. Department of Commerce, *Census of Agriculture 1974* (Washington, D.C.: U.S. Department of Commerce, 1974), vol. 4, pp. 1–9.

5. Earl O. Heady, Howard C. Madsen, Kenneth J. Nicol, and Stanley H. Hargrove, *Agriculture and Water Policies and the Environment: An Analysis of National Alternatives in Natural Resource Use, Food Supply Capacity and Environmental Quality* (Center for Agriculture and Rural Development, Iowa State University, June 1972), p. 17.

6. Frederick, p. 17.

7. U.S. Department of Commerce, *Census of Agriculture, 1978*.

8. U.S. Department of Agriculture, *Soil and Water Resources Conservation Act* (Washington, D.C.: U.S. Department of Agriculture, 1980).

9. U.S. Department of Agriculture, *Field Crop Estimates by States* (Washington, D.C.: U.S. Department of Agriculture, Crop Reporting Board Statistical Bulletin no. 582, December 1977).

10. The Working Group on the Ogallala, *Report on the High Plains Study* (Walthill, Nebr.: Center for Rural Affairs, 1983), p. 3.

11. David Sheridan, *Desertification of the United States* (Washington, D.C.: U.S. Council on Environmental Quality, 1981), p. 25.

12. High Plains Study Council, *Bulletin* 1, no. 10 (October 1981): 1.

13. Working Group on the Ogallala, *Report on the High Plains Study*, pp. 2–3.

14. *Ibid.*

15. E. Phillip LeVeen, *Water Water, ... It Isn't Everywhere* (Berkeley, Calif.: Public Interest Economics West, Spring 1980).

16. Center for Rural Affairs, "Uncle Sam Subsidizes Erosion," *Newsletter*, June 1982.

17. Lyle Schertz, *Another Revolution in U.S. Farming* (Washington, D.C.: U.S. Department of Agriculture, Agricultural Economic Report no. 441, 1979), p. 346.

18. Sloggett.

19. U.S. Department of Agriculture, *Agricultural Statistics* (Washington, D.C.: U.S. Department of Agriculture, various years).

20. U.S. Department of Agriculture, Firm Enterprise Data System.

21. Working Group on the Ogallala, *Report on the High Plains Study*, p. 6.

22. U.S. Department of Commerce, *Census of Agriculture 1974*.

23. Working Group on the Ogallala, *Report on the High Plains Study*, p. 1.

24. Sloggett.

25. Department of Agricultural Economics and Rural Sociology, *Prospective Cost of Adjusting to a Declining Water Supply* (College Station, Texas: Texas A and M University, Technical Report no. 71–3, 1971).

26. U.S. Department of Commerce, *Census of Agriculture 1974*.

27. Center for Rural Affairs, *Wheels of Fortune* (Walthill, Neb.: Center for Rural Affairs, 1976).

28. U.S. Department of Agriculture, *Soil and Water Resources Conservation Act*, vol. 1, p. 53.

29. U.S. General Accounting Office, *Federal Charges for Irrigation Projects Reviewed Do Not Cover Costs* (Washington, D.C.: Government Printing Office, March 13, 1981), p. 43.

30. Working Group on the Ogallala, *Report on the High Plains Study*, p. 4.

Chapter 9

1. Henry John Frundt, "American Agribusiness and U.S. Foreign Agricultural Policy" (Ph.D. diss., Rutgers University, May 1975).

2. See Mitchel B. Wallerstein, *Food for War, Food for Peace* (Cambridge, Mass.: The MIT Press, 1980) for the history of PL–480.

3. Richard Gilmore, *Poor Harvest: The Clash of Policies and Interests in the Grain Trade* (New York: Longman, 1982), p. 92, emphasis added.

4. Wallerstein, p. 37.

5. U.S. Department of Agriculture, *New Directions for U.S. Food Assistance: Report of the Special Task Force on the Operation of Public Law 480* (Washington, D.C.: U.S. Department of Agriculture, May 1978), p. 101.

6. *The Economist*, January 5, 1980.

7. Barry Commoner, *The Poverty of Power: Energy and the Economic Crisis* (New York: Alfred A. Knopf, 1976).

8. Frundt, pp. 129–30.

9. U.S. Department of Agriculture, *Farm–Retail Spreads for Food Products* (Washington, D.C.: U.S. Department of Agriculture, Economic Research Service, April 1965), p. 13.

10. *Daily Bread: An Abdication of Power*, The Joseph Project Report on Hunger, Grain and Transnationals, sponsored by the Senate of Priests of St. Paul and Minneapolis, 1982, p. 44.

11. Eldridge Haynes, president of *Business International*, in testimony before the Senate Committee on Agriculture and Forestry, *Policies and Operations Under P.L. 480* (Washington, D.C: Government Printing Office, 1957), pp. 92–93.

12. U.S. Congress, Senate Finance Committee, *Multinational Corporations: A Compendium of Papers Submitted to the Subcommittee on International Affairs of the Committee on Finance*, February 21, 1973, pp. 837–48.

13. *Business International*, August 18 and August 25, 1972.

14. For a fuller account of these events, see Ernest Mandel, *Decline of the Dollar* (New York: Monad Press, 1972).

15. U.S. Commission on International Trade and Investment Policy, Albert Williams, chairman, *United States International Economic Policy in an Interdependent World—Report to the President* (Washington, D.C.: Government Printing Office, July 1971), p. 11.

16. *Ibid.*

17. U.S. Department of Agriculture, *U.S. Foreign Agricultural Trade Statistical Report, 1975* (Washington, D.C.: U.S. Department of Agriculture, Economic Research Service, 1975).

Chapter 10

1. *World Press Review*, October 7, 1982.

2. United Nations Food and Agriculture Organization, *State of Food and Agriculture* (Rome: United Nations, 1978), pp. 66–71.

3. Dale Adams and Donald Larson, "What Cheap Food Does to Poor Countries," *Wall Street Journal*, November 19, 1982, p. 30.

4. *Daily Bread: An Abdication of Power*, The Joseph Project Report on Hunger, Grain, and Transnationals, sponsored by the Senate of Priests of St. Paul and Minneapolis, 1982, p. 44.

5. U.S. Department of Agriculture, *Foreign Agricultural Trade of the U.S.* (Washington, D.C.: U.S. Department of Agriculture, September–October 1982), p. 24.

6. Gunilla Andrae and Bjorn Beckman, *The Wheat Trap: Bread and Underdevelopment in Nigeria: Project, Proposal and Outline* (Stockholm: University of Stockholm, January 1981), p. 4.

7. *Ibid.*, p. 8.

8. U.S. Department of Agriculture, *Review of Agriculture in 1981, Sub-Saharan Africa* (Washington, D.C.: U.S. Department of Agriculture, E.R.S. Supplement 7 to W.A.S. 27, 1981)

9. U.S. Department of Agriculture, *P.L.–480 Concessional Sales* (Washington, D.C.: U.S. Department of Agriculture, Foreign Agricultural Economic Report no. 142, E.R.S., 1977), p. 11.

10. Beverly Horsley, "Korea: Billion Dollar U.S. Farm Market Today, Multi-Billion Dollar Market Tomorrow," *Foreign Agriculture*, February 1980, p. 7.

11. Personal correspondence from Shirley Dorow, Lutheran missionary in South Korea, 1981.

12. Maurice Brannan, "Trade Patterns," *Feedstuffs*, September 1, 1980.

13. Erik Eckholm and Frank Record, "The Affluent Diet: A Worldwide Health Hazard," in *Sourcebook on Food and Nutrition*, Dr. Loannis S. Scarpa and Dr. Helen Chilton Kiefer, eds. (Chicago: Marguis Academic Media), p. 20.

14. World Bank, *World Tables*, second edition, 1980, pp. 120–21.

15. *Amnesty International Report 1981*, p. 229.

16. John Sayer, *South Korea Report*, unpublished report to the Institute for Food and Development Policy by John Sayer of the Hong Kong–based Asia Monitor Resource Center, 1981.

17. *KIMAMPI, Voice of the People*, February 1979.

18. *Shin Donga*, December 1977, cited in David Fleishman, "South Korean Agriculture: A Poor Model," *Korea Report FON, no. 8, American Friends Service Committee, 1980; Donga Ibo*, January 24, 1979, cited in Fleishman; David Nesmith, "Food Aid for Economic Dependence: P.L. 480 and South Korean Agriculture," *Korea Commentary*, September–December 1977, p. 4.

19. Sayer.

20. *Ibid.*

21. *Ibid.*

22. Marcellus P. Murphy, "Cooperator Programs Change Far West Diets," *Foreign Agriculture*, January 29, 1979, pp. 10–11.

23. Nesmith.

24. Horsley.

25. Sayer.

26. United Nations Food and Agriculture Organization, *Trade Yearbook* 34 (1980), table 39.

27. Mitchel B. Wallerstein, *Food for War—Food for Peace* (Cambridge, Mass.: MIT Press, 1980), p. 153.

28. Ministry of Agriculture and Fisheries, Republic of Korea, *Yearbook of Agriculture and Forestry Statistics, 1978*, cited in Sayer.

29. U.S. Department of Agriculture, Foreign Agriculture Service, *Korean Agricultural Situation Report* (Seoul: Agricultural Attaché, U.S. Embassy, 1979), cited in Sayer.

30. *Daily Bread*, p. 44.

31. Press release from Korean Federation of Trade Unions, cited in Sayer; *Dong-A Ilbo*, October 21, 1976.

32. Don Long, "Repression and Development in the Periphery, *Bulletin of Concerned Asian Scholars* 9, no. 2 (April–June 1977).

33. *Amnesty International Report 1982*, p. 210.

34. *World Development Report*, quoted in Ken Cook, "Surplus Madness," *Journal of Soil and Water Conservation*, January–February 1983.

35. Frances Moore Lappé and Joseph Collins with Cary Fowler, *Food First: Beyond the Myth of Scarcity* (New York: Ballantine Books, 1978), p. 387.

Chapter 11

1. Earl Butz, "A Policy of Plenty," *Skeptic*, no. 10, November–December 1975, p. 57.

2. Thomas A. Miller, Gordon E. Rodewald, and Robert G. McElroy, *Economies of Size in U.S. Field Crop Farming* (Washington, D.C.: U.S. Department of Agriculture, Economics and Statistics Service, Agricultural Economic Report, no. 472).

3. U.S. Department of Agriculture, *A Time to Choose: Summary Report on the Structure of Agriculture* (Washington, D.C.: U.S. Department of Agriculture, January, 1981), table 24, p. 58, indicates that 100 percent of the economies of scale are, on average, reached when sales average $133,000.from table 5, p. 43, one can calculate that roughly 50 percent of sales are from farms above this size. Using lower estimates of the point at which all economies of scale are reached, given in note 2, well more than half of sales are from farms larger than efficiency justifies.

4. Winrock International Livestock Research and Training Center, *The World Livestock Product, Feedstuff, and Food Grain System: An Analysis and Evaluation of System Interactions Throughout the World*, with projections to 1985 (Winrock, Ark.: Winrock International, 1981).

5. Ballantine Books, New York, revised 1979; also available from the Institute for Food and Development Policy. See the list of publications at the end of this book.

6. 1981 figures: *San Francisco Sunday Examiner and Chronicle*, April 25, 1982, p. A15. 1982 figures: telephone interview with spokesperson for W. Grimm Co., Chicago, January 1983.

7. For documentation on agribusiness' use of federally subsidized irrigation water, write to National Land for People, 2348 N. Cornelia, Fresno, CA 93711.

8. Milton Moskowitz, Michael Katz, and Robert Levering, eds., *Everybody's Business: An Almanac* (New York: Harper and Row, 1980), p. 643.

9. Joseph Halow, speech presented at the Annual Convention of the Texas Plant Food Institute, San Antonio, Texas, October 6, 1978.

Bibliography

Books

Aronowitz, Stanley. *Food, Shelter, and the American Dream*. New York: Seabury Press, 1974.

Baran, Paul. *The Political Economy of Growth*. New York: Monthly Review Press, 1957.

Barnet, Richard J., and Muller, Ronald E. *Global Reach: The Power of the Multinational Corporations*. New York: Simon and Schuster, 1974.

Burbach, Roger, and Flynn, Patricia. *Agribusiness in the Americas*. New York: Monthly Review Press, 1980.

Buttel, Frederick H., and Newby, Howard. *The Rural Sociology of the Advanced Societies: Critical Perspectives*. Montclair, New Jersey: Osmund, 1980.

Commoner, Barry. *The Poverty of Power: Energy and the Economic Crisis*. New York: Alfred A. Knopf, 1976.

Daily Bread: An Abdication of Power, The Joseph Project Report on Hunger, Grain, and Transnationals. Sponsored by the Senate of Priests of St. Paul and Minneapolis, 1982.

Dowd, Douglas. *The Twisted Dream: Capitalist Development in the United States since 1776*. Cambridge, Massachusetts: Winthrop, 1977.

Fellmeth, Robert. *Interstate Commerce Omission: Ralph Nader's Study Group Report*. New York: Grossman, 1970.

Gates, Paul. *The Farmer's Age: Agriculture 1815–1860*. New York: Holt, Rinehart and Winston, 1960.

George, Susan. *Feeding the Few: Corporate Control of Food*. Washington, D.C.: Institute for Policy Studies, n.d.

Gilmore, Richard. *Poor Harvest: The Clash of Policies and Interests in the Grain Trade*. New York: Longman, 1982.

Goodwyn, Lawrence. *The Populist Moment: A Short History of the Agrarian Revolt in America*. New York: Oxford University Press, 1978.

Green, Mark, with Moore, Beverly C., and Wasserstein, Bruce. *The Closed Enterprise System*. New York: Grossman, 1972.

Hamilton, Martha. *The Great American Grain Robbery and Other Stories*. Washington, D.C.: Agribusiness Accountability Project, 1972.

Kirkland, Edward. *A History of American Economic Life*. Fourth edition. New York: Appleton Century Crofts, 1969.

Kolko, Gabriel. *Wealth and Power in America: An Analysis of Social Class and Income Distribution*. New York: Praeger, 1965.

Lappé, Frances Moore. *Diet for a Small Planet*. Tenth anniversary edition. New York: Ballantine, 1982.

Lappé, Frances Moore, and Collins, Joseph, with Fowler, Cary. *Food First: Beyond the Myth of Scarcity*. New York: Ballantine, 1978.

Lappé, Frances Moore; Collins, Joseph; and Kinley, David. *Aid as Obstacle: Twenty Questions about Our Foreign Aid and the Hungry*. San Francisco: Institute for Food and Development Policy, 1980.

Mandel, Ernest. *Decline of the Dollar*. New York: Monad Press, 1972.

Mills, C. Wright. *White Collar: The American Middle Class*. New York: Oxford University Press, 1956.

Morgan, Dan. *Merchants of Grain*. New York: Viking Press, 1979.

O'Connor, James. *The Fiscal Crisis of the State*. New York: St. Martin's Press, 1971.

Paarlberg, Donald. *Farm and Food Policy: Issues of the 1980s.* Lincoln, Nebraska: University of Nebraska Press, 1980.

Perelman, Michael. *Farming for Profit in a Hungry World: Capital and the Crisis in Agriculture.* Montclair, New Jersey: Osmund, 1977.

Rasmussen, Wayne D., ed. *A Documentary History of American Agriculture.* 4 vols. New York: Random House, 1975.

Sampson, R. Neil. *Farmland or Wasteland: A Time to Choose, Overcoming the Threat to America's Farm and Food Future.* Emmaus, Pennsylvania: Rodale Press, 1981.

Scarpa, Dr. Loannis S., and Kiefer, Dr. Helen Chilton, eds. *Sourcebook on Food and Nutrition.* Chicago: Marguis Academic Media.

Soil Conservation Policies: An Assessment. Ankeny, Iowa: Soil Conservation Society of America, 1980.

Steinhart, Carol, and Steinhart, John. *Energy Sources, Use, and Role in Human Affairs.* North Scituate, Massachusetts: Duxbury Press, 1974.

Sweezy, Paul. *Theory of Capitalist Development.* New York: Monthly Review Press, 1942.

Wallerstein, Mitchel B. *Food for War, Food for Peace: United States Food Aid in a Global Context.* Cambridge, Massachusetts: MIT Press, 1980.

Wasserman, Harvey. *History of the United States.* New York: Harper, 1972.

Young, John, and Newton, Jan. *Capitalism and Human Obsolescence.* Montclair, New Jersey: Osmund, 1979.

Articles, Pamphlets, and Papers

Agricultural Council of America, *U.S. Farm Export Strategies for the Eighties.* Washington, D.C.: Agricultural Council of America, February 1981.

Buttel, Frederick, and Larson, O. W. III. "Farm Size, Structure and Energy Intensity." *Rural Sociology* (1979).

Center for Agricultural Science and Technology. *Energy Conservation in Agriculture*. C.A.S.T. special publication no. 5, October 1977.

Cory, Dennis. "Estimation of Regional Planted Acreage and Soil Erosion Losses for Alternative Export Demand Projections and Conservation Technologies: A Macro-Economic Approach." Ph.D. dissertation, Iowa State University, 1977.

Flinn, William L., and Buttel, Frederick H. "Sociological Aspects of Farm Size: Ideological and Social Consequences of Scale in Agriculture." *American Journal of Agricultural Economics* (December 1980).

Frederick, Kenneth D. *Irrigation and the Future of American Agriculture*. Washington, D.C.: Resources for the Future, 1980.

Frundt, Henry, John. "American Agribusiness and U.S.-Foreign Agricultural Policy." Ph.D. dissertation, Rutgers University, May 1975.

Hantman, Mort. "Export Agriculture: An Energy Drain." San Francisco: Institute for Food and Development Policy, unpublished, 1982.

Heady, Earl O.; Madsen, Howard C.; Nicol, Kenneth J.; and Hargrove, Stanley H. *Agriculture and Water Policies and the Environment: An Analysis of National Alternatives in Natural Resource Use, Food Supply Capacity, and Environmental Quality*. Ames, Iowa: Center for Agriculture and Rural Development, Iowa State University, June 1972.

Hirst, Eric. *Energy Use for Food in the United States*. Oak Ridge, Tennessee: Oak Ridge National Laboratory, 1973.

Larson, W. E. "Protecting the Soil Resource Base." *Journal of Soil and Water Conservation* 36:1 (January/February 1981).

LeVeen, E. Phillip. *Towards a New Food Policy: A Dissenting Perspective*. Berkeley, California: Public Interest Economics West, April 1981.

LeVeen, E. Phillip. *Water, Water . . . It Isn't Everywhere*. Berkeley, California: Public Interest Economics West, Spring 1980.

Long, Don. "Repression and Development in the Periphery: South Korea." *Bulletin of Concerned Asian Scholars* 9 : 2 (April–June 1977).

Pimentel, David. "Land Degradation: Effects on Food and Energy Resources." *Science* 194 (October 1976).

Sheridan, David. *Desertification of the United States*. Washington, D.C.: U.S. Council on Environmental Quality, 1981.

Working Group on the Ogallala. *Report on the High Plains Study*. Walthill, Nebraska: Center for Rural Affairs, 1983.

Zwerdling, Daniel. "The Food Monsters: How They Gobble Up Each Other and Us." *The Progressive* (March 1980).

Government Documents and Publications

U.S. Department of Agriculture, Washington, D.C.:

Connor, John M. *Structural Adjustments of the Food Industries of the United States*. Staff Report of the National Economics Division E.R.S., July 1982.

Connors, John M. "U.S. Food and Tobacco Manufacturing Industries: Market Structure, Structural Change, and Economic Performance." Agricultural Economics Report no. 451, March 1980.

Horsley, Beverly. "Korea: Billion Dollar U.S. Farm Market Today, Multi-Billion Dollar Market Tomorrow." *Foreign Agriculture* (February 1980).

Lewis, James A. *Landownership in the United States, 1978*. Agricultural Information Bulletin no. 435, Economics, Statistics and Cooperative Service (E.S.C.S.),1980.

Lin, William; Coffman, George; and J. B. Penn. *U.S. Farm Numbers, Size, and Related Structural Dimensions: Projections to the Year 2000*. Technical Bulletin no. 1625, E.S.C.A., 1980.

Miller, Thomas A.; Rodewald, Gordon E.; and McElroy, Robert G. *Economies of Size in U.S. Field Crop Farming*. Agricultural Economic Report no. 472, E.S.S.

Schertz, Lyle. *Another Revolution in U.S. Farming*. Agricultural Economic Report no. 441, E.S.C.S., 1979.

Agricultural Prices. Annual Summary (various years), Crop Reporting Board.

Agricultural Statistics. (Various years.)

Economic Indicators of the Farm Sector. (Various years.)

Foreign Agricultural Trade Statistical Report. (Various years), E.R.S.

Handbook of Agricultural Charts. (Various years.)

National Agricultural Lands Study. With the Council on Environmental Quality, 1981.

Natural Resource Capital in U.S. Agriculture: Irrigation, Drainage, and Conservation Investments since 1900. E.S.C.S., March 1979.

New Directions for U.S. Food Assistance: Report of the Special Task Force on the Operation of Public Law 480. May 1978.

P. L. 480 Concessional Sales. Foreign Agricultural Economic Report no. 142, E.R.S., 1977.

Potential Cropland Study. Statistical Bulletin no. 578.

Soil and Water Resources Conservation Act. 1980.

Status of the Family Farm. Second Annual Report to Congress, Agricultural Economic Report no. 438, E.S.C.S., 1979.

Structure Issues of American Agriculture. Agricultural Report no. 438, E.S.C.S., 1979.

U.S. Food and Fiber Sector: Energy Use and Outlook, 1974.

What Farm Exports Mean to You. Office of Governmental and Public Affairs, May 1981.

U.S. Department of Commerce, Washington, D.C.:

Bureau of the Census. *Census of Agriculture.* 1974 and 1978.

Bureau of the Census. *Census of Manufacturing 1977.*

Bureau of the Census and E.R.S. *Farm Population of the United States: 1981.* Series P–27, no. 55.

U.S. Congress, Washington, D.C.:

Alternative Futures for U.S. Agriculture, Part I. Office for Planning and Evaluation for the Committee on Agriculture and Forestry, U.S. Senate, September 1975.

House Committee on Small Business. *Export Grain Sales.* 96th Congress, June 1979.

Office of Technological Assessment. *Impacts of Technology on U.S. Cropland and Rangeland Productivity.* August 1982.

Senate Finance Committee. *Multinational Corporations: A Compendium of Papers Submitted to the Subcommittee on International Affairs of the Committee on Finance.* February 21, 1973.

Senate Subcommittee on Antitrust, Monopoly, and Business Rights of the Committee on the Judiciary. *Impact of Market Concentration on Rising Food Prices.* 96th Congress, 1st session, April 6, 1979.

Other (Washington, D.C., unless otherwise noted):

Commission on International Trade and Investment Policy, Albert Williams, chairman. *United States International Economic Policy in an Interdependent World—Report to the President.* July 1971.

Duncan, Marvan, and Adair, Ann Laing. "Farm Structure: A Policy Issue for the 1980s." *Economic Review*. Federal Reserve Bank of Kansas City, November 1980.

Executive Office of the President, Council on Wage and Price Stability. *Report on Prices for Agricultural Machinery and Equipment*. May 1976.

"Farm Real Estate: Who Buys and How." *Monthly Review of the Federal Reserve Bank of Kansas City*. June 1977.

National Advisory Commission on Food and Fiber, Sherwood O. Berg, chairman. *Food and Fiber for the Future—Report to the President*. July 1967.

United Nations Food and Agriculture Organization. *State of Food and Agriculture*. Rome (various years).

United Nations Food and Agriculture Organization. *Trade Yearbook*. Rome (various years).

Organizations Working on Agricultural Issues

Agricultural Marketing Project   (615) 292–5401
Center for Health Services
P. O. Box 120495
Nashville, TN 37212

American Agricultural Movement   (202) 544–5740
100 Maryland Avenue, NE
Washington, DC 20002

American Agricultural Movement   (303) 787–2468
Campo, CO 81029

California Agrarian Action Project   (916) 756–8518
P. O. Box 464
Davis, CA 95617

Center for Farm and Food Research, Inc.   (203) 824–5945
P. O. Box 88
Davis, CA 95617

Center for Rural Affairs   (402) 846–5428
P. O. Box 405
Walthill, NE 68067

Center for Studies in Food Self-Sufficiency   (802) 658–3890
362 Main Street
Burlington, VT 05401

Community Access to Media
2524 Hennepin #6
Minneapolis, MN 55405

Coordinating Committee on Pesticides   (415) 543–3706
88 First Street, Suite 600
San Francisco, CA 94105

Emergency Land Fund   (404) 758–5506
564 Lee Street, SW
Atlanta, GA 30310

Institute for Alternative Agriculture   (301) 441–8777
9200 Edmonston Road, Suite 117
Greenbelt, MD 20770

Kansas Rural Center   (913) 873–3431
P. O. Box 133
Whiting, KS 66552

National Catholic Rural Life Conference   (515) 270–2634
4625 NW Beaver Drive
Des Moines, IA 50322

National Farmers Organization   (515) 322–3131
Corning, IA 50841

National Land for People   (209) 233–4727
2348 N. Cornelia
Fresno, CA 93711

National Sharecroppers Fund   (704) 334–3051
2128 Commonwealth
Charlotte, NC 28205

North American Farmers Alliance
P. O. Box 8445
Minneapolis, MN 55408

Rural America   (202) 659–2806
1900 "N" Street, NW
Washington, DC 20036

Rural Coalition   (202) 338–4630
1000 Wisconsin Avenue, NW
Washington, DC 20007

U.S. Farmers Association   (712) 658–2515
P. O. Box 5496
Hampton, IA 50441

Index

Institute Publications

Now We Can Speak: A Journey through the New Nicaragua, features interviews with Nicaraguans from every walk of life telling how their lives have changed since the 1979 overthrow of the Somoza dictatorship. Frances Moore Lappé and Joseph Collins, 124 pages.   *$4.95*

What Difference Could a Revolution Make? Food and Farming in the New Nicaragua, provides a critical yet sympathetic look at the agrarian reform in Nicaragua since the 1979 revolution and analyzes the new government's successes, problems, and prospects. Joseph Collins and Frances Moore Lappé, with Nick Allen, 185 pages.   *$5.95*

Diet for a Small Planet: Tenth Anniversary Edition, an updated edition of the bestseller that taught Americans the social and personal significance of a new way of eating. Frances Moore Lappé, 432 pages with charts, tables, resource guide, recipes, Ballantine Books.   *$3.50*

Food First: Beyond the Myth of Scarcity, 50 questions and responses about the causes and proposed remedies for world hunger. Frances Moore Lappé and Joseph Collins, with Cary Fowler, 620 pages, Ballantine Books, revised 1979.   *$3.95*

Comer es Primero: Mas Alla del Mito de la Escasez is a Spanish-language edition of *Food First*, 409 pages, Siglo XXI—Mexico.   *$9.95*

Food First Comic, a comic for young people based on the book *Food First: Beyond the Myth of Scarcity*. Leonard Rifas, 24 pages.   *$1.00*

Aid as Obstacle: Twenty Questions about our Foreign Aid and the Hungry demonstrates that foreign aid may be hurting the very people we want to help and explains why foreign aid programs fail. Frances Moore Lappé, Joseph Collins, David Kinley, 192 pages with photographs.   *$4.95*

Development Debacle: The World Bank in the Philippines, uses the World Bank's own secret documents to show how its ambitious development plans actually hurt the very people they were supposed to aid—the poor majority. Walden Bello, David Kinley, and Elaine Elinson, 270 pages with bibliography and tables.   *$6.95*

Against the Grain: The Dilemma of Project Food Aid is an in-depth critique which draws extensively from field research to document the damaging social and economic impacts of food aid programs throughout the world. Tony Jackson, 132 pages, Oxfam—England.   *$9.95*

World Hunger: Ten Myths clears the way for each of us to work in appropriate ways to end needless hunger. Frances Moore Lappé and Joseph Collins, revised and updated, 72 pages with photographs.   *$2.95)*

El Hambre en el Mundo: Diez Mitos, a Spanish-language version of *World Hunger: Ten Myths* plus additional information about food and agriculture policies in Mexico, 72 pages.   *$1.45*

Needless Hunger: Voices from a Bangladesh Village exposes the often brutal political and economic roots of needless hunger. Betsy Hartmann and James Boyce, 72 pages with photographs.   *$3.50*

Circle of Poison: Pesticides and People in a Hungry World documents a scandal of global proportions, the export of dangerous pesticides to Third World countries. David Weir and Mark Schapiro, 101 pages with photos and tables.   *$3.95*

Circulo de Veneno: Los Plaguicidas y el Hombre en un Mundo Hambriento is a Spanish-language version of *Circle of Poison*, 135 pages,Terra Nova—Mexico.   *$3.95*

Seeds of the Earth: A Private or Public Resource? examines the rapid erosion of the earth's gene pool of seed varieties and the control of the seed industry by multinational corporations. Pat Roy Mooney, 126 pages with tables and corporate profiles. *$7.00*

A Growing Problem: Pesticides and the Third World Poor, a startling survey of pesticide use based on field work in the Third World and library research. This comprehensive analysis also assesses alternative pest control systems. David Bull, 192 pages with charts, photos, and references. *$9.95*

What Can We Do? An action guide on food, land and hunger issues. Interviews with over one dozen North Americans involved in many aspects of these issues. William Valentine and Frances Moore Lappé, 60 pages with photographs. *$2.95*

Mozambique and Tanzania: Asking the Big Questions looks at the questions which face people working to build economic and political systems based on equity, participation, and cooperation. Frances Moore Lappé and Adele Negro Beccar-Varela, 126 pages with photographs. *$4.75*

Casting New Molds: First Steps towards Worker Control in a Mozambique Steel Factory, a personal account of the day-to-day struggle of Mozambique workers by Peter Sketchley, with Frances Moore Lappé, 64 pages. *$3.95*

Agrarian Reform and Counter-Reform in Chile, a firsthand look at some of the current economic policies in Chile and their effect on the rural majority. Joseph Collins, 24 pages with photographs. *$1.45*

Research Reports. "Land Reform: Is It the Answer? A Venezuelan Peasant Speaks." Frances Moore Lappé and Hannes Lorenzen, 17 pages. *$1.50*

"Facts Behind Famine: The Horn of Africa." Nina Friedman, 15 pages. *$2.00*

"Export Agriculture: An Energy Drain." Mort Hantman, 50 pages. *$3.00*

"Breaking the Circle of Poison: The IPM Revolution in Nicaragua." Sean L. Swezey and Rainer Daxl, 23 pages. *$4.00*

Food First Curriculum Sampler offers a week's worth of creative activities to bring the basics about world hunger and our food system to grades four through six. 12 pages.
$1.00

Food First Slideshow/Filmstrip in a visually positive and powerful portrayal demonstrates that the cause of hunger is not scarcity but the increasing concentration of control over food producing resources, 30 minutes.
$89 (slideshow), *$34* (filmstrip)

Write for information on bulk discounts.

All publications orders must be prepaid.

Please include shipping charges: 15% of order for U.S. book rate or foreign surface mail, $1.00 minimum. California residents add sales tax.

Food First Books

Institute for Food and Development Policy
1885 Mission Street
San Francisco, CA 94103 USA
(415) 864–8555

volunteers and staff, but on financial activists as well. All our efforts toward ending hunger are made possible by membership dues or gifts from individuals, small foundations, and religious organizations. We accept no government or corporate funding.

Each new and continuing member strengthens our effort to change a hungry world. We'd like to invite you to join in this effort. As a member of the Institute you will receive a 25 percent discount on all Food First books. You will also receive our triannual publication, *Food First News*, and our timely Action Alerts. These Alerts provide information and suggestions for action on current food and hunger crises in the United States and around the world.

All contributions to the Institute are tax deductible.

To join us in putting Food First, just clip and return the attached form to the Institute for Food and Development Policy, 1885 Mission Street, San Francisco, CA 94103, USA.

☐ Yes, I want to ensure that the Institute for Food and Development Policy continues to be an independent and effective voice in the struggle against hunger and food problems. I have enclosed my tax-deductible contribution of:

☐ $20   ☐ $35   ☐ $50   ☐ Other $_____

☐ Please send me more information about the Institute, including your publications catalog.

Name _____

Address _____

City_____State_____Zip_____Country_____

Institute for Food and Development Policy
1885 Mission Street
San Francisco, CA 94103 USA

About the Institute

The Institute for Food and Development Policy, publisher of this book, is a nonprofit research and education center. The Institute works to identify the root causes of hunger and food problems in the United States and around the world and to educate the public as well as policymakers about these problems.

The world has never produced so much food as it does today—more than enough to feed every child, woman, and man as many calories as the average American eats. Yet hunger is on the rise, with more than one billion people around the world going without enough to eat.

Institute research has demonstrated that the hunger and poverty in which millions seem condemned to live is not inevitable. Our Food First publications reveal how scarcity and overpopulation, long believed to be the causes of hunger, are instead symptoms—symptoms of an ever-increasing concentration of control over food-producing resources in the hands of a few, depriving so many people of the power to feed themselves.

In 55 countries and 20 languages, Food First materials and investigations are freeing people from the grip of despair, laying the groundwork—in ideas and action—for a more democratically controlled food system that will meet the needs of all.

An Invitation to Join Us

Private contributions and membership dues form the financial base of the Institute for Food and Development Policy. Because the Institute is not tied to any government, corporation, or university, it can speak with a strong independent voice, free of ideological formulas. The success of the Institute's programs depends not only on its dedicated